# BOB FLOWERDEW
# going ORGANIC

## the good gardener's guide to solving the problems

### with photography by Francesca Yorke

For those who would be organic, or at least want to be more natural and gentler gardeners – but fear problems – here are your answers

Kyle Cathie Limited

Thanks to my loving wife, Vonetta, who has helped me so much by keeping our twins at bay while I wrote this book. And thanks to all those who have suffered having to work with me.

First published in Great Britain 2007 by
**Kyle Cathie Limited**
122 Arlington Road
London NW1 7HP
general.enquiries@kyle-cathie.com
www.kylecathie.com

10 9 8 7 6 5 4 3 2 1

ISBN 978 1 85626 714 4

Project Editor **Sophie Allen**
Design **Mary Evans**
Photography **Francesca Yorke** *
Copy editor **Annelise Evans**
Proof reader **Jane Struthers**
Indexer **Helen Snaith**
Production **Sha Huxtable** and **Alice Holloway**

* Full photographic acknowledgements on page 222

A Cataloguing In Publication record for this title is available from the British Library.

Colour reproduction by Sang Choy
Printed and bound by snp Leefung, China

# contents

Gathered here is a lifetime's knowledge and all the tips you should ever need to solve almost every garden problem, while becoming a more competent and successful gardener, more naturally and more organically.

I've been gardening for most of my life. And over those years I have had successes, and failures, with almost every thing I have ever grown. Each year, and the conditions it brings, is different from all others and so necessarily different plants do well or poorly. Yet despite this, every year almost everything in the garden does do fairly well and the real disasters are rare – and to be fair those are often weather or owner related. Pests and diseases come and go, and a few years gardening soon gives most gardeners enough experience to learn which need dealing with, and how to avoid the commonest cultural mistakes.

But it is better to avoid those mistakes if possible, and I trust this book will guide the novice past all the pitfalls and traps, which I have delighted in springing upon myself in the guise of experimentation. I also suspect some folks feel more comfortable believing they can reach for a bottle of pesticide and zap whatever they think might be troubling them. But there is no need for such action – often such pests and diseases are of no great importance, only signs that nature is about. They may even change over the years – some pests and diseases are rife for a decade and then become unknown. New problems appear, and then disappear; only a few remain a constant threat and for these organic gardeners have developed effective remedies.

Indeed, it is not at all difficult to be an organic gardener as it is all about being a good gardener, working with nature rather than fighting her, using good techniques and making our plants strong enough to shrug off diseases and pests rather than regarding these as enemies to be eliminated. As fighting nature is never easy, organic gardeners use their wit and cunning to get nature to do the hard work for them. After all, seeds want to grow, flower and fruit, it is their whole raison d'être. And remember although every plant may have a pest to bother it, every pest has a predator looking for it for their dinner. So, by simply aiding the pest's enemies we help our plants.

And you don't actually have to become a totally committed organic gardener to use the same natural remedies, nor do you have to break your back or your bank balance. Organic solutions are simple, usually natural and often remarkably cheap alternatives. The vast number of pests and diseases you may ever come across can be outmanoeuvred using these simple safe remedies instead of reaching for a bottle of poison.

But perhaps the most important part for the newer gardener is understanding how to avoid the commonest mistakes and which problems must be identified and dealt with. Well I've made those mistakes and had those problems so you never need discover them for yourself without having the remedy to hand. Have a great time gardening, and don't get too bothered about all those bugs!

Bob

# don't make a rod for your own back

Be positive, be realistic ● Don't draw attention to faults ● Your garden is better than you think ● Distinguishing big problems from little annoyances ● Doing a proper job only once and without problems ● The importance of planning to avoid unnecessary errors ● Better to do nothing than the wrong thing! ● Doing the right things at the right time ● Avoiding taking on

too much in a new garden and spotting white elephants ● Renting instead of owning
● Realistically estimating your resources: labour, expense, time, help and skills ● Avoiding
mistakes with storage, tools, hardware, water supplies, paths and plants ● Essential skills
required for simply tending or improving what's already there

# gardening ought to be enjoyable

Much of the skill in becoming a 'good' gardener is simply learning not to become a plant hypochondriac and to distinguish real problems from little annoyances.

## the ideal is not real

Too many of us imagine making over our gardens into an ideal picture that is hard to ever bring into reality. Perhaps the perfectly manicured gardens on television, in books and magazines, and at major flower shows are to blame. Raising an entire garden to perfection is possibly achievable for just one day or three, as you may indeed see at flower shows. But to keep a garden display immaculate for any longer is near impossible, even if it's a very simple and basic design. Visit the Royal Horticultural Society's Chelsea Flower Show on the first and last days and you will see exactly what I mean.

Perhaps the grass is greener on the other side of the fence. Well, it's all to do with geometry: when you look straight down at your turf you see the weeds and bare spots. When you look through a fence you see the grass blades at an angle so they nearly always look fuller and richer. Maybe your neighbours' flowers look better than yours, but if you had super eyesight you'd probably see aphids over there too. It is hard enough to make even a window box look superb throughout the entire year. To fill a bed or border with random choices and expect year-round, problem-free flowering is a tad unrealistic.

## don't draw attention to your faults!

This is an important rule in getting a reputation as a successful gardener. The old advice was not to cry 'stinking fish' if you want to have any hope of selling them. Rather like that eternally foolish conundrum too dangerous to answer, 'does my bum look big in this?' Well it didn't until you asked me, but now thinking about it... So if you take someone, even an esteemed expert gardener, around your garden and point out every failure, they will come away with a different view than if you had selected only your successes.

Another pitfall to avoid: you may find yourself uttering the words, 'you should have seen the garden last week, it was...' Fine yourself a donation to charity on the spot! Once you admit that currently your garden is not exactly as you wish it to be, the visitor will look at everything more critically instead of savouring your present triumph.

Tutor yourself in selective positivism. No matter how good you become, you cannot maintain perfection. In each and every year, different plants prosper, and others fail, according to the vagaries of the seasons – that is gardening. Each year the weather is slightly different and occasionally favours a plant that may never have done well before. And in most years there will be reliable performers, plants we often regard as commonplace. Dwell upon these successes, enthuse on their gorgeousness and the 90 per cent you have achieved. Simply refrain from taking much notice of the miffy and the 10 per cent you've not yet done, and most others will not notice them either.

## parable of the engineer's car

There is an urban myth that the motor engineer's car is the worst pile of junk on the road. Well, this may be true: the engineer will know exactly what is wrong, if and when it is likely to fail and, if so, what to do to fix the situation. In the same way, professional gardeners, such as busy writers scraping a living, often have apparently appallingly maintained gardens at home, unless they take in help. (Yes, that is a plea in mitigation!) Equally, the best vegetable grower in the village may have a plot thick with weeds. These situations exist because the owner knows exactly what is going on, how long it can be left and, most importantly, what to do when it needs to be done. This is where a few years' experience pays – you just 'know' what to do when.

## your garden is better than you think

All real gardens always have something that has still to flower or has gone over, a patch that needs weeding and, without doubt, a plethora of pests and diseases if you make the effort to look for them. Yet these same gardens are beautiful and beloved, productive of fruit and flower; many are considered superb by most of their visitors. The point is: a garden is surely to be enjoyed, not fretted over.

Unless you take part in competitions or sell your produce, everything doesn't need to be manicured beyond perfection, treated with pesticide or fed until it bursts. Serious control freaks can indulge themselves in areas of gardening such as topiary and training fruit and, if they want, they can enter shows to exhibit their massive perfections. But for the rest of us it really helps to be more relaxed. The missing pounds of yield per square yard or the odd bug or blemish should not matter much in the grand scheme of things.

## no problem

Indeed much of the skill acquired in becoming a 'good' or problem free gardener is simply learning to tell apart which are the real problems from what are no more than little annoyances.

Weeds are not necessarily a problem. Not every bug is bad. Indeed most pests and diseases are often inconsequential. With both crops and blooms, it is surprising that as many

What do you really want? An immaculate construction or something more comfortably rustic?

problems may come from nature's generous over-production as from her failure. This means for example that great improvements can be made by judicious fruitlet thinning or dead-heading as easily as by wholesale destruction of hosts of minor pests and diseases.

True, there are a few situations that require prompt action, but most plants make it through relatively unscathed even when we do nothing at all. Just look around you.

Annoyingly, most of the really irksome things that bother our plants can have nothing done about them anyway – or are as rare as five-legged cows. It is not a good plan for the novice gardener to dwell too much on pests and diseases rather than enjoying the truly amazing vitality and vigour of the natural world. Still, for the curious, almost every bug or blight you are likely to come across, and the remedies, are dealt with in this book.

# doing a proper job

## do it only once

In gardening, as in life, there are three parts to any task: the first is knowing what to do, the second is knowing when to do it, and the third is knowing what not to do. Only then can we consistently do a proper job – one that works, is neat and efficiently done and economic with materials. We may make mistakes but we must learn from them. An old carpenter friend once told me that he considered that there were three important parts to every task: thinking it out thrice, measuring it up twice, and then doing it but once – properly. He applied this philosophy to almost everything in life as he did to his woodworking. His whole point was that we too often skip the planning, rush the measuring and end up having to do much more work putting right the inevitably bodged results. Gardening is just the same.

## the importance of planning

Better do nothing than the wrong thing! Think things through. Put them down on paper. Be sure of what you have in mind before you start. When I laid up my garden a quarter of a century ago, I spent months working it out first, walking through it in my mind season by season, year upon year. Of course I still made more than a few errors, but I also avoided a great deal of wasted or wrong work by doing all that planning first.

I cannot emphasise enough how well plants get on without us interfering. Most of the worst gardening disasters are caused by someone doing the wrong thing, or even too much of the right thing. I once rushed to a 'sick' garden where everything was dead, dying or in the throes of such strange

Letting this climber choke this pear may not be a good plan, unless intentional – it depends how many pears you want?

growth that everyone assumed some ghastly spray had blown in on the wind. It turned out that the new owner, having little knowledge of application rates, had applied fertiliser to everything far too liberally. In dry places, it could be seen lying thick on the ground like a fall of hail. Where it had dissolved into the soil, the plants were dead or suffering terribly. The concentration of fertiliser was every bit as poisonous as a herbicide. The only 'cure' was to scrape up what we could and to wash through the rest.

Most of the plants needed replacing. The same has been done with natural fertiliser such as poultry litter.

Likewise fruit trees and flowering shrubs that left alone would do reasonably well may fail simply because someone chopped the wrong bits off, or cut the right bits off but at an inappropriate time. And we ought not to have to lift and move something bulky and heavy several times, all through a lack of planning. Yet I have seen it happen so often – and sometimes done it myself!

Zucchini/courgettes can crop prolificly BUT ONLY if all are picked as they swell – not long after the flower fades.

## timing is everything

Do the right things at the right time! Get the timing wrong and you almost might as well not have bothered. The old saying, 'There's a right time for everything in gardening and it was a couple of weeks ago', always rings true. This is where experience really helps. There are books and tables of jobs through the season, but these are true only for a given time and place and don't fit every garden, with its different mix of plants and microclimates. The most useful aid to effective garden management is a spare diary. Whenever you notice you forgot to do some task at the right time, make a note of it, but in the correct week, in the form of an instruction to do that task. So next year when the appropriate week comes around again, the task will get done spot on time. Of course every year varies, so the diary date for any given task may still be slightly earlier or later than the weather and the particular season dictate, but the order of tasks in your diary should remain remarkably consistent and can serve as reliable prompts as the years go by.

## don't take on too much

Unless you have years of experience, a large garden can grind you down. The initial digging and clearing of a flower or vegetable bed is almost thrilling compared to the subsequent hours of patient sowing, watering, weeding, thinning and then picking. If the area was a lawn, it would take half an hour to manage once a week, but as a vegetable bed, it's half a day – and another half-day for processing and storing the produce. I love all of this, but be sure that you do.

Likewise with any large project, be it orchard, water feature or greenhouse, think it through thoroughly before you order the trucks! Consider the time, effort and expense not just of the creation but also the maintenance. You may want a grand sweep of lawn, but are you prepared to cut it weekly for most of the year? Or can you afford to pay someone else? A generous border of delightful plants does not take much more time than a smaller one, but let it get out of hand and it does. A huge old greenhouse may look appealing, if restored, but will need repainting every other year or so, as will any outside paint, on shed or roof. It is easier if you have only a small area and not too much hardware to tend. Start too many projects or tend too large an area with many compartments and some surely get neglected before you even notice it. Then pests and diseases get out of control, pruning and trimming is neglected, weeds consolidate their hold, gutters block and before you know it the jungle is reclaiming your living room. Perhaps I exaggerate, but be warned: 'only bite off what you can chew.'

# recognising white elephants

## what to avoid

The old books often say something like: 'choose an open, warm, sunny slope with a rich, loamy soil for your garden, with a well, stream or spring to hand.' Oh, if only we could. The primary problem is finding an affordable home at all. Any preference about the garden usually has to come a long way down the list. Most modern gardens are far too small for a keen gardener and certainly for anyone seriously into growing food crops. But size is not everything.

Do beware of taking on a grand garden that will be far more than you can keep up with, especially if you are a suburbanite moving to the country. Do not be beguiled by first impressions into buying a garden that may be very expensive to maintain. Larger gardens, especially those with imposing drives, lawns and hedges, usually require a lot more work and expense than small ones. Many outbuildings could be useful storage – and yet more repair bills. Big trees, while beautiful to behold, can be a never-ending source of revenue for arboreal surgeons. Meanwhile, their canopies shade and dry out everything underneath and provide vantage points for those worst of thieves, wood pigeons and grey squirrels. Established trees are much more problematic than most estimate; better choose the open, windswept site any time.

## mature means challenging

Beware the estate agents' phrase, 'with large, mature [or well established] gardens'. They may look lovely, but will almost certainly be in need of an overhaul, and are likely to be shady underneath and drip in the wet. A setting of mature trees and shrubs is better suited to those who wish to merely have a garden and a jobbing gardener rather than serious gardeners who want to grow plants for themselves. Mature gardens age, go over and lose their interest. A garden that is obviously in decline cannot be made back into the manicured film set it may once have been, and will be difficult to change, unless you really know what you're doing. Although it is an interesting challenge to take on another's garden and keep it unchanged, you will probably want at least some of it another way. In almost every case, the less 'mature' the garden, the less work it will be to make over or even

'Taking an albatross for a garland of flowers I hung it round my neck
Imagining its scent and form could my life and soul bedeck.
Instead it robbed me of my hours and drove me mad with flies
But rather than admit mistake; I still listen to its lies...'

maintain. Large trees, shrubs and hedges take more effort to eradicate than a patch of bedding plants or lawn; but the real problem is the shade and competition, so don't take on a garden nestling in a little glade among big trees – unless that is exactly what you wanted already.

### hollows and frost pockets

Gardens set in hollows can suffer from another difficult problem. Cold air runs and pools like water, so any low spot has colder, damper nights and a shorter growing season. Similarly, a site in a pretty valley may seem appealing, but remember that the sun must come up later and set earlier than for another place on the flat. A garden set on the shady slope of a valley may never get any direct sun in summer and, worse, it will be a very dark, shady spot in the winter months. This will cause the gardener many more problems simply because many plants can't grow well without some direct sun and a very restricted range of plants has to be grown to avoid weak and sickly growth and all its resultant woes.

### shun the shade

Although it seems obvious to avoid shady gardens in the country, it is even more important in built-up areas. Suburban gardeners should be especially careful to visit prospective homes both in the morning and late afternoon to ensure that they are not too heavily shaded by some large building or trees for too long. This effect is worst in winter when the sun is low, but direct sun is needed more during the growing season, so low shade is annoying but not as bad as tall shade. Since a small city garden will have houses very close by, it is important to find one with as much sunlight as possible. It may even be worth the gain in light to endure a site next to a wide road or parking lot, if the garden is on the sunny side.

Indeed, light is so important that it should really be the major factor in choosing almost any garden. Soil may be improved or imported, planting containers made, bought or found, water piped in or rainfall stored, but you can't easily replace the sun. (You could install towers with electric floodlights, but that's not going to be popular with neighbours.) So beware: if a garden is heavily shaded, or likely to become so, then your gardening will be beset

a challenge (although it will aid a few plants in summer); it is likely to be a serious handicap in winter by drowning roots, to say nothing of any actual risk of serious flooding!

### other problematic sites

Rocky sites with thin soils, gardens on chalk with barely any topsoil, and any garden that is overrun with pernicious weeds such as horsetail (*Equisetum*) or bindweed (*Convolvulus arvensis*) will all be very challenging. These might be turned into attractive gardens, especially if food crops are not required, but they will not be problem-free and will demand well-planned, hard work.

Although it is not the worst site, you should also beware the very open, windswept site with not a tree in sight, especially if it is high up on a hillside. Yes, you have grand views, but you will need shelter belts, hedges, walls and so on. Most plants give up growing actively in winds of more than just a few miles an hour, so such sites are naturally handicapped. If they do grow, the plants are inevitably lop-sided. Even so, windy and windswept is still far better than a shady spot; you can get the plants out of the wind under glass or plastic and then grow almost anything. Remember to ask yourself this question with any prospective garden: is this a white elephant? If so, don't buy into it.

### renting instead of owning

Every size of garden has some drawbacks: if you want fewer problems, choose a slightly larger than average garden, never a huge one. For many, there may be another solution: rentable allotments or collective garden plots are ideal for those with no or only a small garden. The main disadvantage of an allotment is that all visits need planning; you can't just pop out to get some fresh herbs or flowers. The fellowship of other gardeners makes up for some of the inconvenience and the occasional theft. These communal gardens often have an advice service – apart from the unofficial service from your fellow gardeners – and a shop or a discount on seeds and products. If no allotment is handy, why not look for someone nearby who cannot tend their entire garden; perhaps they'd let you take on a part of it? Giving them back a share of the bounty seems a small price to pay for a bit of good earth.

with problems, unless you go with it and live in a ferny grotto – very nice and cool on hot days, but a bit short on flowers and crops, and depressing in darkest winter.

### watery places

Also to be avoided are gardens directly by a river or stream. These may look quaint, picturesque and very appealing. Certainly water casts no shade, in fact, it reflects considerable light up onto plants nearby. And of course you imagine that there will be no water shortage. You may be surprised to learn that you will probably need a licence and have to pay to extract any water, and you may be charged for your rainfall draining into the watercourse. Most importantly for the gardener, water nearby in any great amount, be it river or pond, makes the air cool and damp and causes increased problems with moulds and mildews. Fogs and mists will abound. The high water table will present

# assessing your resources

Better to make one strong frame of two posts and a good crossbar than a dozen wobbly canes.

## the pitfalls

I have always repeated to customers something I learned years ago from an older colleague: he said, 'You can have a cheap job or you can have a quick job or you can have a proper job; I can even do you two out of the three but never all of them together.' Time, labour and expense are not interchangeable, but very much inter-related. Short cuts may be taken, but they almost always cost hugely or cause trouble. A proper job takes time. It is expensive or demands that you work very, very long hours. I have already emphasised the problems that come from taking on too much. Now some need further explanation.

### labour and expense

Firstly, it will never be easy to do hard, physical work for hours at a time unless you are already halfway fit. If you have gardened only a window box and take on a large suburban plot, you may find even mowing a lawn more than enough exercise. Don't take on too much at once. Break jobs down into smaller ones and do a bit at a time. Otherwise you will have all sorts of aches and pains and be discouraged from gardening altogether.

Secondly, consider the expense, which in gardening can be quite small if you do it all yourself, but quite different when you subcontract. Here the smaller garden wins every time since an amount of cash spent on quality paving to floor an entire patio would not pay for even a gravel path to the front door of a larger plot. Many problems of cost shrink if you plan ahead and especially if you sow, root and divide plants for yourself instead of buying in bigger ones. However, although these are not difficult procedures, they are inherently more complicated than simply putting in a load of ready-grown plants and so may give rise to more potential problems.

### time and help

Thirdly, and importantly, is time. Once again I must stress that it is unwise to want results too quickly or to take on schemes, especially unwittingly, that will require too much maintenance time. Here is where labour and expense

Not the very best formed espalier in the world – BUT MINE OWN!

come in; subcontracting some of the garden chores may be money well spent if it frees up enough time to enjoy your garden. Do not rely on friends or family; they may help clearing the jungle or possibly with big, easily defined jobs such as laying a lawn, but you will never get them to mow it for you week after week or regularly trim your hedges. These are obvious jobs for professionals; whatever they charge should be worth it, but make sure that they are properly insured to avoid real problems!

Finding someone who can and will weed a border properly is much harder; many jobbing gardeners apparently can't tell a weed from a valuable plant. The best place to ask is at your local horticultural society or allotment group; their recommendations may be safely followed because they probably not only understand what is required but will also know who is a reliable hand in your area.

## pruning and other skills

Pruning falls into several types: tidying deadheads and shoots as on roses and soft fruits; training frameworks, as on grapevines and espaliers; tree surgery, removing dead, decayed and overgrown branches, from shrubs to large trees. Arboreal or tree surgeons specialise in the latter type of pruning; employ one who is qualified and insured and preferably one who has advertised for some time in your local phone book. However, they are unlikely to be good

at other types of pruning because they are outside their field. Proper pruning, particularly summer pruning of trained subjects, is a complicated affair and surprisingly few, not even many professionals, perform it well, especially on plants with which they are unfamiliar. It all goes with experience: with a good, specialist book and a couple of years' practice, anyone can become expert on his or her own plants.

Until then, if you have choice shrubs and trained fruit, avoid creating long-term problems by getting the best professional help that money can buy. Ask for recommendations from your local horticultural group or horticultural college. Best of all, find a local, skilled amateur and get them (*pay them*) to teach you how to prune by doing it with you. If you can't find anyone who inspires confidence, leave it alone until you've read the book.

Indeed skills such as pruning successfully are what divide the good from the problem-beset gardener. Skill is simply being able to do a job effectively, without stumbling over the common pitfalls. Practice makes perfect and if at first you don't succeed, try and try again – these are clichés but in gardening so true. We all make mistakes, causing avoidable problems for our plants and ourselves. The plants usually forgive you, so have another go, but learn as you do, read more books, practise, and you will soon have the skills.

# mistakes to avoid

## siting garden structures

We often forget that a garden does not exist
in isolation. There are all the ancillary bits
that have to be fitted in. They seem to forget
in 'designer' gardens about where the lawn
mower lives, where the tools go, where you
do the potting and store the sticks, pots and
compost. Storage is essential and needs to
be well placed; otherwise you create the twin
problems of difficult and distant access. A
potting shed/tool store is so useful and frees
up the greenhouse, if you have one, to make
better use of that space. Don't place the shed
too far from either the vegetable bed or greenhouse or it will be inconvenient. The shed
can go in the shade whereas the greenhouse
must have as much sunlight as possible. It is
barely worth having a greenhouse in a shady
place because the plants will grow so badly.
Under a tree is not good, but please don't
put it under an apple or pear tree unless you
reinforce the roof. Water butts and compost
heaps can also go in shady places, as can
stores of almost anything, from wood to bricks
or bags of compost. Save all the sunniest,
lightest places for plants.

Make sure that getting to storage locations
is easy. Doors and gates should open in a
convenient way, hinges be oiled, and the
catches simple to use. Do not make it a battle
to get at your mower, spade or whatever.
I used to visit a man who kept his heavy,
petrol-driven mower in a shed, up some
steps with a high threshold at the top. The
mower had to be manhandled out and back
almost every week of the year! This took as
much effort as cutting the grass did.

## essential tools

We all get loads of tools that we never use. Beware of gadgets! They rarely do the job any quicker or easier than the standard tools that have been developed over centuries – except we have become taller than our ancestors. Most tools are still made as they always were, but now their handle shafts are too short and give us backache from bending over them. Rakes, spades, forks and hoes should have longer shafts for all except the shortest of us. You don't need many other tools to do most jobs – a good pair of secateurs, a garden knife, perhaps a pair of shears, a trowel, broom, coarse sieve, wheelbarrow and a pair of watering cans. (Two cans are best so that you can carry twice as much water per journey, but in a more balanced way that is better for your back.)

Buy these as second-hand, well made or new, middle-of-the-range models. Expensive tools are not much better than moderately priced ones, but the cheapest are no good at all. Tools should last a lifetime and be comfortable to use; it is very important to make sure that the handles fit your hands well to avoid unnecessary aches. Tools that have a cutting edge such as trowels, spades, hoes, shears and secateurs need to be kept sharp, making them so much easier to use; therefore invest in a good file or sharpening stone.

Get a tough wheelbarrow like a steel builder's barrow with a pneumatic tyre and avoid those stylish, plastic toy models because they will soon break. A good wheelbarrow makes moving heavy objects light work, a bad one makes it tedious or difficult and even painful.

A remarkably common problem with many gardeners is blisters and calluses; the answer is to wear gloves! Gloves may keep the dirt off and possibly stop thorns, but their main function is to reduce damage to tender skin, so wear a pair for long or heavy work. Especially useful are those cleverly designed ones, known in the UK as brickies' gloves, which are made of stretchy cloth covered in a soft plastic web; these give even the weakest hand a stronger grip and make work much pleasanter and easier. Rubber gloves are excellent and stop stinging nettles hurting you when weeding, but not thorns. For pruning thorny plants, invest in a pair of long, leather gauntlets – and don't forget the goggles.

Nearly the same age as me, we're both easier to push around if kept well oiled.

if you have to have a lawn then you need a mower, preferably a green one – unfortunately that's probably a sheep

Such a a snailery has to be home-made.

### the real hardware

If you have to have a lawn then you need a mower, preferably a green one – unfortunately that's probably a sheep. Ideally and more safely for the survival of the rest of your garden, you can have rabbits or guinea pigs in wire cages that are moved daily (really, it is being done!). There are also countless hens in mobile arks cropping lawns. Sadly, the majority of gardeners seem to want to gaze upon an empty, green desert and are prepared to put a lot of time, effort and expense into making one. Your choice, although have you considered a wide, shallow pool instead? It is perfectly flat and green all summer and it will never need cutting.

Anyway, if you are into exercise there are push mowers available, but unless the sward is already excellent and the mower is used frequently, a push mower will simply not work (if you are a Hercules, go ahead). For most gardens, the mower must therefore be electric or petrol-driven. Obviously, the former is more

suited to a smaller lawn that is close to the house or to another, safe source of power. It is essential to have all the safety devices possible for an electric mower. Also, get a more powerful model than you think you need, for all but the most tokenised patch – in general electric mowers tend to be underpowered and a bigger model will last longer and be better when conditions are tough. Go for one with wheels and a roller, and preferably one that collects the clippings since these can be useful elsewhere. Leaving clippings on the sward regularly leads to problems.

### big boys' toys

With larger areas, the petrol-powered mower is almost obligatory, but does not have to be a huge machine or ride-on tractor unless you really do have an estate. Those toys consume a lot of energy for a simple task that could be done more peacefully by a much smaller machine. The smaller mower will do the job without hurting your wallet, your back or

compacting your soil. Beware of salesmen; they will always try to sell you a bigger machine. They also won't like you buying an inexpensive rotary mower (the speed of the rotating blade tears off the ends of the grass leaves) when you could get one with a cylinder (rotating, curved blades slice off the grass against a fixed blade, just like scissors) that is more suited to maintaining a bowling green than a domestic lawn. Similarly, if you go for a hedge trimmer, you may end up being sold something powerful enough to double as a chainsaw.

Gardening ought to be pleasant, light work, unless you are doing it for a living. Only then is it worth getting powerful machines to do the job quickly. A huge, petrol-driven hedge trimmer will finish the job faster, but you will be more tired than if you had taken twice the time and done it with shears. (Also, with shears you can pause and chat to neighbours and passers-by, whereas they are unlikely to want to stop if you look busy with a noisy, dangerous machine.)

Similarly, an electric shredder to chew up compost material is a noisy, dangerous aberration. By the time you have finished, you will have consumed kilowatts of electricity in turning stuff that would have composted anyway into smaller pieces. Why bother? Compost the soft stuff, which needs no shredding; put the dry and twiggy stuff underneath a compost heap to rot down slowly; and if it is really solid and woody, save it for a celebratory bonfire, a wildlife pile or for a friend with a wood stove.

### collecting water

Water is crucial to gardening and it's important to have a sufficient supply. Water from the tap

This artificial pond and 'log wall' fosters numerous predators to patrol the garden nearby.

is for household use and is often too cold and full of salts to be the first choice for watering the garden. It has its uses, but most of us need to save and store whatever rain we can. This means investing in better guttering and more water butts. One or two butts will not suffice; you need a whole bank of them connected together to store enough water for the average garden. Do try and save every drop that falls on any roof, including the greenhouse and even the dog kennel. Common errors to avoid are setting water butts so low that you can't get a watering can under the spout, or having butts with tops too narrow to get the watering can in.

More worrying are water butts without an overflow. Ideally, overflow water would top up another butt. However, at some place it needs to run off during heavy downpours. This run-off must be to a drain, ditch, pond or soakaway and certainly must be taken well away from the house and other buildings. Never ever allow a butt to lean on a wall; the lowest side will overflow and make the wall deteriorate rapidly.

To avoid mosquito and gnat larvae breeding in butts and stagnant pools, float some vegetable oil on the surface – this suffocates them and won't hurt most plants if it gets mixed into their irrigation water. Alternatively, keep goldfish: they do a really good job and add fish fertiliser to the water for free. A nylon stocking on the end of every downpipe will stop too much detritus going in the butt, which ought to have a lid to exclude blown leaves – and of course animals, birds and kids.

You can almost feel it catching your legs as you go by...

## path pros and cons

Paths are another feature likely to trip up the unwary gardener, literally and metaphorically. Good paths, wide enough for two to walk side by side or one person pushing a heavily laden wheelbarrow, are essential. Paths that are narrow, awkward or slippery will slow down your work and be irksome. Concrete, either poured or as slabs, is excellent if roughly surfaced; gravel is much cheaper; either is far better than grass. Grass paths are fine in the dry where there is no heavy traffic, but soon turn to mud and become dangerous. If a grass path must be kept but wears bald, replace the middle with a row of slabs to give a more solid footing. Square slabs may be placed corner to corner to give an economic but still continuous run for the wheelbarrow; this is better than setting the slabs square with gaps between.

In between trees or shrubby borders, you could use paths of chipped bark or a similar material; these are fairly dry and slip-proof but, like gravel, can be hard work to push a heavy wheelbarrow over. Never place vigorous plants next to paths because they will soon flop over and get in the way and be unpleasant when wet. However, small plants flopping over path edges do soften them and may be allowed – as long as they are trimmed whenever they start to spread and before they trip you up.

Be careful too of paths under trees; if wet leaves build up on them, they can be as slippery as ice. Frost makes wet paths into death traps – a simple way to avoid problems, and medical bills, is to scatter sharp sand on top. This gives a secure footing and also tends to help wear away algal and mossy growths from the surface, which although pretty do make the path slippery. In among

Again – it's pretty, but a pretty unusable path after rain – and you can't walk side by side.

sell more of them. The longer-lived of them soon become seen almost everywhere. Thus our gardens are often full of good plants, which we tend to be a bit snobbish about. Do not spurn the commonplace – this just indicates the plant's vigour and virtue. Grow what already does really well in your neighbourhood, but give each plant more space and better conditions and you will rarely ever have many serious problems. Look carefully at neglected gardens; look at what is doing fantastically well with no attention at all and note its soil and position – this is what it really likes. When you see any plant doing phenomenally well, especially if there are several in an area, make a note of the local conditions. This sort of observation will enable you to choose and place your plants in appropriate situations.

## basic plant needs

Of course there are idiosyncratic plants, with strong preferences such as the legendary lime-hating calcifuges, or ericaceous plants. All plants have a preference for a particular balance of acid or alkaline (soil pH) in their soil. The calcifuges particularly resent lime and alkaline conditions; other plants, such as most vegetables, prefer lime and alkaline soils and do badly in acid conditions. If you are not aware of a particular plant's needs, check the label, which may carry a warning, but double check by always looking up the requirements of unfamiliar plants in a reference book. See whether they like acid or alkaline soil, sun or shade, wet or dry conditions – follow these indications and you are almost guaranteed success. Ignore such basic preferences and, although they may survive, the plants are unlikely to thrive.

larger beds and borders, where there is no room for a path, it is worth placing stepping-stones so that you can gain access without treading on the soil and compacting it. Stepping-stones also act as mulches, keeping the soil beneath cooler and moister and preventing weeds from coming up.

## right plant in the right place

Plant problems come from the choice of plants as much as anything else. Fashion, economics and chance result in many plants being put in the wrong place. Plants in the right situation flourish; in the wrong position, they sulk and get attacked by pests and diseases. It takes several years of living with a garden to understand how each has special spots that favour this or that plant. Even with house-

plants, you soon appreciate how each may suit a different windowsill. So read the labels (although it is not always easy to interpret instructions on a label), check in a book and observe what already does well where in your garden, to avoid a lot of problems later.

It's important, when planning, to spend as much time on the choice of plants as on the shape and form of a garden. Obviously some problems start when you are a novice and we all learn by mistakes. Later, different challenges occur. As we try more unusual plants, some will fail more frequently than the tried-and-tested ones.

Fortunately the commonest plants on offer are generally also among the most reliably successful plants. We buy more of what succeeds for us and nurserymen naturally

# essential gardening skills

Once upon a time even I didn't know when to gather a globe artichoke.

## tending what's already there

The first requirement for an easy life of problem-free gardening is to acquire the basic skills needed to look after an existing garden. After all, that is the way most of us start; we move into a new home and take on a garden that is either neatly maintained or, more challengingly, abandoned and overgrown. In most cases, no more is required than mowing grass, watering, weeding, tidying and cutting back but, the closer to a jungle it has become, the harder work is needed to restore a garden. Tending such a garden is mostly a matter of common sense, and easier than looking after a pet – and you have most of the skills already.

## improving the garden

There are not many more skills needed for improving what's already there, by making sensible design and functional changes. Indeed any fool can make a rushed makeover of a garden look good. It takes a bit longer to create a garden to the point where it's beautiful every day of the year without it becoming too much work. But gradual re-planning and replanting can slowly work over a plot into a superb garden in a few seasons. This longer process of improving a garden is not necessarily a total makeover, but a slow campaign to make it your own paradise. This sort of improvement takes place more effectively if you make notes of little jobs to do at another date as soon as they have been spotted. Sketches and plans of beds and borders, lawns and paths, real and projected, all help to reduce both the actual work and unforeseen problems later. After all, as my carpenter friend said, 'Think it out thrice'; the more we plan on paper, the less sweat, blood and tears we have to expend.

You can teach an old dog new tricks but my cat is very dubious.

# gardening skills

How to avoid the commonest pitfalls ● What you need to know, what to do and, more importantly, what not to do ● Looking after plants outdoors and in pots indoors ● Watering, feeding, general weeding, mulching ● Tidying, deadheading and trimming, ties and supports ● Hospitalisation-free grass cutting ● Compost, wormeries and snaileries ● Choosing, buying and positioning plants ● Plants that are really weeds ● Whether to move plants, moving turf

● Potting on plants as they grow ● Planting and transplanting, from young plants to trees
● Sowing seed successfully ● Mistakes to avoid with propagators, frames and greenhouses
● Weeding more effectively ● Pruning – how not to cut the wrong bits off ● Plant propagation
that works: division, taking cuttings, layering and saving seed

# what you need to know

Thinning fruits leaves the best to get bigger.

## what to do and not to do

As I just said, much of 'all the gardening knowledge and skill you need' for any task is made up of three parts: knowing what to do, knowing when to do it, and knowing what sort of thing not to do. This last element is always going to be difficult to give advice about, since as well as the many errors I have committed myself, heard of or witnessed, there is undoubtedly a herd of other possibilities.

As a general rule, don't do anything unusual or wildly hopeful. For several years I threw every spare packet of seed, both flowers and vegetables, onto one bed that was initially clean and then left it to itself. In a few years, there was almost nothing but stinging nettles. Do not expect to establish a beautiful flower, or even wildflower, garden merely by scattering seeds. Simply expecting plants to survive, and maybe prosper, is reasonable if the conditions are suitable for the plants, and nothing else is trying to survive there. But you must remember that all plants compete for light and water and all except a very rare few need a soil-like material around their roots. Some need sun, some like or need some shade, a few like drought, even fewer prefer waterlogging and many die or become dormant in cold. Each plant has a particular set of preferences and very few tolerate very extreme conditions.

If most of the plants in your garden are reasonably happy, things can't be too bad. Don't be alarmed by the odd problem if everything else looks fine. In fact, given a period of slow adjustment, plants can perform well in quite a wide range or in less-than-perfect conditions – as long as these don't alter suddenly. In other words, 'if your garden isn't broken don't fix it'. Just keep on with the same treatment.

## plants indoors and outdoors

The main difference between indoors and outdoors is that plants have to endure neglect indoors whereas outdoors they may suffer more from well-meaning but inappropriate attention. Plants grown under cover and in containers are subject to our whims and need diligent care to be at their best. Not only do they need us to provide water, food and ventilation for them, but they also require a suitable medium

Stones make great mulches and suit some plants.

to grow in. The soil outside may not be perfect, but there is an awful lot of it, whereas the amount of compost in a pot is relatively tiny and the roots cannot travel elsewhere. Outdoors, the annoying fact is that, except in times of drought, plants generally do well without us, provided that they have been planted in a reasonable site and are already established.

## composts

The most important rule for growing any plant in a pot, cell or container is not to economise on the compost. Use the best, freshest composts you can every time; avoid any that are cheap, remaindered or damaged since they are likely to have gone off or be too wet. Choose sowing composts for seeds, potting formulations for bigger plants. Avoid multipurpose, cheap or homemade composts (unless you are experienced in mixing your own) and do not ever use garden soil, molehill soil, muck or anything else that is handy. Do not re-use compost in planters and hanging baskets and so on. I repeat: one of the commonest and most foolish mistakes is to 'economise' with the compost that you put around your plants' roots. Remember that some plants such as orchids need special composts, and of course lime-hating plants like heathers and azaleas need lime-free or ericaceous compost.

# doing the basics

Use a rose to sprinkle, not jet, water if you want to wet compost or little plants.

## watering

Watering is probably the most crucial thing we do for our plants, especially those under cover and in containers. Plants in the open ground can at least hope for some rain, and soil moisture is available during much of the year for established plants, although it may be inaccessible to younger plants with undeveloped root systems.

### watering outdoor plants

The general rule for plants in the ground is that you will rarely hurt them by overwatering. There are a few plants that resent wet roots, but during the growing season excess watering will do little harm even to most of these because the surplus can drain away. However, having soggy, wet roots in winter can harm many more plants. More tender plants also survive much better through cold periods if their roots are relatively dry. The commonest mistake outdoors is watering too little too often: this just wets the topmost soil, evaporates away and in doing so makes the soil temperature drop, encourages moulds and mildews and is possibly as bad as no water at all. Better then to water plants by soaking the soil thoroughly but less often. This can be done with a watering can or hosepipe but to achieve a thorough soaking, water into shallow trenches and depressions alongside the plants or into half-buried funnels made from plastic bottles.

Drip irrigation and seep hoses are other possibilities, although expensive in cost and time to set up, adjust and check. Investing in these is often pointless because they do not suit the amateur as much as the large-scale, professional grower. Also plants need more or less water depending on the stages of growth,

Stand thirsty plants in trays to water them.

Pour water into a hole beside the roots.

weather and so on, and any mechanical system tends to deliver the same amount of water continually, whereas the gardener can adjust the watering to each plant's current needs. (True, we do guess a lot, but you know what I mean.) Sprinkling may suit a lawn, but for most plants wetting the leaves is usually a mistake and also poor value because much of the water evaporates and – worse – definitely encourages moulds and mildews if the roots are still dry.

## watering appropriately

When we water, we generally tend to water too little; more water would usually give better results in most regions – obviously not in naturally wet areas. We may also water indiscriminately, which is a serious error. New plants need plenty of water until their root systems establish; this would be for the whole of their first growing season. Similarly, little plants, especially wee seedlings, suffer

most when the top soil layer dries out. Plants with big, lush leaves tend to need much more water than wiry, small-leafed plants, while silver-foliaged and downy plants usually detest excess water and often thrive in drier conditions. Watering all plants in the same way does not give good results. Therefore we usually divide plants up and put them in different areas, such as the herb bed and salad bed, depending in the main on their requirements for water.

## watering pots and under cover

Watering has to be even more systematic for pots and plants under cover. In general, we probably kill plants mostly by overwatering in winter and underwatering in summer. Plants under cover do not use much water in the low light of winter, although dry air can cause them and their compost to dry out. Because the roots are not working hard in winter, they are easier to drown and great care should be

taken not to waterlog the compost, particularly for seeds and seedlings in late winter and early spring. In the hotter, drier air of summer, plants need much more water.

Ironically, the signs of both drying out and waterlogging are similar: the plant looks dull and limp. And do not assume that because the surface looks wet that the roots are! Often a dried-out rootball will not soak up water and, if you water it from the top, all you achieve is to rot the neck. Always water into a saucer, allow the water to be sucked up by the compost, then empty out any remaining water. In good growing weather, fill up the saucers, return a quarter or a half hour later and refill any empty ones, then come back within the hour to empty them all. (Although some very thirsty plants such as tomatoes could be left with water in their saucers, it is safest never to leave plants in such a state.) Of course, using warm water is better than chilling the plants with cold.

Two are better than one.

## using rainwater

It is also a good idea to use rainwater whenever possible because the salts that are dissolved in tap water will build up in the compost. Bring filled watering cans indoors the night before watering, so they have time to warm up. Avoid wetting little seedlings, especially early in the year, with stale, dirty rainwater: it can cause damping-off disease, where the seedlings simply wither away, so use sterile, warm tap or even bottled water. Do not however use fizzy or carbonated water: although the carbon-dioxide bubbles would benefit the plants' leaves, they would asphyxiate the roots, which breathe oxygen.

## when to water

As for the centuries' old argument 'do you water morning or evening?' – either is better than not at all. Plants get used to a watering regime and may tolerate less than perfect conditions if these do not vary much, but will surely suffer and expire in conditions that are poor and randomly variable. Try to get a regular routine going so that the plants can adapt. If you water often and in quantity in some weeks and barely at all in others, plants will soon bolt or die. Personally I prefer watering morning and evening and even in the heat of the day if the plants need it.

A big one outside keeps a small butt inside full, saving me carrying the water about.

## waterlogging

The outdoor problem of waterlogging, or even flooding, may be resolved with draining and soakaways and is essential since few plants cope with waterlogging for long. Raised beds can give some relief. Temporary waterlogging, especially of new plants in heavy clay soils, is a common cause of failure. Improving the humus and grit content of soils helps to alleviate it.

## general feeding

Fertilisers and plant foods may often cause more problems than they cure, whether in pots or outdoors. I knew a man who had a special formulation for almost everything, but his crops never did particularly well compared to those of his neighbour, who used nothing but muck and water. The really important factors that make plants grow are light, water and air; after that the improvement gained by adding fertiliser to the soil or compost is almost irrelevant. However, some feed is still essential when growing plants long-term in pots and containers. After a few weeks or months in a pot, tub or even barrel of compost, no matter how good it was, most plants will run out of some nutrient and give a less than adequate performance.

To feed potted plants, we can add fairly large amounts of slow-release fertilisers as top dressings, but these soon use up all available space. We can add much smaller amounts as liquid feeds in every watering and this regime suits pot plants well. Remember it should be little and often – a cupful in a watering can, no more. I use a mixture of comfrey, borage, stinging nettle, urine, seaweed and fish emulsion, rotted down together and then very well diluted.

### feed less rather than more

While farmers and market gardeners need to get the maximum return to every bit of ground, the amateur does not. Of course we want good crops and beautiful flowers, but these are improved less by adding fertiliser and more by better watering and tending. Most garden soils are fertile enough for the majority of plants and will be more so if they are kept moist, mulched and well weeded. Additional fertiliser will often just make the plants overly lush and more prone to drought, pests and diseases.

That does not mean we cannot use fertiliser sensibly for some plants and situations. Some crops and flowers are known to be hungry for certain nutrients and adding such elements,

Adding some top dressing to a big plant that can't be repotted easily.

It's easier to add feed little and often with water.

Any organic mulch not only suppresses weeds and keeps moisture in, but turns into fertility.

Wood ashes are fantastic for fruit trees.

in moderation, is worthwhile. However, overdo it and the plants may suffer from the excess, even dying as a result – just like us and alcohol; a little improves things, excess does the opposite. This is why fertiliser, and especially homemade fertiliser 'potions' such as mine, are inherently risky; it may be too strong and burn the roots, along with disrupting all the micro-life in the soil and ending up in our drinking water.

Soluble fertilisers, usually whitish crystals, are the most hazardous. Most of these are not permitted under organic standards; however, if they are highly diluted in water they become relatively innocuous. Most powdered and pelleted fertilisers may be added to the

soil but are best if they are first incorporated into a compost heap, as are all manures and other wastes – they make the compost 'cook' better and once mixed in together, the fertilisers become less fierce and nicer for the plants. It's a bit like making a cake; it's more pleasant and digestible than the flour, fat, eggs and sugar were individually and tastes better the more ingredients you add in.

## sources of plant nutrients
If your plants require extra nitrogen, then dried blood, blood, fish and bone meal, pelleted composted manures and all animal manures, worm casts, urine, feathers, and fresh green borage, comfrey, stinging nettles and grass

worm casts, urine, feathers, and fresh green borage, comfrey, stinging nettles and grass clippings are all good sources of nitrogen

Claytonia, one of the best green manures and very tasty.

clippings are all good sources. All plants crave nitrogen, like we crave sex or cream cakes or whatever, but keep the plants lean and trim with just enough to keep them strong and not a drop more. Extra potassium or potash to make them more resistant to diseases and to taste better is best added as wood ashes, although seaweed solution has some too; comfrey and borage leaves are rich sources of potassium and especially useful as teas.

Extra phosphorus or phosphate is produced from old bones, which you bake on a bonfire, then pound to a dust or just keep passing through compost heaps until they break down. (Cooked bones take longer than raw ones, which disintegrate very quickly.) You can also get a ground, mineral, rock phosphate, which is very slow acting but effective. Datura weeds accumulate phosphate to high levels and can be gathered, composted and fed back into the soil.

Calcium is found in lime or chalk and is important for keeping the soil and compost heap sweet, and suited to vegetables especially, but of course lime-haters such as heathers and azaleas detest it in their soil. Dolomitic limestone is often the sort of lime dressing used in the garden because it provides both calcium and magnesium. Magnesium is also found in quite high levels in borage leaves, along with potassium and other nutrients, so borage makes, like comfrey, a useful tea. The leaves rot to a thick, glutinous paste, which dilutes down to a smelly, yellow feed that appears remarkably similar to stale urine and is loved by tomatoes even more than comfrey tea.

Seaweed solution contains most trace elements and may be added to other liquid feeds or well diluted and watered or sprayed on as a foliar feed. It seems to encourage healthy growth and discourage pests and diseases. But remember, in the ground there is little to beat adding well-rotted manures and garden compost – except that is for green manures.

### green manures

These are plants sown in empty ground to be used as compost material or dug in where they grow. This is a way of growing your own soil fertiliser and works well, with a couple of minor glitches. Firstly, the usual green manures offered – clover (*Trifolium*), grazing rye (*Secale cereale*), tares (*Vicia sativa*), vetches (*Lathyrus vernus*) and so on – are all pernicious weeds that are hard to eradicate and more suited to a farmer with a tractor and plough. They are hard to dig under and often spring back up.

Choose instead from these softer crops, which are easier to pull or kill: beans, peas, mustard (*Sinapsis alba*), *Phacelia tanacetifolia*, poached egg plant (*Limnanthes douglasii*), borage (*Borago officinale*), miner's lettuce (*Claytonia perfoliata*) and corn salad (*Valerianella locusta*). The last two are also handy winter salads and chicken fodder.

Secondly, if you dig under a green manure, allow at least a month or two for it to rot before you plant or sow, otherwise you may experience problems. It is better to incorporate it *in situ* and cover it with a plastic sheet, which is quicker, or pull the plants and compost them elsewhere – the roots that are left are unlikely to regrow. Unless you want seed, it is a mistake to let green manures go to flower, or worse, seed; it's also better to grow several, short-term green-manure crops than one long-term one.

## general weeding

Any bare soil will become weedy. Fill the ground with other plants and there is no space for weeds. Green manures work well, but in some ways native weeds that rush to cover the ground are as good – *if* they are dug under or hoed off and composted and never allowed to establish, flower and seed. Plants grown to fill the ground permanently, called ground cover, must be evergreen or so vigorous that they swamp all else. Do not make the mistake of planting roses or other thorny subjects as ground cover if there is much likelihood of either weeds or litter, since these are both difficult to extricate.

It makes sense to cover as much ground as possible with mulches. These not only look nice, save water and add fertility, but they suppress weeds. Few weeds come from seed up through thick mulches. Weeds that grow from perennial roots may get through and

*must* be eradicated first; it is a serious error to leave any alive. Even if ground-cover fabric is laid under the mulch to suppress weeds, the creeping, rooted weeds must be dealt with before they spread. Several layers of newspaper laid under mulches improve their effectiveness in suppressing weeds, but will not stop the most pernicious ones such as bindweed or stinging nettles.

### weeding techniques

Without doubt, the most effective weeding among growing plants is done by hand, using a sharp knife to slice through roots and a pail or bowl to collect the bodies for the compost heap. However, where there is bare soil that cannot be mulched, hoeing it regularly will ensure that it never gets weedy. Hoeing an area once weekly kills weeds before they are big enough to be noticeable and also liberates the nutrients locked up in their seeds for our

plants. It is a big mistake to weed but seldom because the weeds then have big roots and resprout, whereas weeding little and often keeps them under control.

An oversight too often made is with the hoe; it ought to be light, strong, with a long handle and, crucially, a thin and very sharp blade. I sharpen mine before I commence hoeing and then again every ten minutes or so with a stone that I keep in my pocket. Little weeds can be left to wither; bigger ones must be raked and composted. Weeds with seed heads and those pernicious ones with fleshy roots are best drowned under water for a month or more before they and their slurry can be safely added to the compost heap. Do not assume that weed seeds falling on mulches or even lawns will not germinate – not true, all seedling weeds, and garden plants, should be deadheaded and never allowed to seed anywhere, especially not onto mulches, soil or gravel paths.

Daisy grubbers get other tap rooted weeds.

Most valuable tool – the sharpening stone for my hoe.

# keeping a garden at its best

### hide the clutter

Tidying – getting rid of all the little eyesores, the toys and tools lying around, empty pots and so on – is a vital task. It helps to have plenty of storage space just to hide all the detritus we accumulate. If you don't have a shed, an old caravan is a remarkably cheap alternative and needs no erecting, but is a bit of an eyesore in itself.

### deadheading and trimming

Along with tidying goes the task of cutting off all the blooms that have finished so that the plants do not waste energy on producing seeds. You can deadhead by cutting just below the flower, but with most plants, it's better to cut a bit lower down the stem because this more often encourages new flowers. Now although neatness and perfection are nice, sometimes time is short; in practice most deadheading – and quite a bit of pruning – may be done with a pair of shears. The majority of perennials will cope with a light haircut after flowering

**Getting rid of the old encourages the new.**

and this is one way of keeping them both floriferous and compact. It is not the best, but it works in the majority of cases. Do put down a sheet to catch the trimmings; it's easier than raking them up afterwards.

### ties and supports

These are often overlooked and should be attended to when tidying. Supports give untold trouble and often look unsightly into the bargain. The idea is to hold a branch in position against its will in order to 'train' it; to support a heavy crop; or to stop the trunk of a newly planted shrub or tree moving in the wind so that its roots can establish.

A tie is meant to provide a firm but flexible grip, not a stranglehold. Too loose and it will move and rub, too tight and it will choke. Thus ties need to be both adjustable and adjusted over the years. A professional tree tie comes with a spacer to place between the limb or trunk and the support, such as a tree stake: this helps the tie to keep a firm grip

and stops the support and trunk from coming into contact and rubbing. An old pair of nylons or a bicycle tube makes an acceptable tie, but wire (plastic-covered or not), thin plastic string and so on do not.

If a tree has grown large enough to support the stake rather than be supported by it, take the stake and tie away. If it is a weak tree or poor graft, replace a single stake with two uprights driven in well away from the trunk, which you then support against a cross bar; this is more effective than a single stake for supporting heavy crops or top-heavy trees.

### setting up supports

When tying in plants to wires or metal rails, it is best to first fix canes to the wires and then to tie the plants to them. Metal can get very hot in summer and freeze in winter, damaging plant tissues that are in contact with it. If fixing supports against a wall, do not make the gap too small to allow air to circulate – although if the gap is bigger than about a hand width, almost all the benefit (of warmth) from the wall will be lost. For strings to support plants such as tomatoes, it is best to use natural-fibre ones that can be cut off to go to compost with the haulm, taking any pests and diseases with them. Using plastic twine will invariably occasion reuse and re-infestation on a grand scale; I know, I've done it – little is better for overwintering red spider mite, mealy bug, aphids and diseases by the million than the recycled farm-binder twine which I use all the time.

Taller, herbaceous plants often need support and there is little better than short canes, stuck in a ring and connected with twine. If it is done early enough in the season, the plants will grow through and conceal their supports. Top the canes with plastic caps (old bottle tops will do) to prevent you from poking out your eyes when tending the plants, and to stop water getting into and rotting the canes.

# ties and supports

**1** **A standard tree tie** in soft plastic does an excellent job.

**2** **A clothes peg** can be quite handy if used without crushing the stem.

**3** **String** is fine for loosely tying things but must never be made tight.

# raspberries can be treated in different ways

**1** Wound down to one strong wire.

**2** Tied loosely together, here with an old bicycle tube.

**3** Or wound in around a vertical support.

# tending your sward

Mow often and mow early.

## the best mower for the job

Most difficulties with lawn mowing come from having the wrong or an underpowered mower and consequently having to get too vigorous with it. The minority of people who have cylinder mowers can do the neatest job because these machines cut precisely. However, the downside is that the grass must be cut at least weekly, sometimes more often, and must be fairly flat and stone- free, like a bowling green. Most people now use rotary-bladed mowers. These do a rougher job, but cope with much worse conditions and are not ruined by a minor scuffle with a molehill.

## hospitalisation-free mowing

Whereas getting it wrong with most garden tasks may result in the odd bruise or scratch, getting it wrong with a lawnmower is likely to result in serious injury and involuntary amputation. Think safety. Do not put any bit of you near moving blades or engines and if using electricity beware the extra hazards. If you do choke up your mower, do not clear the blockage until you have disabled it by disconnecting either the electric or the spark plug lead. Blood and bits of flesh are good for fertility, but will attract vermin and are best retained by the owner!

Likewise, never walk in front of a mower that has the engine running; be careful also behind the machine and at the sides since small stones may be picked up and flung out. Be sensible: wear safe clothes, boots and goggles, and don't expose yourself, especially your eyes, to the ejection zone. Be even more careful when using a nylon line trimmer because this can fling objects violently some distance. (I know, I've damaged some of my windows.) So always keep pets and children well away, otherwise they may rush in and get hurt before you can stop them.

## when to mow

It really helps to cut grass regularly but lightly almost every month of the year, otherwise tussock-forming, weedy

Don't throw away your grass clippings, use them as a mulch, very good amongst raspberries.

grasses and some weeds may get a hold. But do not cut when frost is about. Most people don't cut in winter and start again in early spring. However, many leave it too late when they do that first cut, with poor results. Underneath the overgrown top, the grass will be yellow and dead and the mown lawn will then look scalped and bald for weeks. Cut early and cut often. Cut high initially in spring and slowly reduce the height of the cut until early summer when the grass is growing fastest. From early summer, start to cut higher again to allow the grass a deeper pile, which will stay greener in the heat of summer. You may cut it shorter again in early autumn but then, as the leaves fall, let the height of cut rise so that the pile is at its deepest in winter.

## cutting long grass

Sometimes, say the first dry day after three weeks of rain in early summer, you have to cut grass up to your knees. In such tough cases, it is not the cutting ability of the mower that is stretched but its throughput. It will choke up with all the cut grass. Leave the box off so the grass will blow through more easily. Once you've cut it all, don't rake up the clippings straightaway – leave them a day or so to wither and it will be much easier. Alternatively, the clippings can be more easily picked up after withering with another cut.

When first cutting overlong grass, set the mower as high as possible and cut the grass off in narrow strips, never cutting with the full width of the mower. A half-width cut will allow more airflow to carry the clippings through, whereas a full-width cut would just choke the mower. After cutting very long grass, give it a day or two to recover after raking up the mowings and then cut it again, this time moving crossways to the first mowing, but still set as high. After another few days, cut once again, this time with the height lowered somewhat and the box on – you should now be back in control. (If the grass, or rather weeds, are head-high, hire a professional with a nylon-line trimmer or even a flail mower for that first cut.)

## using grass clippings

Do not return the clippings to the lawn because this makes a thatch and wastes material, although returning the odd cut will feed the worms. I often leave the box off for a few of the first and last mowings, since the shredded leaves are so good for the worms. But I collect most of the autumn leaves for leaf mould – once well shredded by the mower and mixed with grass clippings, the mixture rots down in bags within a year or so into a superb material for adding to potting composts (I improve most bought-in potting compost by adding up to a fifth of well-made leaf mould). Never wastefully burn leaves that fall on grass, although they must be cleared or they will kill off the grass through lack of light. And never dump grass clippings – use them in thin layers each time as mulches around trees, soft fruit, shrubs, roses and potatoes where they will do the power of good.

# tending your sward - the perfect finish

Sward can look good from a distance, even if not close up.

### achieving a perfect finish

This is a minor problem for some. Well, cutting too close does not do it: that lets in too many weeds, handicaps the grass and is a serious error. A slightly deeper sward will stay greener and stronger. Equally it will be better if the species of grass is a strong sort suited to the conditions, so over-sow in autumn and spring with suitable grass seed. Do it just before mowing with the box off to help get the seeds into gaps in the turf. Regular cutting is crucial, as is rolling; you don't need a separate roller, just a mower with a roller and make extra cuts with it set at the same height. Infilling hollows and lowering humps are worth it if you are fastidious. Simply pare back the turf in autumn or early spring, add or subtract soil until it is level, replace and firm the turf, and water until it re-establishes. It's no more difficult than that.

Feeding your lawn is not so important as many think, although it's a good way of recycling urine – this is usually sterile; if not, see your doctor! – and rarely gives any odour or hygiene problem if well diluted and watered on turf in the evening since it will be absorbed by morning. Grass loves urine (diluted) and grows emerald green, yielding more clippings to be used as fertility-enhancing mulches. But don't tell the neighbours.

Otherwise, apply organic, slow-release lawn fertilisers or liquid feeds that are well diluted when watering. Spread lime every winter to discourage most mosses and acid-loving weeds, such as buttercups, speedwell and veronicas, except on fine, acid-loving, bowling-green grasses, or if you grow ericaceous plants. Add clover to get a greener sward for free: clover is leguminous, so fixes nitrogen in the soil and feeds the grass. And just keep cutting, cutting, cutting.

### don't forget the edges

Edges maketh a lawn. Neat edges are as necessary as a shave to a well-dressed man. But do not use a half-moon edger or ever pare away at them; in a few years, you will have nothing left. Use a pair of old shears, or the specially offset ones, and trim the edges by hand. You can do it somewhat dangerously with a nylon-line trimmer; this is fast but risks every window in the vicinity. (I've racked up three house and two car windows and a door panel so far.) Setting silly little plastic or aluminium edging is tedious, looks tacky and it invariably degrades while providing hiding places for numerous pests. Wood edges rot, but at least look decent. Stones, bottles, bricks and tile edgings are insane – they create work by providing hiding places for pests and crevices for weeds.

Do plan to maintain the minimum length of edging: amalgamate beds and borders, use curves instead of square corners and eliminate small paths of turf with stepping stones. The less edging, the better! Rake up all the trimmed off edges – there will almost certainly be some rooted bits among the clippings and you don't want them to establish. These small bits are handy for patching damage, for instance where dandelions have been pulled.

### if you want stripes...

It helps to have a mower with a roller, although all mowers create slight striping if driven in alternate directions. To make the neatest job, go around the edges and odd paths first, leaving the main areas until last. Then cut the longest way up and down to make stripes. Whenever possible, mow in other directions (crosswise and at an angle), week by week, to give a better overall finish. If you want a really neat finish, use a rotary mower for all the brute work but get a fine, old-fashioned cylinder mower for the finishing cut in the most important areas.

Unless you have a large area to maintain, would it not really be better to have that flat, green pool or a bark or gravel garden? Or how about a meadow garden with long grass to lie on during hot summer days? Go on, you know you'd love to give up all that mowing; think of saving the space where the mower lives, all those peaceful days without panicking to cut the grass before the rain comes!

# making garden compost

Looks good enough to eat.

## what is compost?

More questions get asked about this than any other gardening topic. One problem is that we are often talking about different things. John Innes loam-based sowing and potting composts are specialised, sterile mixtures made up for those specific purposes. Other bagged composts, which are called anything from ericaceous (for lime-haters) and multipurpose to peat-free and orchid compost, are all types of potting mixtures. All of these are best bought fresh from fast-moving stacks since they go off with age and become problematic. Garden compost is completely different; it is the rotted-down remains of last year's surplus and wastes usually combined with kitchen waste in a compost bin (not a heap). The idea is to rot everything together to get a soil-like, humus-rich additive to your soil that can take the place of bought-in manures. The bad news is that it sometimes goes wrong; the good news is that this may be corrected with only exercise or a long waiting time.

## speeding up the rot

In a compost bin, the warm, damp conditions and mixture of materials allow a multitude of microbes to accelerate the slow rot of time. The temperature can become as hot as an oven in a well-mixed heap of different materials that are moist and insulated. In a well-made bin, the heat can be extreme but usually subsides after a fortnight or so. A bin may be left to mature for about ten months or turned to save time and improve the product. If the bin is emptied, mixed and refilled (or moved to another bin), turning the inside to the outside and vice versa and kept just moist, it will re-cook and then subside and mature in only a few months.

## sieving compost

1 Chopping the compost in the matured heap.

2 Moving chopped compost, sieve fitted on top of wheelbarrow.

3 Pushing composted material through sieve.

4 Detritus – stones, plastic, glass – to be binned. Roots etc. for next heap.

Unfortunately we mostly have materials to add to the bin in small amounts, and by the time it is full all the lower wastes have degraded too far already to cook the top. Sure, it will eventually compost, but very slowly and not awfully well – good enough to put under runner beans, but not a pleasant thing to handle. Most bins are also too small and lose any heat before enough compost is made. The answer is firstly to have a bigger bin. Secondly, continue adding materials a little at a time and cover each batch with a sprinkling of earth (or preferably some compost from a previous heap, or wetted sawdust or wood ashes). Too much or too little soil will slow it down; just a sprinkling is needed on each layer, as an inoculation of micro-organisms.

### turning the compost

When the bin is full, acquire as much fresh, green material as possible, such as grass clippings and stinging nettles. Empty out the bin onto a plastic sheet, mixing it as you go. Then repack the material in the bin – or make a new bin out of pallets of wood or something similar. Fill around the edges first as you go, making sure that the compost is well wetted; be creative – urine, ditch and tank dredgings, rotten wine and sour milk all add fertility. Keep packing until you have a tall stack, and then cover it with a plastic sheet to keep in the steam. Add insulation such as more plastic sheets or old carpet. After a few weeks, mix and restack the compost again, or just leave it to mature. The advantage of turning the heap is that it can be made to cook if it has not already done so, and you don't wait a year to find out. Turning or refilling a bin will always cook the contents.

Anything that has once lived that will rot can go in the compost.

Sieved compost makes an excellent neat mulch.

## what can go in

Not everything will rot, but most things that were once alive will, given time and damp, warm conditions. Thicker, more solid things take longer than the soft and fresh. Some stuff, such as cooked bones or timber, may last for decades, but they break down eventually. However, it helps to leave out logs, as well as inorganic objects like stones and bottles. Meat, oil and cheese attract vermin and are better fed to the birds or pets. Diseased, woody and thorny material may be better burnt and the ashes added instead.

Everything else will rot quicker if broken up and mixed well. Roots such as carrots and fruits like apples have skins that are designed not to rot, so they need chopping to speed their breakdown. Dry stuff such as cotton and woollen clothes, paper and cardboard should be wetted with something disgusting, put in the bin in thin layers, and covered with plenty of fresh, green material and old compost. Pets and road kill will compost readily; green bones compost much quicker than cooked ones and add much value to the compost. However, I can't recommend it unless you are a skilled and practised composter and local by-laws permit.

In the absence of bodies, other activators will enrich a bin and accelerate the break-

The rough stuff – put it back in the next heap.

My home-made snailcatraz composter because snails make manure too.

down, for example blood, fish and bone meal, seaweed meal, urine or any manure such as that of horse, cow, sheep. Poultry manure is especially powerful.

Other things that people worry about but can go on the heap include poisonous plant material such as rhubarb leaves; these pose no problem since the poisons degrade. Soot is okay as long as it's from a clean fire that burned no plastic or painted wood or such material. Wood ashes are wonderful as long as they constitute no more than 10 or 20 per cent! The same is true for leaves or grass clippings. In fact, any one ingredient should not make up too large a percentage for the best compost.

## composting problems

If a bin full of material does not compost, then remaking it and adding more activators should do it. Too wet a compost is usually foul and claggy and obvious, so mix in more dry material. Too dry a compost may be obvious, but mild cases often have a white fungus (called firefang) running through everything that is only partly decayed. Add not only more water but disgusting, smelly stuff with a drop of detergent or washing up liquid in it to help wet the dry stuff and as much urine as you can obtain.

## maturing the compost

This means letting it stand for months. I find it does best if the sides are removed and a lid left on. Then it almost dries to the core, but remains slightly moist. Once it is in this ideal state, I dig it out, recycle the top and sides, and pass the composted middle through a sieve. After sorting out the glass, metal, plastic and stones, the lumpy spoil is put into the next heap as an inoculant. The sieved material is like rich, brown, loamy soil. This can be used as a neat and effective mulch or top dressing anywhere in the garden or mixed in with potting composts and into the soil when planting.

## wormeries and snaileries

For gardeners with very small amounts to compost, a worm composter may be more suitable. This is essentially a large, plastic drum with aeration and drainage holes. You put wastes in (preferably chopped) and little red brandling worms eat them. Every so often, you empty out the worm casts and replace the uneaten fraction and the worms; the casts are excellent as a top dressing for plants in pots or added to potting composts. You also get a liquid draining out, which dilutes to make a liquid feed – and free worms for fishing. Too much stuff overwhelms

the worms, as does anything that is too acid, such as citrus skins; add a light dusting of wood ashes and soil or lime every so often and this will also discourage gnats and flies.

A snail composter also uses an aerated drum, such as a perforated laundry basket, that is equipped with old pots for the snails to hide in, a saucer of water and more waste. The snail casts drop to the bottom and may be removed every so often, to be used like worm casts, or washed out to give a sludgy liquid feed. Snails and worms eat almost everything except bones, which can be burnt on a bonfire, powdered and then composted. Woody stuff may also be burnt.

However, worms and snails can't get through much bulk. Snails eat woody stuff and paper slowly and eat rather fewer things than worms. The two work best together, with the snails as pre-processors before the worms. I've been informed that you can have a combined composter, with worms below and snails above. Hens are even better as pre-processors, having a go at the waste before the snails or worms; they eat seeds and high-value items such as bread crusts, turning them into eggs and manure. They can also eat any surplus snails and worms!

# getting plants for the garden

Herbaceous plants may get wider but they never get taller and so need no pruning to keep them in place.

Hellebores planted in the sunny side will not look as happy as those planted in the moister shadier side.

## choosing and buying

We buy too many plants on impulse. It is far wiser to choose at leisure, bearing in mind your soil, site and local conditions. Three tips: choose smaller, slower-growing forms of shrubs; evergreens (not conifers) for year-round value and shelter; and herbaceous plants, which need no pruning and rarely get too tall. Do not insist on a rare cultivar because it will probably be expensive and short-lived.

Illustrated books and catalogues give some idea, and you could visit good gardens each month or garden centres, where many specimens will display flowers and typical foliage and are well labelled. Once you know what you want, everything else is easy.

We often pay too much at peak times in garden centres, whereas you can get everything by mail order from catalogues and through the Internet. Remember that if you can't see it for real, the colour may never be the same, nor is the scent describable in words. Fruit is an especially personal choice; it is best to taste cultivars first – go to a tasting at an autumn fruit show. If you want something unusual, you could buy it from a stall in an open garden, order it from a garden centre or visit a specialist nursery. Beware of descriptions in advertisements and don't be too disappointed with your blue rose or black tulip, and oh yes, Pharaoh's pea was not!

## positioning plants

Don't leave plants to deteriorate but get them planted straightaway, but after a thorough inspection for pests such as scale insect and vine weevil. You should know if the plant likes sun or shade, moist or dry, and have chosen a site. Set the plant there and try to imagine it when it has grown bigger. Often it looks better to have three, five or seven smaller plants than one or two bigger ones. The best ornamental and vegetable beds often have just a few, large blocks of the same well grown plants. Repetition, repetition, repetition. Too many different plants can look bitty and in the vegetable garden means few will get appropriate attention.

## plants that are really weeds

We all know the common weeds, but some garden plants such as poppies can soon become weeds. Deadhead anything with a seed head before it self-seeds everywhere. Big hedges, especially x *Cupressocyparis leylandii*, are weeds to whoever lives on the shady side. Rambling roses are too vigorous for most gardens. Other plants such as mints (*Mentha*), many bamboos, alstroemerias and raspberries (*Rubus idaeus*) send their roots and shoots up all over the place, as do trees such as *Populus* x *jackii* 'Aurora' (a seriously bad choice within running distance of any building), stag's-horn sumach (*Rhus typhina*) and cherries. These are all best contained in beds in the middle of regularly rough cut grass. These spreaders can sometimes penetrate concrete but that is the next best choice as a barrier; asphalt or slabs will not stop them.

# moving plants about

There is an advantage to moving some things about such as citrus, which need to go under cover in winter.

## leave well alone

One of the more foolish errors in gardening is to move plants about unnecessarily. They do not move in nature; the sun always comes up the same side and goes down on the opposite one so each seedling 'knows' its orientation. Some people believe that it is important to maintain this orientation when you move a plant. Others practise daily rotation of houseplants in windows with the idea of giving all sides the same light. I'm on the side of leaving them alone since some do not like moving anyway. I place the tag or label on the shady side and nearly always try to keep it so throughout a plant's life. If the plant is in a container with a handle, I also ensure that the handle can come upright to lift it without impinging on the plant; the plant is slightly offset towards one face. I usually make that face the sunny one so I can easily lift the plants from behind to put them in and out of position.

Really heavy plants such as old citrus trees may be better taken out of their pots and moved separately, then repotted. Sack barrows and trolleys can make life much easier, as can boards and rollers – or get more hands and have a plant-moving party.

## hardening off

When plants come from a protected, dim environment under glass or plastic or from a supermarket or garden-centre shelf, they are tender. They cannot happily survive cold, windy conditions and especially not in cold, wet soil. They need to be hardened off, by standing them out in a sunny warm spot during the day and bringing them under cover at night. The minimum period is for three or four days. However, longer is better. I stand my citrus plants together in a clump for the first few weeks outdoors, so that they shelter each other and can all be covered with a sheet on colder nights.

And bringing peaches and apricots under cover for spring and summer keeps earlier crops free of a multitude of problems.

# moving turf

**1** I'm removing some weedy turf from the path.

**2** Cutting the same size and shape of good turf.

**3** After fitting, and firming new piece in where poor turf was, I water well.

Do not forget that, no matter how well you harden off plants, if they are tender they cannot stand a frost and need bringing into the warm under cover. Larger, older plants withstand more cold than small ones, so you need to panic slightly less. If the leaves drop, you have not hardened them off enough; scorch or bleaching results from too much sun too soon.

Bringing plants under cover can also be a shock because it is dim, warm and the air is somewhat stagnant. Never bring in damp plants since they may mould; take care to keep the air dry. These plants need hardening off in reverse, so be sure to keep them ventilated and, if the weather is fine and your back strong, stand them outdoors during fine days – they'll love it.

## moving turf

Turf is one of the few plants you can move easily. In early spring or autumn, whenever it is moist and not frosty, you can slice off the topmost layer of a turf sward and move it to a new position. Do it methodically in small, neat slices and you can transplant a large area very quickly. Place the turves so they alternate like bricks, press them down, brush soil into any cracks and water them well. That's it. Of course, you can do a better job by preparing the new site really well, but for a roughly good result, rough measures do with turf – it's very forgiving. Thus you can easily re-route grass paths and the shapes of beds and borders set in lawns. One of the best ways of recovering a weedy area is to move the valuable plants into a new bed made in the middle of a lawn and use the turf to cover the old beds after levelling them. After a few years under turf, the old beds can be cut out again from the lawn; they will have no weeds left in them and may be replanted with the multiplied stock. (Weed seeds may be another matter; although regular mowing kills the weeds, their seeds mostly remain viable for half a dozen years or more.) Bought-in turf is not as easy to lay because it's not as fresh and not used to the conditions in your garden, but it is still easier and quicker than sowing. If the turves you laid shrink, they are drying out and need watering; if they are yellowing, they have been kept dark too long and were almost dead when laid.

# repotting and moving plants

## repot plants as they grow

Every time you move a plant you check it; sometimes this helps ramify the root system or spread the season of flowering and cropping compared to unmoved plants, but it is a check. The easier you make it the better, so don't repot and move plants at the same time. Repot and return them to the same conditions, then move them later, or vice versa. Also, do not repot too often since plants need time to adapt to each new condition.

The common error, especially with houseplants, is to fail to give them enough space or compost. It is true that a very few need cramping to make them flower, but even those plants do not like ten years of neglect. Every year or so, perennials need a bigger pot, whereas annuals and fast growers such as tomatoes may require repotting every few weeks. Do not wait until the plant gets so big it may never make it.

Too small a pot will increase the tendency to dry out, but will also dwarf most plants – if it doesn't cause them to bolt and die. Do not over-pot by giving a plant something that is far too big so that the unused compost goes stale; if you want to use a huge container, plant in a smaller pot held inside the container with packing and then gravel over the surface to hide the 'join'. (Do remember where the real pot is when you water!) Never plant in something with a narrow neck like a jug or teapot unless the plants, such as annuals, will never need repotting. It's surprising how many small trees, especially oaks and avocados, are doomed from the start to short lives as bonsai!

## use proper potting compost

Specialised composts such as orchid and ericaceous are a good investment, John Innes type formulations are trustworthy, but avoid indiscriminate multipurpose types. Many plants in pots are killed or made to perform badly by people economising with cheap or homemade composts and then not even repotting the poor plants as they use up what little resources were in the compost. If you can't repot, then either liquid feed as you water or top-dress with slow-release, organic fertiliser. Worm casts are excellent.

And most important of all, *do not forget* to put some drainage material in the bottom of the pot and check that the drainage holes are clear every so often. Be firm when repotting; loose composts do not suck up water and you will never harm roots by over-firming the compost.

why sieve? ● Use good, fresh seed compost. Nothing else will do. Coarsely sieve it, not to remove lumps or bits but to re-introduce air.

# repot as they grow

**1** It doesn't need extra drainage, just needs to be put into a bigger pot.

**2** The compost is worked around it and then firmed in.

**3** Note the difference in size of the two pots before and after potting up.

**1** **Clay pots** are often used for plants more sensitive to drainage, and are usually given a crock in the bottom to improve the drainage tremendously.

**2** The crock is covered with lumpy compost to improve drainage before the plant is inserted.

**3** Then fill with compost and firm really well.

# planting outdoors

1  Water well well before planting.

2  Firm in well after planting.

## planting in the ground

Indoors or out, planting in the ground is much the same as it is in pots, but we have to remember to add pest protection, especially from slugs and birds, both of which love the soft growths of transplants, whether they are hardened off or not.

Pre-warming the site with plastic sheet or cloches helps wonderfully, but plant out in cool, cloudy weather; you do not want fierce sun, wind, cold or wet because all these conditions will be hard on your transplants. Make sure that the plants and the planting site have been well watered in the previous days. Do not rely on last-minute watering since this leaves the holes cold and anaerobic (lacks oxygen), and hostile to roots. Ideally dig planting holes in advance, fertilise with gentle, slow-release feed, if necessary, and water the holes a day or two before, stirring up and mixing the soil to make it warmer and more friable. Then plant out the hardened-off plants. Never leave roots exposed to sun and wind, but cover them with a wet sack.

We do not plant in waterlogged or muddy soil because it is anaerobic and kills roots,

then it later dries, cracks and tears roots apart. Frozen ground stays frozen in lumps and should never be dug or mixed. Powder-dry soil is obviously no good. Plant always in friable soil that can be packed firmly around roots; mix in potting compost to help small plants, but not strong fertilisers and never raw manures because these burn the roots.

## the planting hole

Trees obviously need the biggest hole, but smaller plants like big holes too. A great many problems come from cramping roots in small holes, so be generous – wider is much better than deeper. Do break up the subsoil and sides roughly since smooth surfaces can deflect roots from spreading outwards. If the subsoil holds water, break it up more – the plant will never survive in a pocket of water. Always tease out roots and spread them in different layers and directions, depending on their natural tendencies. For reasons of hygiene, cut off badly damaged roots, but don't remove the majority, except maybe the taproot on fruit and other trees if you want these trees to be smaller and more fruitful

earlier. When planting, be very careful not to damage the stems near ground level because so many troubles start there.

Planting at the wrong depth is an error easily made. Little seedlings need burying not as deep as the first leaves or they may surely rot; older plants need their roots and stems to remain at the same point as they were before, even big trees retain that same point of vulnerability at ground level. Bury plants too deep and they suffer and die; most of their roots need to be in warm, aerated topsoil and few roots go deep, except for water or a foothold. However, too shallow and they risk drying out, but may still survive if mulched or they can root deeper in time.

So, on the whole, it is safer to plant shallower rather than deeper; this is especially important for fruit crops. Mulching and watering overcome many problems and keeping the bulk of the roots in fertile, warm, moist soil promotes fruitful rather than rank growth. (Blackcurrants and clematis are notable exceptions and are planted extra deep.)

Bird guards – wire basket, cold guards – cloche, and weed guard – carpet.

### plant firmly, very firmly

Provided that you have packed the roots in their layers surrounded by friable soil, you should not be able to hurt a plant by compressing the soil around the rootball. Under-firming is a common problem. Seriously: after planting, take hold of a small piece of leaf proportionate to the size of plant and slowly pull until the leaf tears or breaks off; if the plant moves instead, it needs firmer packing! If the plant is bigger, then be firmer.

Give trees and big shrubs, especially evergreens, a stake to hold the roots in place – if the top rocks, the roots never establish well. And put the stake in first so that you don't damage the roots. In a pot, use the previous hole for a cane or, after repotting, push it in the new compost by the edge to avoid the rootball.

### after planting

It helps smaller plants if you give them shelter when they are planted out; a bottle cloche or similar really helps for the first few weeks. Do not water after planting because this just attracts problems. However, do start watering soon after and keep doing so until the plants are well established. Annuals should take in a matter of days, but some trees may take two growing seasons or more before they can do well enough without extra water. Evergreens are safest transplanted in early spring, as are herbaceous subjects, but then need careful watering all through the first few seasons. After planting, do not allow weeds to crowd around seedlings, plants, shrubs or trees; weed or mulch them away.

# successful seed sowing

## where to sow?

Outdoors everything is at the mercy of the weather and wildlife. It is truly educational to see a self-sown seedling growing next to similar seedlings that you have carefully raised. Invariably, you soon see your seedlings totally outclassed by the outsider. However, such self-sown plants are only a few among countless others that did not survive. A deliberate sowing produces far more plants in the right places.

Although seedlings sown *in situ* usually produce better plants than transplanted seedlings started in pots or a seedbed, the latter are more easily guarded and looked after, especially if they are tender. In other words, we sow in pots under cover to be sure, and to protect small plants while they are tender and the weather is too cold out-doors. Creating this longer season means that we can grow such crops as tomatoes – these will grow from self-sown seedlings outdoors on their own, but they rarely crop soon enough in the average summer. Sweetcorn and other crops often do better from being started in pots so they hit earlier ripening windows, when the sun is hotter. But later crops that are sown *in situ* make bigger, stronger plants with larger yields, even if they do not ripen well every year. You takes your choice: in pots for certitude, *in situ* for larger, stronger plants.

## sowing in pots

You can also sow in multi-celled trays, which are just like miniature pots and very convenient. Use good, fresh seed compost. Nothing else will do. Coarsely sieve it, not to remove lumps or bits but to re-introduce air. (To economise, I will half-fill a pot with my own mixture of sieved garden compost, but seed is sown on a bed of John Innes formula because this gives me the best all-round

performance.) Check whether the seeds need to be sown on the surface or at what depth, and see if they prefer dark or light by reading the packet. All these elements must be done correctly:

● Sow evenly, thinly and properly spaced – crowding is worse than weeds.
● Do not sow or cover too deeply. Firm well.
● Do not water from the top. Moisten the compost by standing the pots in warm water until it shows on the top of the compost, and then drain the pots well.
● Do not stand the pots in a cold place: it has to be warm enough for germination.
● Don't forget the label.
● A final mistake to avoid: do not forget to move the seedlings on into pots of their own as soon as they are big enough to handle. Leaving them all together checks their growth.

## sowing in the ground

This requires even more care, particularly to be sure that no pests, especially slugs and birds, or diseases make off with the seed or seedlings. Be sure to avoid the errors of sowing too deeply, too early, too thickly and of forgetting the labels. Water holes and drills well before time, so they can warm up and the water can permeate the soil.

Cover the seeds with warm, friable soil or a sterile, sowing mixture. This avoids several mechanical problems, such as capping (where the surface forms a crust) and hinders weeds, diseases and some pests. Best of all, it marks where you've sown, preventing you from accidentally weeding out the seedlings and also facilitates faster weeding around the seedlings. This is especially important with odd-shaped patches of flower seeds, whereas rows of emerging vegetable seedlings can be spotted unaided. Firm the soil or compost. If it's too loose, the seeds may not germinate; too hard and the seedlings will not break

Sweetcorn, buried at least its own width deep.

through. When the seedlings do emerge, thin to the best ones at a good spacing – if you overcrowd them, they will all be poor.

If you have problems sowing, thinly mix your seed with sand or some other inert stuff of the same size as the seeds. For widely spaced plants, don't sow rows but a few seeds at each spot; cover and firm them and thin to the best seedlings when they emerge. Try sowing more tender seeds such as sweet-corn on small hills or ridges, to give them a better microclimate.

Annuals and especially carrots seem to do well when sown broadcast; rows don't always suit. Rake the moist soil as a seedbed (preferably several times in the weeks beforehand to get rid of flushes of weeds); broadcast the seed in several passes in different directions; gently sprinkle the bed with a mixture of sharp sand and old potting compost until just covered; firm and add protection, be it wire cage, cloche or fleece.

## sowing seeds in multi-celled trays

1　Having filled the cells and firmed them down, the seed is sown in depressions.

2　Sowing compost sieved over the top.

3　Surplus compost being scraped off.

4　Firming down really well.

5　Standing the tray in water to soak up from the bottom.

# propagators, frames, greenhouses

And people think I don't grow flowers!

### errors to avoid under cover

The first problem to avoid is not to get too small an item. Nobody ever complains that their propagator, cold frame or greenhouse is too big, except maybe when they look at their heating bills. Any propagator the size of a seed tray is quite large enough to germinate all the seeds for the average garden, but where do you keep the tender plants when they get bigger than matches? Even a huge greenhouse or polytunnel soon gets full. A cold frame outside can be a useful halfway house for tender plants on their way to the garden. Similarly, another in the greenhouse provides a good place to move plants from a heated propagator, before they are strong enough to take an unheated greenhouse.

Don't use any light space under cover as storage; this is a waste and harbours pests such as woodlice and rodents. Get another place to store things – say a couple of plastic rubbish bins with lids, a shed, defunct caravan or a dead freezer unit...

## light and heat

It is a huge mistake to site any cover, from propagator to tunnel, in shade; if it is not in full sun you may as well not have bothered. It will be of some help, but shaded cover is like a car with a wheel missing. Except for propagation in midsummer, there is little need for shade and it can always be created. Put the door on the shady end if you can so that it wastes the least sunny space. Do get safe electric light; it is so useful, as are fan heaters and soil-warming cables. Power makes a covered area into a kingdom of your own where you really can look after your plants properly. But don't waste energy by heating too much; have an inner, warmer enclave, double and triple insulate in winter, and be abstemious. With sense and a little warmth, you can get better flowers and crops all year round. Thermostats on fan heaters work wonderfully and these are essential. Soil-warming cables and hotbed thermostats have invariably failed me after a year or two; they corrode and are uneconomic so I put soil-warming cables on time clocks instead to warm at night on economy power – after all, that's when it's most needed.

## ventilation

Plants are handicapped by a lack of air faster than a lack of light, so it is unwise to have insufficient ventilation. You can't have too much, but if you've bought already it is worth finding a similar, scrap greenhouse to cannibalise for extra roof and side vents.

Ventilation is crucial. Notice the self-actuating ventilator.

Propagators and cold frames must also be opened before they cook the plants; even on winter days they can get too hot and sweaty. Greenhouses can have automatic vent openers, which are almost an essential, as are easily fitted clips to hold winter insulation.

Fit slatted, not solid, shelving to allow more internal ventilation. Slatted staging is probably best because it raises plants up and allows more airflow. However, make sure that there are few unwanted and un-closable gaps in the walls and roof, so you can shut up the greenhouse on cold days. Also, fix net over all vents and the door, to keep out flying pests before they come in and damage your plants.

## floors and walls

Keep out most ground-level pests and weeds with solid foundations; moles will be kept out only if you lay galvanised netting from wall to wall. Solid floors are not often the best choice: soil may be temporarily covered with

The only place for decking is the greenhouse border so you don't compact the soil.

slabs and is often the best choice for crops and flowers. If it gets worn out, it can be dug out and replaced with some small effort, whereas a solid floor means that you must grow in containers.

A bad mistake is to allow the glass or plastic to get dirty because it cuts down the light very dramatically and reduces plant growth and vigour. Worse is to try and pressure-wash it... Soapy water and a sponge will do. A plastic label will get algae out of the gap where glass overlaps. Big polytunnels may be cleaned with a soapy blanket on two ropes, pulled to and fro over the top. Clean inside with a squeegee foam sponge on a stick. Use soapy water first, and then rinse it off. A drop of bleach in the rinsing water will sterilise the glass and prevent the algae from growing away again quickly.

# weeding more effectively

A daisy grubber is a really handy tool for evicting all sorts of weeds.

## first, choose the tool

We all weed, but some of us make hard work of it, especially if we do not change our ways according to the situation. Weeding is more effective if done in different ways for different places. For keeping large areas of soil clean, there is little to beat a hoe. The old saying was, 'hoe every week and you'll never see a weed'. The worst mistake is to have a blunt hoe! A hoe is a knife with which you sever weeds from their roots, so it must be sharp and smooth when you start and be sharpened as you work, and any accumulation of mud or fibres scraped off. A heavy or cumbersome hoe is also a mistake, as is too short a handle.

Most prefer a swan-necked or draw hoe for most work since this can draw soil up around stems and so on. For cleaning larger areas, a Dutch or push-and-pull hoe demands least effort. The blade should be thin, springy and hard. It is so difficult to find a really good, new hoe blade that I now find worn-out hoes and fix pieces of scythe blade to them. There are many idiosyncratic hoes on the market, some with moving parts, but most are no improvement and indeed make the job harder.

## how to hoe

You don't have to hoe backwards, I prefer mostly hoeing forwards, but in either case try to change hands every so often if you can; it is very unbalanced work and bad for the posture. The hoe works best in the dry – wet soil makes it stick. The best way is to hoe through the topmost fraction of soil and rarely dig down into it. The idea is to cut through everything, churning the topmost soil and weed seedlings as you go. First carefully work

**1** Cutting through the weed's root with a sharp knife.

**2** Picking it up gingerly as it's a stinging nettle.

**3** Dumping it in the bowl, which is lower, so much easier than a bucket.

around the plants you want and then chop up everything in-between those cleared spots. In hot or windy weather, most small weeds will shrivel away, but in wet weather they may re-root. Bigger weeds may set seed even while lying on top of the soil. So it is best to rake away the larger weeds afterwards, which of course doubly troubles the ones that are left to wither.

If the ground is too heavy or too stony to hoe easily, consider levelling it carefully, then sowing and planting through a 'hoeing mulch', a thin layer of sieved topsoil or potting compost or of sharp sand that only just covers the surface; any of these can be quickly hoed. On stone-free soil there is a trick worth knowing: when the ground has frozen solid but the topmost layer has started to thaw, you can hoe at amazing speed

because everything underneath is solid, roots are held in an iron clamp, and the top growth and surface layer of soil scrapes away incredibly easily.

### hand weeding

Much weeding has to be done by hand, though; for example among seedlings and in dense plantings. The usual tools such as an onion hoe are not as handy as an old-fashioned, steel knife, which can be used to snick individual weeds or slice sideways through many of them like a hoe. An old washing-up bowl – not a bucket – is better for collecting the weeds because it is low down. Hand weeding requires being on one or both knees; those firm, sponge knee protectors that are worn by skaters make it much more comfortable. An old rug, or even a newspaper,

will make your knees last longer, but do not kneel unprotected on wet ground, otherwise you will have problems as a result, to say nothing of soil compaction.

### weed-suppressing mulches

Dense mulches kill weeds by burying them so deeply that they give up. It works only on the smaller weeds, but does suppress any weed seeds in the soil from germinating. Thick mulches are useful almost everywhere, except among low-growing, carpeting plants such as thymes and chamomile (*Chamaemelum nobile*). Repetitive mulches, where more is added regularly, usually only on top of any emergent weeds, are a very effective way of control where there are only a few weeds. Grass-clipping mulches are perfect for this method as extra material is produced weekly.

Planting out followed by a mulch of newspaper and then a mulch – it looks neat and keeps the plant's roots moister longer.

When you've made your cup of tea, kill a few weeds with the rest of the hot water.

The mulches may be placed to smother any new weeds in previously mulched spots rather than just added broadcast in some place or the other by turn. The biggest problem is caused by applying mulches too thinly, which allows the soil to mix in and weeds to germinate. Mulches may also be scattered by birds scratching about in them. Creeping weeds will encroach and other weeds seed onto the mulch and germinate in carpets, but these are easily pulled.

### sheet mulches

Plastic sheeting and permeable synthetic fabric may be used in place of deep mulches, or under them for suppressing weeds and retaining moisture. They work extremely well except against creeping underground weeds such as bindweed, which can cover a large area and come up for light only at the edges or through the odd tear. Great care must be taken to deal with any such invasive weeds. Be careful also with sheet plastic; it can suffocate the soil, if too wide an area is covered, and

shoot water off alarmingly, so get the fall and drainage worked out. Sheets can also blow up in high winds and do a lot of damage as they snag and flutter so fix them securely.

However, putting down a sheet of black synthetic fabric for a fortnight or more does kill almost everything underneath and is a simple way of killing weeds on a drive, patio or vegetable bed, or even for making a new bed from a lawn.

### using groundcover

Mulches and sheets suppress weeds and save water, but simple, dense planting, especially of evergreens, does much the same and looks better. The same problems of creeping under-ground weeds apply though, and some such as ivies and brambles sneak in and need evicting. One of the best plants for covering large areas are stinging nettles since they make some of the best compost material, but I can see their drawbacks. A choice selection of evergreens, planted in groups of five or seven through landscape fabric in weed-free ground

and mulched afterwards, should need almost no attention for years. Done badly and let go, however, it will be difficult to reclaim because the fabric will get in the way of weeding.

### thermal destruction

As anyone who has ever left a cold frame or greenhouse tight shut on a hot day will know, you can kill plants remarkably quickly with heat, just as quickly if not more so than with cold. Cooking kills everything eventually, but even a little too much heat can 'boil' the roots in a pot, scorch leaves, seeds or fruits, or simply wilt a plant. We can turn this weakness to our benefit to get rid of unwanted seeds by heat-sterilising composts. And with some cunning devices we can kill weeds in our gardens every bit as effectively as with chemical herbicides.

Most seedlings and small plants expire with one heat treatment; a few take more. It is foolish to keep cooking the freshly emerging leaves of a plant that has roots maintained by other untreated leaves elsewhere. A few deep-rooted weeds may take several

**1** For weeds on paths or rockeries, a small flame gun or paint stripper can be effective.

**2** Where there are many established weeds it is better not to char the leaves to an ash on the first pass but to cook them all lightly.

**3** The damaged leaves weaken the root systems so the second pass a week later finishes more of them off.

## flame-gunning

Do think safe and have water and a fire extinguisher nearby, wear sensible clothes and do not use near cars, oil tanks or woodpiles.

treatments, but the great advantage of the thermal methods is that they kill what they touch and that includes the seeds.

### boiling water and steam

An old gardener's trick was to use the spare boiling water each time tea was made and pour it over any weeds in the paths. Few survived a second or third dousing! Although it would be expensive to boil water just to kill weeds we can adopt the old practice and use up any spare boiling water. This may be sufficient to keep quite a large area weed-free, for free.

A powerful jet of steam is even more effective at killing plants and will cook plants faster than boiling water. Steam generators for all sorts of uses are available for hire and will rapidly kill every leaf and seed in sight, and are good for sterilising greenhouses. (Better than a pressure washer, which pushes the panes out!) Of course, some deep-rooted weeds throw out new leaves a week or so later, but a second or third steaming does for them. For small patios with only a few weedy cracks to

deal with, try a redundant steam iron! (Avoid using your partner's one without consent.)

### flame-gunning

For the weedy problem of an infested rockery or crazy paving, a small, hand-held hobby blowtorch or hot-air paint stripper does a surprisingly good job. It's simpler to kill off the weed tops rather than try to excavate all the roots disrupting the rocks. Obviously some perennials regrow, but these may be dealt with in turn until their roots expire. Few plants throw out new flushes of leaves more than three or four times. Where there are many established weeds, it is better not to char the leaves to an ash on the first pass but to cook them all lightly. The damaged leaves weaken the root systems so that the second pass a week later finishes off more of them. The second pass also cooks any regrowth and any more seeds that have become exposed and burns to an ash any leaves that have shrivelled already. A third pass may be needed to deal with very tough weeds, but these may be so

few that they could be treated by other means.

The fierce flame does of course kill any soil creatures it touches but does not penetrate far into the soil, so the vast majority are safe. The deadly effect does though make a flame gun more applicable to paths, drives and non-cropping areas and less suitable for dense weed clearance on new ground, where more spiders, beetles and so on may be harmed.

There is a range of bigger, boys'-toys flame guns available to cope with bigger areas. Although older versions were powered by paraffin, modern flame guns run on gas and are big blowtorches. Some come with hoods and wheels: these make short work of big drives, paths and gravelled areas. Any leaves and detritus are shrivelled and burnt so there is no build-up of humus to encourage any weeds ever to germinate.

When using flame guns, it is vital to think of safety. Have water and a fire extinguisher nearby, wear protective clothes and do *not* use the flame gun anywhere near cars, oil tanks or woodpiles.

# the dangers of pruning

Summer pruning with shears.

## do you need to prune?

In an ideal world, we would never prune. Our shrubs would be so compact and well spaced that they would not outgrow their positions and we would leisurely push off buds rather than allow them to develop into shoots that need to be cut off with secateurs. And of course, there would be no damage or infection to take out. In the real world, we prune, but too much pruning often produces the wrong result, with rampant regrowth, few flowers and no fruits, and a lot of prunings to dispose of. Less is better and the least pruning is best; if you do prune, it is often better to remove one entire branch than two dozen smaller shoots.

Pruning is one of the skills that demand most learning: practise on soft fruits because they respond quickly, forgivingly and cheaply. The commonest method, much tut-tutted about, is the lollipop or haircut approach – a short-back-and-sides all round. This is not so bad as is often made out; if done after flowering, it may actually work.

The wrong time is often chosen: pruning in summer is better for checking growth than pruning in winter, but the latter is most often done, misguidedly, in an attempt to control excessive growth. Winter pruning encourages replacement growth so is best done in the early days of establishing a tree and forming its framework, which you want to spring up quickly. Once the tree or plant is mature, you want the flowers or fruits and not much more growth; these aims are achieved most efficiently through summer pruning and disbudding, not by winter pruning. Indeed, most fruit trees actually crop heavier and earlier when left entirely unpruned.

### how not to cut the wrong bits off

The skill in pruning is not knowing what to cut off, but being able to see how it will regrow when you do. That does take experience. There is more to pruning than almost any other horticultural subject. Many plants have their own specialised pruning regimes, which may even differ again according to the species. You can find many books, some disagreeing with others, on pruning plants such as clematis, grapes, pears and roses. Really, it is best to leave all alone, except for a few. Trained fruit trees such as cordons and espaliers and soft fruits, especially grapes and raspberries, really need pruning; almost everything else may be deadheaded a bit ruthlessly with that despised lollipop cut. Even the trained fruit may be pruned with shears rather than secateurs; some growers use hedge trimmers! The same goes in the flower garden: just deadheading is much more important for improving performance than pruning. A proper job is lovely, but just trimming back to let in air and light works.

### which plants when

In general, most plants flower in spring or summer and fruit or seed in autumn. Some from foreign climes get out of step. Many Mediterranean plants used to a warmer winter expect that they can flower in autumn and early winter and carry crops through the rest of winter into next year, to ripen, often, with the next flowering. Plants from more severe continental climates, which have more clear-cut springs and autumns, suffer in the damp shilly-shallying of the UK weather. The pruning of all these plants comes back to the principle of 'leave well alone', but if you must then do so just after flowering. This gives the plant the maximum amount of time to make the next crop of flower buds and removes many of the seeds or fruits, concentrating its energy on the remaining ones.

Of course some plants are very particular: stone fruits such as the plum and their ornamental cousins (all *Prunus*) must be cut or pruned only in the summer – the deadly silver leaf, a fungal disease, enters the wounds at any other time.

Hollow-stemmed shrubs are pruned in spring because leaving hollow stubs in which water can freeze all winter may kill off the plant. Evergreens are normally pruned in spring so that new growths don't suffer from winter cold. Gooseberries are left until late so that the birds don't steal their buds. Some shrubs, such as daphnes and tree paeonies, are best never pruned at all.

### pruning tips

When you prune, or even just deadhead, wipe the blades with methylated or surgical spirit between plants to kill diseases. In general, it is wise to cut out damaged, diseased, rubbing and in-growing wood. Paint over wounds with a wound sealant to stop water and big pests getting in. Burn out cankers and cauterise over stumps cut at the 'wrong time' with a small gas blowtorch and then use sealant. Do not leave little stumps or snags unless these have live buds on them; otherwise, they will die back and let in disease.

**The main aim of pruning is to remove dead, diseased and congested growth.**

# plant propagation that works

## worth the effort

Multiplying your own plants is satisfying and economic, and remarkably easy with some plants. However, others are more than difficult to propagate, even for professionals; but we amateurs have a big advantage. To the professional who sets 100 cuttings, anything less than 80 or 90 per cent take is a failure and uneconomic. But to you or me, ten or twenty rooted cuttings are probably more than we can ever use. Since failure is not a big problem, have a go.

If you want exactly the same offspring from a perennial flower or fruit, you have to propagate it vegetatively; that is, a bit of the original has to be got onto new roots. If you want to be really successful, go for plants that you can divide.

## division

This is the easiest propagation method with plants that readily regrow if you break up their root systems into smaller pieces, each with some buds, such as raspberries and delphiniums. Simply tease apart the dormant plants, making sure that each part has some roots with fat buds, and you have as many identical new plants as you want. You can try separating the rootstocks with two forks back to back, as they show in some books, but I find that useless. If I dig up the clumps and immerse them in a bath of water, I find them easy to pull apart, using secateurs or a knife to cut any connecting roots. Much neater!

One group of plants, the herbaceous perennials, with the exception of plants such as *Eremurus*, hellebores and paeonies, actually benefits from being divided and replanted every few years, giving better clumps of flowers with fewer dead centres.

You can divide most herbaceous plants in spring, just before they start into growth.

Common mistakes are to make the chunks too big, with too much old, woody growth, or too small with no decent buds. A healthy set of roots and some good buds on youngish growth is usually better. Dry the wounds and dust them with wood ashes or sulphur to avoid rot. Small divisions are best potted up and housed under cover, say in a cold frame. Larger examples may be put either in a nursery bed or in their final places straightaway. Do not propagate many more than you need.

Vegetative reproduction is also easy with plants that have bulbs or tubers, such as daffodils (*Narcissus*), gladioli and potatoes. Choose wisely: don't propagate from miffy plants and if increasing bulbs, divide off the smaller offsets, not the fattest, which are probably ready to flower. Propagating many of these plants causes the problem of what to do with all the new plants, so produce only what you *really* want; otherwise, all may be neglected.

## taking cuttings

Many plants root easily from cuttings. Almost every climber, rose, shrub and soft fruit may be propagated from autumn or hardwood cuttings. These need to be about a foot long and from strong, young, unflowered wood; many of them root most easily and rot least if cut near a leaf node. Cut these when the leaves start to fall, stick them the right way up in reasonable, moist soil and, in a year's time, a goodly number will have become new plants and may be dug up. Sure, it helps to put them in a moist site with a sandy-bottomed slit trench, but some take anyway.

If you take a hundred cuttings, fifty or sixty roses take and maybe ninety-nine currants, but

It's easy to have too many.

only five figs or one gingko – and in theory you shouldn't have them anyway. So set large numbers of cuttings and be ruthless in choosing from the survivors. If you don't want shrubby plants with many shoots, but single-stemmed ones, remove all buds from the cuttings below ground level before you set them. That's it; if it works, it's easy. Weeding and watering the cuttings will of course help and increase the take.

Tender plants and soft ones such as pelargoniums are easier to multiply by softwood cuttings if you have a propagator to provide some bottom heat and you root them in pots of gritty compost. Make sure that everything is sterile since warmth and moisture cause problems to multiply. I never use rooting compounds, but you might dip cuttings in sulphur dust to stop rot and leave cuttings of plants like pelargoniums to dry for a day or two before setting them.

tender plants and soft ones such as pelargoniums are easier to multiply by softwood cuttings

## splitting plants (division)

**1** Soak the whole plant in water…

**2** It's much easier to pull the roots apart.

**3** Putting each division into its own pot.

**4** Firming in well with compost.

**5** Gently inverting plant, but not pot or compost, in water to wash off compost from leaves.

**6** Draining off pots after they have been allowed to soak up water into the compost.

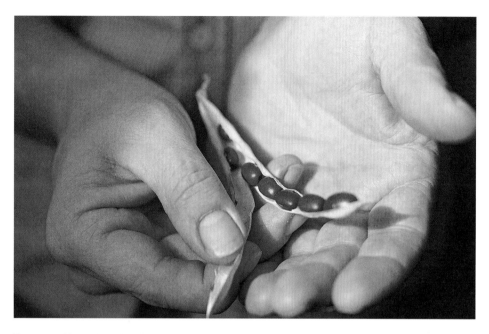

Few vegetable seeds, other than peas and beans, are worth saving.

A dead fridge makes an ideal seed store.

However you will find that cuttings of most fruit trees, rhododendrons and some few others are hard to root, even with bottom heat. These might root from softwood cuttings taken in summer and set in a propagator with warmth and shade, but they go mouldy overnight if you don't get it right.

### layering

If cuttings don't work, try layering. This is often used on plants reluctant to root by other means. Bend down a pliable shoot so that you can cover it in sterile, sharp, gritty compost, either on the ground or in the air in a pot. If you wound the bark and surround it in damp compost, you can often get the shoot to root, although this may take a rather long time, often up to a year or more. Still, it is worth it because choice, quite large plants can often be got this way. Keep the compost moist; on the ground, pin the shoot down, cover it with compost and place a stone on top to keep it cool and moist. Eventually, when the stem sends out new roots, you can detach the new plant.

If you can't get a plant to layer, you may be able to graft it, but although it is essentially easy, take it from me that you need to read a whole new book before you start on it. So why not just sow a seed?

### to collect seeds or not?

Well, if you sow seeds, you may get something like the parent, or maybe not. Most annual flowering plants and some vegetables will produce almost identical offspring from seed, but others give a range of weird variety. Sweet peas (*Lathyrus odoratus*) notoriously degenerate rapidly to scrappy, purple-blue flowers and hyacinths to dodgy, ersatz bluebells. It all depends; old-fashioned and wild-flower species usually give seed that comes true, but highly bred flowers, soft fruits, fruit trees, and everything called an F1 hybrid will not come true and will produce mixed offspring. It is rarely worth saving vegetable seeds because too many are grown, and most are promiscuous cross-breeders anyway, but certainly choice annuals are often easy and worthwhile, as long as you grow only one cultivar.

Again, don't save or sow seed you don't really want. It is fun, but essentially only fun, to grow citrus from seed (ten to twenty years

to crop), apples and pears (five to ten years to crop) and avocados (will never crop) and so on. But do not let me stop you. Of course there is always that exciting chance of getting a new and different plant, but sadly they are not usually an improvement on the parents. So please, do not imagine great wealth from any new findling; a few hundred, or maybe a thousand, pounds sterling is all that awaits most raisers of new plants. Believe me, I wish it were otherwise.

### saving seed

Seed for collection must be ripe, but there is a danger of losing it from the plant, so often nearly ripe seed heads are cut together with their stalks and ripened under cover, to shed their seed where it can be caught. Often seed stays freshest in seed heads that are stored in paper bags in a dry, airy, pest-free place. Seed shaken out of the pods may take up less space, but may be more subject to attack from pests or disease. Make sure that the seed is well dried. I store it in paper envelopes in wooden boxes in a defunct refrigerator. Do label each batch correctly to avoid confusion later.

# things that may still go wrong

Spotting problems on plants ● What has happened ● Why has it happened ● Is it worth fixing?
● How to identify problems and what you can do about them ● The commonplace and therefore
most likely problems ● Cultural disorders: incorrect watering, drainage, soil pH, feeding and nutrient
deficiencies ● Beware of chemicals ● Seedling failure ● Pot binding, root strangulation and

isolation ● Stem strangulation, over pruning and owner's itch ● Microclimates: what can go wrong ● The weather: lightning, hail, frost, snow, sun scorch ● The commonest pests and diseases – what they look like, what they do to plants, and what to do about them

# spotting problems on plants

The odd spot on an apricot is not worth worrying about...

## assessing the symptoms

Most of the time, most plants do well, maybe not as well as they could, but well enough. Then we notice this or that does not look so good, investigate and find something 'wrong' and, we hope, clues to why it is wrong. Only then can we ask: are the symptoms serious and do they indicate a simple problem such as wilting from lack of water or something more complicated, such as wilting of leaves that are mottled by a virus?

Only once the cause has been ascertained can an effective remedy be applied. Unfortunately, a remedy may not be available to save the plant in this year since it will often be too late by the time the damage is seen. We may however be able to prevent a problem from spreading and forewarned is forearmed; we can make sure that the plant does not suffer the same again next year, by taking precautions in good time.

### is it worth doing anything anyway?

Much of the time in gardening, we may be in pursuit of perfection and miss the point. There is no sense spending a fortune to save a cheap plant or crop; sometimes things have to be regarded as expendable, past their useful life, not worth saving. It is hardly worth spending a small fortune on pheromone moth traps to ensure your apple tree has nearly 100 per cent clean apples when you could probably pick a neighbour's surplus for free or even buy fruits more cheaply.

We do not expect a bouquet of flowers to last more than a week or so, so why should a decorative pot plant or even a flowering basket live forever? Some may last a lifetime, but most are better regarded as dispensable and younger, prettier replacements best obtained. Of course, if you want a challenge, then try to make your amaryllis flower a second time, get your poinsettia to show crimson bracts next year and stick the flower buds back on your Christmas cactus (*Schlumbergera*). Remember: sometimes there is no point – bin it.

### the obvious suspect

Most of the time, when our plants do badly it's simply because they are not comfortable with their physical conditions. It is then that they may also succumb to pests and diseases so, above all, we must always try to keep plants healthy and growing without check.

So if a plant does not look well, say dull and flagging, and you think it is worth the effort, first check for over- and under-watering, now and in the recent past, and for poor drainage or an unhappy root system. Then check whether it could be damage from heat or cold, wind or draughts. Maybe, just maybe, the plant might have the wrong sort of compost, soil or pH or a serious nutrient deficiency, these are not common with most plants. Even less likely is that the plant could be suffering from a wilt or root infection, a virus or other disease, but these are relatively scarce, except for a few troublesome ones.

So the majority of problems are often initiated, and could be prevented or even rectified, by the growing

...However, cabbage caterpillars are a serious problem and need dealing with straightaway.

conditions and cultivation. These errors are automatically avoided as the gardener becomes more experienced but often catch the novice unawares. However, acquiring the skills does not grant immunity and I must confess to causing my plants distress often but only inadvertently.

## pointing to pests

Another obvious way that plants look distressed is when bits go missing or their leaves get folded up, wrinkled and bent over, which are all common signs of pests at work. (A few diseases can cause holes in leaves and some viruses will distort, variegate or mottle leaves.) Great numbers of any insect living on a plant are probably going to be pests because useful creatures occur far less numerously. You can usually tell the predators from pests because they move about more rapidly; after all, they have to move more quickly than their prey or they would never catch it. Plants succumb more to pests if they are not healthy and resilient, so outbreaks often appear on specimens that are already poorly. Therefore, as with diseases, making physical conditions more comfortable for your plants may be necessary before some pest attacks can be eradicated.

# first aid for plants

## commonplace or likely

The vast majority of potential gardening problems may never happen, but a certain, few others are almost as guaranteed as night follows day. Human error and misguided good intentions create many a minor problem and some huge ones. Thus plants in our care in pots and tubs are far more prone to cultural problems than those in the ground, which are more likely to suffer from common pests and diseases.

Such pests and diseases are usually so widespread that, even if you could start off without any of them, some would soon find a way in. Their survival rate is often so good simply because they are able to attack a wide range of plants. They are the most likely culprits and need to be eliminated from suspicion before other less likely sources. Most commonplace problems exhibit slightly different symptoms and may be diagnosed and treated. Fortunately plants are tough, so it's often possible for them to make a full recovery.

## keeping a balance

Most problems may be broken down into one of three sorts: is it something cultural in the plant's environment, or an attack by pests or by disease? First eliminate the cultural, and then if no pests can be seen wandering about the plant, it is probably a disease. But do not assume that if you find a symptom, you have found a problem. Most of us have a medical file full of ailments, we carry millions of parasites and yet we probably consider ourselves to be in moderately good health. Our garden is similar: it naturally will have all sorts of pests and diseases present; these populations should not be increasing or threatening our plants, but living in harmony with them. They can be regarded simply as curiosities of nature.

Rarely does anything get out of control, except when the weather or other conditions temporarily favour them, but very soon order will return. Years of plagues of aphids are followed by years without any; often ladybird plagues interact with them and occur in alternating years. The same goes for almost all natural problems; if left alone, they come and go. If we intervene and use chemicals, we risk destroying the controllers along with the controlled and causing worse fluctuations.

## the most likely offenders

Slugs and snails, woodlice and earwigs, ants, aphids, scale insects and mealy bugs, capsid bugs and cuckoo spit, vine weevils, swift-moth caterpillars, cutworms, chafers, wireworms and leatherjackets, millipedes, eelworms and nematodes, symphalids, flatworms, caterpillars, maggots and 'worms', thrips, sciarid flies and flea beetles, psyllids and leafhoppers, spider mites and other mites, whiteflies, leaf miners, wasps, flies, mosquitoes and gnats, galls.

Birds, moles, cats, dogs and foxes, badgers, squirrels, deer, rabbits and hares, mice, rats and voles, two-legged rats.

Mildews, rusts, grey moulds, coral spot, fireblight, leaf spots, rots, moulds and wilts, viruses, cankers, mushrooms and worse.

Flowers are usually problem-free and most bugs, if not friends, are certainly not enemies, just curios of nature.

Purely man-made problems occur randomly, and sometimes more often when a gardener shares the workload. Do it all yourself and you can be sure it's done properly.

## how to spot the signs

It is a process of elimination: firstly, ascertain the general health and well-being of the subject – is it being looked after properly? So we look for signs of common cultural problems, starting with input from humans since they are often at fault. Is there evidence of bad practice in watering or feeding for example (see pages 78–83)? Then we turn to more tangible aspects of the plant and check whether it could be suffering from mechanical problems such as pot binding or over-pruning (see pages 84–6). We can then consider the plant's microclimate, that is the conditions specific to its planting site (see pages 88–9), or if the weather could have caused the problem (see pages 90–3).

If the growing conditions are appropriate, then we should examine whether the plant is under attack from the commoner pests (see pages 94–115), which may or may not be present at the time, and diseases (see pages 116–121). The most likely offenders could be found in most gardens and may attack almost any plant. Once you have pinpointed the source of the problem, you can take action to remedy the situation.

# the cultural problems: water and watering

These planters will need careful watering because the foliage will throw so much of the rain off, and yet these are drought-loving plants.

Pots where the plants have been killed by standing in water all winter.

## under-watering

This is a classic mistake, but not the worst. It is true that it results in poor growth and soft, matt, pale leaves that brown at their tips, wilt and eventually die. But plants on the dry side tend to evade death for a long time, especially in winter when cold and mould would almost certainly have got them if they had been 'better' looked after! If the plant is dead or nearly so from drought, the rootball will be withered and dry, and the bark firmly attached to the roots and stem. If the leaves remain on when they are dead, the plant may be farther gone than if they had all dropped off...

Plants in the ground survive remarkably well without extra water, but with water almost invariably crops increase, foliage is lusher and flowers are more profuse. Recently planted trees and shrubs also need extra water to establish. Newly emerged seedlings have short roots and need help in dry periods. Most of all, it is pot plants that suffer from water shortages. They are safer being too dry than too wet, especially in winter, but most houseplants, and many others confined to pots indoors and out, are given far too little water too infrequently.

Stand each pot in a bowl of warm water for half an hour, then drain thoroughly, every day of the growing season. If you must splash water around with a can instead, then do so more often, and again let it drain! Rescue a plant that has been grossly under watered by soaking the roots in water (warm is better), for no more than half an hour at a time, but several times over a day or so. Adding a drop of washing-up liquid to the water will help it soak into a rootball of powdery compost. Plunging the plant underwater or misting the tops can also help get water back into the plant, but may cause mould and mildews if the weather isn't warm and sunny.

## over-watering

The symptoms are very similar to water deprivation because waterlogged roots become damaged and unable to take up water. However, a dry rootball looks and smells very different from the decaying mess of a waterlogged

one. The roots will not have withered, but rotted. It is the lack of air that kills roots and they literally drown, and then rot. A few tough or fast-growing plants may take a saucer of water in their stride, but for many it is slow death.

Where over-watering of pot plants has taken place to the point where they have suffered, it is often best to repot in fresh, gritty potting compost that is just moist, after first ruthlessly removing all the rotten roots and stale compost. Also applying bottom heat may often save otherwise doomed victims because it can stimulate rooting.

Over-watering may leach out all the goodness in the open ground or in containers with tough plants, resulting in similarly poor growth. Years of heavy rain have the same effect; often soils and composts lose lime and potash as well as nitrogen (basic element for fertility). They become sour and acid and need treating.

In the open ground, it is hard to cause damage by over-watering, although it could lead to low levels of nutrients. In poorly drained ground, any watering may become a problem. If the leaves drop off suffering plants, then there's a chance of recovery; if the leaves stay on, it's usually over.

Typical problem caused by erratic watering.

## bad drainage

The symptoms of bad drainage are very similar to those of over-watering, but may allow the plant to exist in a parlous state for longer if the plant is big enough in proportion to its pot. It's a race: waterlogging drowns the roots, but if the plant can absorb the excess water fast enough it may survive. Thus large plants in badly drained pots lurch from disaster to disaster and if you feel the compost, it's probably moist, so you add a little more and prolong its anguish.

Indicators of bad drainage are a scummy surface to the compost or a whitish, powdery look where mineral salts are forced to crystallise out because they are unable to drain away. Lots of liverworts, mosses and algae on the soil surface may indicate bad drainage or over-watering, but also often indicate an acid, sour compost. Watch out for roots blocking drainage holes as they get older and expand.

In the open ground, signs of flooding above ground are hard to miss, but in a heavy clay soil only the planting holes may fill up and waterlogging may pass unnoticed. Even when plants are dormant, flooding for only a few days can kill their roots and lead to their demise at a later date when growth resumes. Many plants obviously will grow new roots, but some will continue to rot away to the point at which they cannot regenerate roots. These plants expire in the drier days after their buds have opened into leaves, wilting and dying sooner or later, depending on how large are their reserves.

Evergreens are particularly susceptible to bad drainage because their leaves demand water year round and they find it difficult to survive long enough to grow new roots even after temporary flooding.

## wrong sort of water

Tap water is often too alkaline for plants and full of dissolved salts. Some plants react to water with the wrong pH straightaway. The tips of houseplants' leaves turn brown (which they also do if the compost is too dry), the outsides of clay pots encrust with powdery crystals, and the compost surface gets discoloured and dead. But a more insidious poisoning results from months of applying tap water. When the plants are watered, most of the water evaporates from the leaves, some is taken into the plant, and some evaporates from the compost. All this water leaves its residue of dissolved salts, which build up in the compost until they poison the roots.

Repotting with new compost is better, although deposits may be washed out with copious drenchings. Using rainwater for all plants (other than seedlings,

These contain water but it's full of leaves and fine for tough plants but not for seedlings.

which need sterile water) is more sensible because it carries minimal amounts of minerals and rarely leads to such problems.

## wrong soil pH

Pale, weak, often yellowed growth (chlorosis) is often a sign that the acid or alkaline level in the soil is wrong for the plant. We are usually careful to use an ericaceous (acid) or lime-free compost for potting up calcifuges or lime-hating plants, but then we forget to check the pH of the water and fertiliser. If either of these is alkaline, it will make the plants chlorotic; wood ashes, which are quite caustic, are especially dangerous. Use rainwater and acid feeds only, please. Concrete (alkaline) pots are another error best avoided.

On the other hand, some plants need lime. A pot of old, leached-out compost may be totally lacking in lime and again the plants will show poor growth. The pH of compost or water may be determined with a simple test kit, available from garden suppliers, and the compost may then be either replaced or modified. Extra sulphur will acidify compost; lime will make it alkaline.

In the open ground, it is barely feasible to change the soil pH by much very quickly, so it is easier to grow plants that suit the conditions. Ground that is manured or composted annually can slowly become acid, hence the old recommendation of liming every fourth year instead. Beware of sites near concrete paths and mortared walls, which may become quite alkaline even when all around is acid soil. If a plant is generally happy, it will tolerate a pH that it would not like otherwise. For example a witch hazel (*Hamamelis*) or skimmia will not thrive on a chalky (alkaline) soil in a dry, sunny site, but will be happier – and show it – if the site is partly shaded and the soil moist and rich in leaf mould.

# feeding problems

## over- or underfeeding

Feeding plants is best little and often, with the stress on the 'little'. Neglecting feeding will eventually give poor results, or no growth at all; in practice, this takes considerable time. It is better to err on the side of under-feeding and using too dilute a feed.

Overfeeding either in frequency, or worse in quantity, gives dark green, luxuriant growth but is more quickly dangerous; it makes plants prone to pests, diseases and frost damage and likely to die. Too much fertiliser kills in the same way as any other strong salt would; a strong application kills plants as readily as a weedkiller. To say nothing about the disruption of soil life: the depression of nitrifying organisms (that make nitrates available to plant roots for free) and the growth of denitrifying organisms (that break down nitrates and cause nitrogen to be lost from the soil into the atmosphere). Nor about the fertilisers that leach into our ground water…

Even just a little too much fertiliser and the plants may suffer. Surplus fertiliser can upset the complex chemical balance of the soil, reacting with other vital nutrients so that they become locked up and unavailable to plants. So it is not uncommon to find tomatoes short of iron and magnesium because they have been given too much potash.

It is safest to feed only sparingly and generally only during the growing season. Soluble fertilisers and liquid feeds must be diluted and never applied in any stronger concentration than weak! Do follow instructions, especially for plants in pots. Forget feeding plants in the open ground and stick to forking on barrow-loads of well made garden compost and well rotted manure!

Liquid feed AFTER giving a really good watering.

## nutrient deficiency

This is effectively another form of over- or underfeeding. It is true that almost all plants could grow a tad more if supplied with whatever they are short of. A drop more sun would do in most cases. Also true: nutrient deficiencies to the point of plant damage are rare, except when caused by over-fertilisation with some other nutrient. Nutrient deficiencies do occur, but only a few are common.

For example most old trees need a feed anyway because their soils become impover-ished, but cooking apples especially need potash. They show a shortage of potash with bluish leaves that yellow and brown at the edges and by making small, gnarled fruits. Similarly, if they need nitrogen the leaves are small, growth is stunted and the fruits are really red but, if nitrogen is in surplus, the leaves are lush and the fruit is very green.

A shortage of lime shows up in apples as little brown spots throughout the flesh. Gooseberries need a lot of wood ash or potash and reveal a deficiency in brown margins to their leaves.

Almost all leaves show some nutrient deficiencies at the end of the season, but if they get odd colours earlier on, there is a simple solution. Don't try and work out if a nutrient is in short supply, and if so which. Spray the plants with dilute seaweed solution regularly and the trouble should start to recede in a week or so (provided that the plants are not in a soil or compost with a wildly unsuitable pH). If the plants do not show a marked improvement, the problem must be caused by something other than nutrient deficiency since seaweed provides all the trace elements that could be needed. (Older leaves may never recover, but the new and semi-mature ones should improve.) Seaweed

# seedling failure

Never handle seedlings by stem, only by a leaf – its loss if damaged is repairable, the stem is not.

solution is worth spraying regularly anyway, to prevent nutrient deficiencies. It does no harm if correctly applied; do not apply it in too strong a solution, every day or in full sun.

## beware of chemicals

### inadvertent overdosing
Strange things happen to plants if they are accidentally given an inappropriate chemical. Some pesticides are harmful to certain plants, many more so if they are applied to the correct plants but in too strong a concentration. Some herbicides are so potent that after only one use a watering can, even many times washed and emptied, will still be contaminated and have an effect on some plants. A drift on the air from a spray used by a farmer or neighbour on wasteland can result in twisted, deformed foliage, variegation, chlorosis or distorted growth. Brassicas, cucumbers and grapevines seem most affected. Some have reported plants suffering even after a conservatory or greenhouse has been treated or repainted.

Absolute care should be taken with any chemicals, horticultural or household. Beware of air fresheners, furniture polish, and especially window cleaner inside, obviously, but also outside! Many an odd-spotting problem for plants has come from these chemicals drifting. And never ever use second-hand watering cans, and especially sprayers, unless you can be certain that they have never ever had herbicides or other noxious substances in them.

Just a little note about weed killer damage. Please be aware that weed killer promotes a gross distortion of leaves, stems and flowers in all sorts of strange ways, especially thickening and curling.

## unexplained absence
Seed may not always germinate and, with no evidence of the cause, just sow again but with more precautions. A trial sowing in a pot under cover will prove the viability of the seed, or obtain fresh seed. Check that the soil or compost is suitable, the conditions warm and moist enough, the likely pests dissuaded and exonerated, the sowing depth correct and the covering soil or compost firmed down sufficiently. Correct firming is crucial, so sometimes it is better to substitute a covering of sterile sowing compost that can be sufficiently well compressed and is not prone to capping. Where individual seedlings seldom appear but sometimes entire clumps emerge by pushing up the topmost crust, it is a bad case of capping. For long term prevention, improve the soil structure and more immediately, cover seed with a better-textured material, such as gritty sowing compost.

## identifying the culprits
When emerged seedlings simply disappear, maybe, just maybe, it was a rot, mould or wilt, scorch or frost that got them, but if there are no bodies on display at all it was probably not one of those usual suspects. Check for birds and slugs, then cutworms, and so on. When whole plants, bulbs or fruits go missing it may still be birds – some such as wood pigeons are quite strong – or foxes, badgers, squirrels and so on. These creatures can be playful and destructive to plants for no apparent reason. They may even plant things for you to find; buried eggs are not unknown. You need to look for other evidence; a night-time vigil will soon reveal the culprit or droppings and hair or fur caught on fencing may give another clue. Once the cause has been determined, you can apply the 'cure' (see pages 112–15).

# how plants suffer physical neglect

I think it has been left far too long Bob! Tut tut.

## pot binding

Generally poor growth and flowering and failure to hold most flowers, buds or fruits are signs of pot binding, as is rapid drying out after watering. Although we know that plants need regular potting up into bigger containers, it's amazing how many, especially house-plants, are allowed to suffer for years without repotting. Often the plants carry on looking fairly happy, although they may need watering more and more frequently as the ratio of foliage to compost worsens. Being slightly pot-bound even suits some flowering plants that are reluctant to bloom until they become congested; however, they stop flowering again once they are really cramped. Therein lies the difference: some pot binding good, too much bad. A very similar effect is caused by planting too deep – especially bulbs, which then find the weight of surrounding soil too much to expand against; if it were shallower, they could crack or heave the soil.

When you come to pot up a plant with yards of roots wound in circles, tease them out under warm water first so that they have a chance of getting into the fresh compost. Then firm them in with good, gritty material packed all round the roots. Otherwise, they may be pot-bound forever by the ghost of the shape of the previous pot.

Most pots do not ever break down, although there were once whale-hide pots and other biodegradable pots do exist, such as those you make from newspaper. So do not plant plants in their pots; remove them first. Netting root bags are also best removed before planting because they may strangle the swelling roots later. It is even possible to get symptoms of being pot-bound by putting plants into small planting holes chiselled out

When roots fill the compost, it's time to pot on – though the odd bare bit, as in this third picture, may be where it was getting too hot in the sun.

of hard ground. For goodness sake, break up the surrounding soil well – the bigger the hole, the better the results; wider is more important than deeper. The root systems we want are mostly near the surface in the most active soil; too many deep roots are not always desirable and are often removed from overly strong fruit trees.

### root strangulation

Similar to pot binding (see above), this condition occurs when the roots grow around each other or through holes, then swell and get constricted. This is especially a problem with trees that have been planted out from containers without teasing out the roots. Because the roots went round and round each other on the rootball, they are unable to support the tree as they grow outwards and constrict themselves. This results in the classic example of the tree coming into leaf

and then fading in early summer and undergoing its 'autumn' months early. The only cure is ruthless uprooting and replanting, properly, during the dormant season. Spearing the roots with a cane or stake causes similar injury. You may be lucky and not damage the roots much, but always take care to put the stake in before the tree; in a pot, use an existing hole to insert a new or bigger cane.

### root isolation

Where the roots become disconnected from the main trunk or stem, or do not establish in the surrounding soil, the plant exhibits very similar symptoms to those of root strangulation and pot binding (see above). The collar, where the top of the plant meets the roots, is especially vulnerable to attack and if rot gets in here the plant is doomed. Often this happens because of a lack of staking in a young sapling or even a standard rose or

fuchsia. The top sways round and round; a cup is formed in the soil around the base of the stem and fills with water; and the collar rots. If the plant was pot-grown and planted insufficiently firmly or if it was bare-rooted, unstaked or very badly planted, there might be air gaps around the roots or rootball. Air gaps allow rocking and cause the roots to pull, bend, break and die – with dire results. Again, it is best to lift and replant when the plant is dormant.

## stem strangulation

Surprisingly large numbers of trees and shrubs are badly damaged by ties and labels being left on until they strangle the plant, or cut deep enough into the bark to let in diseases and pests – a sure sign of neglect. All ties need checking every six months or so. Some plants have been damaged by labels spinning around in the wind and winding the ties so that they slowly but inexorably wear away the bark. Beware the inconspicuous but durable tie that has dropped to ground level and been covered in soil while still fast around the stem; it will kill the plant in a few years. Where a tie has grown in, cut it away and extricate what you can, then seal the wound; if it is on the main stem, provide new supports on either side of the stem, which will be weakened.

## over-pruning

Trees and shrubs that have been over-pruned look at first glance relatively healthy, but fail to flower and fruit. They may have many congested, vertical shoots coming from older branches. A keen but novice gardener rarely prunes hard enough; however, a few prune too hard and, worse, treat all subjects in the same way. Incorrect or over-pruning may remove the bits that would flower and fruit or stimulate excessive regrowth by removing too much wood – and when plants grow strongly they are also unlikely to flower or crop. The answer is to stop pruning unless you do it by the book. However, the countless vertical shoots festooning the branches still need clearing; do this in several stages in mid- to late summer to avoid stimulating even more growth. Learn to summer prune, since this controls growth more effectively than winter pruning.

Ivy and lichens do little harm.
Wire ties can cut in and kill.

## owner's itch

Plants just don't do well. So they are moved
from one place to another, to another, and
then yet another... Plants need time to settle,
even if they are well suited and happy. Indeed
some, such as paeonies, are well known to
take several years to settle after a move.
Christmas cactus (*Schlumbergera*) should
never be moved an inch once the flower buds
form or they may fall off. Gardenias like to stay
put. Plants that are not well suited to their
situation may adjust and succeed, if not
thrive, but will take several seasons to do so.
Houseplants especially are often expected to
survive in adverse conditions; they may need
to drop their leaves to grow ones more suited
to the location, but then get moved before the
new leaves have even matured. Give plants
time: do not fiddle impatiently, repot weekly
or move plants often. And stay away from
applying any *ad hoc* 'treatments', especially
any involving unguided use of the saw and
secateurs or strong fertilisers!

Steps are the biggest cause of serious accidents
in the house and garden. More people hurt themselves by foolishly using steps without checking
that they have firm footing and are well set. Or
worse, overreaching, like this foolish man is
doing, which is extremely dangerous.

# microclimates: what can go wrong

The weather in your garden day by day is largely dictated by your local climate, and this mostly depends on your geographical position. Those in temperate, maritime regions must expect a predominance of cool winds and rain, while those with a more continental climate can expect more variation between summer and winter. But within local areas, and again on an even smaller scale within each garden, are microclimates. In each one, local factors such as soil type, aspect and shelter create places where our plants may experience different, and we hope more appropriate, conditions.

## too hot

Such conditions rarely affect plants in the ground outdoors in the UK – although in the odd hot summer exposed bark on tree trunks may bake; paint it with whitewash before this happens. Plants in pots, especially on warm, sunny patios, can get far too warm, those in black plastic pots the most. Indeed I have noticed that some plants, such as sweet peppers, which you would imagine would enjoy warm soil, actually avoid rooting into the compost on the sunny side of black pots! Many houseplants and quite a few patio specimens are wood-land-shade plants, which is why we can get them to survive in our dark rooms and overcrowded borders. In full sun they may not just scorch their leaves but actually bake their roots, especially if they are in dark pots, and even if they are well watered. The answer, at least in part, is to use double pots to create an air cavity, to repot into white plastic or terracotta pots or to provide black pots with aluminium-foil reflectors.

We can apply shade paint or make rollover shading to keep our greenhouses cooler and dimmer. Many seeds and seedlings get baked to death in propagators, cold frames and in greenhouses when the sun comes out unexpectedly. If there is sufficient automatic ventilation there is no problem, but a closed-up cold frame or a seed tray with a sheet of glass over it can steam everything to death in only a few minutes of hot sun. Many times seed is blamed for being poor when it was cooked during a short, sunny period while you were away at work. And some seeds just will not germinate in soil if it's too warm; lettuce, for example.

## too bright

Whereas too much heat bakes leaves and stems, too much light often results in scorching, bleaching or even burnt spots where water droplets once lay. Plants taken from low light conditions under glass or plastic and put outside in the cold air under bright sun can scorch and desiccate in minutes; they must be hardened off first (see page 52). Likewise with houseplants, generally being woodland-shade plants, they naturally do not like bright conditions and so bleach or scorch. In particular, watch out for large-leafed plants since these tend to be shade loving more often than small-leafed plants. Some plants such as gardenias like bright positions that are not in direct sunlight. Azaleas with small leaves may like a bit more sun than their cousins, rhododendrons, that typically have larger leaves.

## too cold

We all know how frost kills plants, but many will withstand a short, rather cold period if it is dry but will be killed by a longer, less cold, but damp episode. Cold, especially combined with low light, reduces a plant's resistance so that every problem is magnified. First up are often grey

Glass sheet in front for winter to protect a nearly hardy citrus hybrid, moved behind for summer.

One citrus here is not meant to be this yellow – suspect scorch.

moulds and rots and, if these girdle stems, they may kill before the plant ever achieves its minimum safe temperature. Generally plants survive better if they are warmer, but many also do really well if they are just drier. Even in the growing season, warm is better than chill; so watering with really cold water may cause distress and then disease to get in. It is better to warm water to room temperature before use. Fill the cans *after* use and stand them nearby in a warm place; the water will warm up to the ambient temperature in a few hours. Be thoughtful when you draw the curtains to keep in the heat – are you shutting a too tender plant out in the cold?

## too dry air

In air that is too dry, plants use up water quickly yet fail to grow strongly, their leaves get thin and curled and finally they dry up, often getting red spider mite (see page 108). A common problem for plants is that our homes are far too dry. Plants prefer it more humid, but with central heating and air conditioning most household air is desiccated. So plants are often happiest in the less well heated rooms or the more humid kitchen and bathroom. Providing houseplants with pebble baths in saucers, misting their foliage and packing the plants close together will all help.

Outdoors, very dry, searing air like that experienced in deep winter can burn and scorch foliage; often in spring this cold, searing air actually does much of what is thought to be frost damage. Windbreaks, especially netting ones, can protect plants more safely than plastic sheeting, which will cause stagnation. Wrapping tender evergreens with a couple of layers of net when cold, searing winds are predicted will often save them from losing most of their leaves. Cloches, plastic-bottle tubes, and other shelters all help to protect young plants from this searing as much as from simple cold. Sweetcorn for example is fairly cold – tolerant, but not very wind-tolerant.

## too moist or stagnant air

In moist air, plants may develop little drops of water along the leaf edges and veins (a process called guttation); they also get turgid, pumped up full of water, because they cannot transpire. If it is also cool with low sunlight levels, as in spring or autumn, they become very susceptible to

rots and moulds, which run though them like a plague. In the open ground, plants develop all sorts of mildews, rusts and rots whenever the air gets damp and humid, especially by rivers and pools. Increase the airflow by cutting down hedges, open pruning and better spacing; add more heat and ventilation under cover, and be careful when watering not to sprinkle it about too much.

## too draughty

Plants may easily suffer in draughts; in fact, even outdoor plants do not like winds and find it hard to function if winds are blowing more than a few miles an hour. Draughts make houseplants look cold, pinched, thin and lacking in vigour – very similar symptoms to those of plants in dry air. Even Swiss cheese plants (*Monstera deliciosa*), aspidistras and spider plants (*Chlorophytum comosum*) sulk in such spots, but they are the most suitable choices.

# the weather

Just a bit of frost and this will be brown pulp.

the weather is something we can do little about but which seriously affects the way our plants grow, or die – day by day

### the wider environment

The weather is something we can do little about but which seriously affects the way our plants grow, or die – day by day. We cannot change it, except by moving to another region, but sometimes with care we may change its action and effect on the plants in our garden. So we may be able to water during a drought, protect some smaller plants against frost or cold winds and generally strive to create more shelter and warmth. However, there is little we can do about some forms of extreme weather such as tornadoes and lightning except observe the evidence afterwards...

### lightning

Trees or even shrubs damaged by lightning can be strangely scarred or split or have whole branches blown off – and these signs are not always accompanied by burning or signs of heat. Lightning strikes are far more common than you care to imagine and, although it is attracted to metal, lightning also hits tall trees, and even low ones, shrubs and water features. Similar damage can be caused by whiplash – when a tree or branch has been blown so hard it has bent over then sprung back; eucalyptus is very prone to this injury.

### hailstones

Striking as it often does in summer as in winter, hail will cause bruising that shows up later, especially on the tops of fruits, and dropped crops, if not a total shredding of leaves, buds, fruits and flowers. Little can withstand a bad hailstorm. Do not forget that, although most of it is small and shot-sized, hail occasionally reaches huge dimensions and can be bigger than golf balls, which will ruin your car as well as your garden. Netting or plastic sheet screens could be erected, if a warning is given in time. A heavy hail fall can also freeze tender plants at times when snow and frosts are unlikely, especially if it builds up in hollow crowns; tree ferns can be killed in that way.

### frost

Frost may just touch the softer tips of growth on the flowers, buds and leaves and yet leave older leaves untouched. The frozen bits change their shade of green and then moulder if it is wet or go grey or brown if it is dry. Flowering parts are often highly vulnerable and frosts may ruin many potential crops in the bloom. Even after fruit set, small fruitlets are still vulnerable to frost for weeks after. Netting, sheets and so on are the best preventatives.

Frosted tissues are damaged further if they defrost suddenly. It is said that you can prevent frost damage if you spray the frozen parts with cold water before the sun hits them, but this is not easy to do. Now we all know how frosts kill tender plants, but you may not suspect how really cold frosts kill many more plants than the ones you would expect. And any plant that ought to be hardy but has been grown soft, is too well sheltered and overfed will be more easily killed by a slightly colder than usual frost. On the other hand, plants grown hard in dry soils may survive colder weather than usually reckoned. But do not be deceived, it is always possible to suffer occasionally much colder weather than usual.

### protecting against frost

We can wrap the most valued plants with layers of leaves, straw or bracken, or sheets of plastic insulation if we are sure that the plants can still breathe. We can cover the crowns of herbaceous plants with thick, dry mulches (bracken is superb), or even dig plants up and bury them in well covered trenches (done with cherry trees in Russia!). But with luck the usual precautions will do. Don't forget that frost loosens the soil so newly planted subjects may need refirming. Frost heave, as it is called, can even eject pot-grown plants from their containers. Of course, anything that can be broken by the expansion of freezing water will be.

Do not move or even touch items such as hosepipes when they are frozen. Check your shed and greenhouse for bottles of liquids and so on before frosts are due. And do make sure that you have no exposed water pipes, or worse a dripping overflow – this will freeze drip by drip until it is blocked, then will back up and flood your home. Likewise, watch for frozen gutters and downpipes if rain is likely before they thaw. Most importantly, never plant into or dig frozen soil because buried bits stay frozen for a long time.

Scorched, shrivelled apple should be removed as it will be a source of infection.

gets. Never walk, or worse drive, on snow; this helps to pack it down to ice, which then lasts longer. Clear your paths and drives by hand as soon as the snow stops falling and before traffic has compressed it. Salt will of course help to melt it – but go on to poison your plants! Using warm water to melt icy paths will be safer for the plants on either side – or just throw sharp sand on the icy bits so that you can work more safely.

### strong winds
These turn foliage brown, even stripping it off. They desiccate as well as chill and are particularly bad for evergreens and newly planted subjects. Strong winds can loosen roots, even pulling out newly planted evergreens. Using windbreaks on stakes and wrapping treasured plants with netting are good plans, just as used to protect plants in dry air (see Too dry air, page 89).

### sun scorch
Sometimes, sudden patches appear of pale, bleached foliage and flowers; the patches then turn brown. Strawberries, apples and other fruits get scalded patches, like soft bruises, which then rot. These symptoms are common in some seasons, when a long, grey period is followed by a few short, bright, hot days. Plants that are well adjusted to cool, dim damp can't cope suddenly with harsh, bright sunlight all day. I've very badly cooked half my lemon crop by simply failing to open the vents on a sunny winter's day. If spotted before the symptoms appear, this problem is easily thwarted; shade, netting or sheets simply hung over the plants will suffice.

### unseasonality
Plants can cope with minor fluctuations in weather, but when we get cool, damp summers and warm, bright autumns, it's not surprising that some plants are fooled into flowering at the wrong time. Also late, mild winters followed by cold springs with hot days and frosts can confuse plants that evolved in an all-on-or-off, stay-cold-then-get-hot, with no shilly-shallying, continental climate. Some plants just fade away; mostly, they rot. Many plants need a certain period of cold to perform well in the next growing season and if winters are too mild they do badly.

### snow
Broken branches and flattened evergreens betray where snow builds up. If it lodges on branches, it can break them off, and it can pull over entire trees. Shrubs have little chance. Evergreens are worst hit since their leaves carry more snow. Similarly, hedges may be crushed or split open by snow building on their tops, which explains the protective value of tapered sides and a narrower top. Even sheds, greenhouses and particularly fruit cages risk damage from snow: clear it off before it builds up too thickly.

Block gaps, especially under the doors, with rolls of newspaper; snow may blow into places where rain never

# the commonest pests

### what you can do

Even if growing conditions are appropriate your plants may still suffer from the commoner pests. The most likely offenders to cause any damage, and to be found in most gardens and on almost any sort of plant, are listed in the following pages. Although there are problems specific to some plants (see pages 122–201), they are not half as likely to occur as this bunch.

## slugs and snails

These are top of the hit list for gardeners almost everywhere. Their appearance and damage hardly need describing, the confirmation of their guilt is the slime trail. Symptoms are well known: bits missing; whole trays of seedlings gone; rounded holes (they eat by rasping) on edges and in middles of leaves; slime trails. Especially prone to damage are wilting soft growths, seedlings and fruits, over-watered and over-fertilised, soft plants and stressed, badly grown plants. Mollusc numbers increase in heavy, wet soils and damp seasons; they almost disappear from dry, sandy soils in hot, dry years. Slugs may live within the soil (like that notorious potato destroyer, the keeled slug) whereas snails need cool, shady places to hide in. Old-fashioned poison pellets spread around the garden rarely succeeded, but are alleged to have decimated our song birds and killed a few pets. There are better ways.

Control measures are especially important when seedlings are emerging or succulent young transplants are moved, and most on warm, wet nights. A classic problem is 'planting out the brassicas or lettuce today, seeing them half-eaten tomorrow and not doing anything'. Molluscs crave succulent,

## defensive methods

1. **Plastic rings or tubes** cut from drink bottles are free and effective in keeping away a host of other problems as well. Although open at the top, few slugs or snails seem determined enough to scale the sides.

2. **Impregnated cardboard rings** are commercially available and claim to be organic and safe.

3. **Ring barriers made of copper** work and deter all but the most intrepid travellers and may be the answer for a loved plant, but don't circle the plant and let the leaves droop down and bridge the protection.

4. **Cocoa shells** are remarkably effective for longer than most mulch type rings as they stick together and their smell seems to repel. Coffee grounds are similarily effective.

wilting leaves of fresh transplants, but after a week or so our plants get tougher and less appealing. So pre-emptive action is required – and effective action: throwing them over the fence does not work. Snails will easily manage to walk home; an hour or two later, they will be back. You are just exercising them and building up their appetites. If you catch them, kill them quickly or release them a very long way off. (I prefer to confine them to my 'snail-catraz' composter (see page 49).

Garden hygiene and trapping are both effective: a night patrol with a torch or a tidy-up produces startling numbers of slugs and snails. They are found in cool, moist places such as in stored pots and pans or a pile of empty bottles – don't allow this sort of 'junk' to accumulate near a salad bed, seedbed, cold frame or in the greenhouse, unless regularly policed. Deliberate traps can be made for them under a bush, hedge or other cover.

### slug and snail barriers

Total exclusion is a most effective technique and a number of barriers may be suitable, according to circumstances. Protect buds and crowns of most herbaceous plants while dormant in winter with a thick mulch of sharp sand to repel the pests. Once plants are in growth, the molluscs may cross sand but will avoid harsher materials. Rings of soot, wood ashes, baked and crushed eggshells and so on are fairly successful if short-lived since rain and birds disturb them. Cocoa shells are remarkably effective, for longer – they stick together and the smell seems to repel. Coffee grounds act similarly. Prickly leaves such as holly are reputed to work, but I don't want them where I hand weed, do you?

Copper ring barriers are more aesthetic and incredibly expensive, but deter all but the most intrepid travellers. It may be the answer for a loved plant, but don't let the leaves droop and bridge the copper barrier. Impregnated cardboard rings are claimed to be organic and copper and zinc tapes are also available. Self-adhesive tapes are especially useful for the sides of propagators and cold frames.

Plastic rings and tubes cut from drink bottles are free and very useful, and keep away a host of other problems. Aluminium drink cans may be cut into protective rings; use pinking shears for a rim so spiky it's impossible for the pests to cross.

A double saucer protects plants in pots; one, for draining and watering as usual, stands in another wider one kept full of water. Plain water is sufficient but salty water is surer. Similarly, a very wide, shallow tray of

water keeps safe plants that can stand having wet roots most of the time, such as young melon, tomato and cucumber plants in the first rush of growth in spring.

### slug and snail distractions

Sacrificial barriers encircling a new crop or transplants give the molluscs something tastier. Use any surplus plants and damaged bits. Why should the pest walk further when a tasty meal is there already? The next step is to grow soft succulent leaves such as lettuce and Chinese cabbage under cover just for sacrificial barriers around other plants. The sacrifice can even be grown *in situ* but you risk it becoming a breeding ground. Sacrificial barriers work best combined with ruthless nightly inspections.

Oatmeal is a favourite of slugs and snails and piles of this, or bran, hidden under leaves can both trap and/or fob them off. Some claim they may explode after eating these as they absorb water. I'm dubious.

Different cultivars are more or less mollusc-prone; some escape damage when others are shot to pieces. This does not always mean that you should not grow them. The onion cultivar 'Buffalo' mixed in with my other autumn-sown onions attracted slugs to the point of extermination, leaving the other onions relatively unscathed and 'auto thinned'.

### slug and snail traps

Baited traps are especially effective against soil-dwelling slugs that bedevil our root crops. Hollow out surplus but sound carrots, apples, potatoes, swedes and turnips and place near an infested crop to lure the pests. Putting bait traps around potato plants in flower eliminates many slugs before the new tubers even finish forming. Hollow traps are also useful in the root and apple store. If you have no vegetables to hollow, household peelings will do. Place the bait in a pot on its side or under an

## a superior slug pub

1 Using a pair of scissors cut crenellations from a plastic bottle. Turn those crenellations on the base inwards to form ramps.

2 Bury the bottom in the soil and pour in your choice of liquid – fruit juice, milk or beer.

3 Slugs and snails are attracted to the liquid and can climb in down the ramps.

4 Push the top over to exclude pets and rainwater.

Soil-dwelling pests can be controlled by parasitic nematodes washed in with water.

A thrush's anvil.

inverted saucer on a stone, so the pests can get beneath, and cover with a cabbage leaf or similar to keep it cool. Buttered cabbage leaves are said to be very efficient although it seems rather profligate. I find citrus shells less good than vegetable peelings. Marrows and squashes make large traps but rot very quickly.

Slug pubs, bowls of beer, milk or fermenting fruit juice, are commercially made, but a saucer is fine. Bury it to the rim near suscep-tible plants or a pest haunt and fill it to the brim. The fermenting smell reminds the molluscs of rotting fruit and they dive in and drown. You may need to empty and replenish it daily. Unfortunately, this trap may also drown useful ground beetles; to help them escape, place some twiggy material in the trap. A superior slug pub may be made from a plastic bottle: divide the bottle in two by cutting a coarse crenellation so that the top and bottom both have largish tabs. Bury the bottom so that it is flush with the soil surface and turn the tabs inwards to form ramps. Fill it with juice, milk or beer, and then cover with the top by slotting its tabs over the bottom and between the ramps. The cover excludes rain and pets, and I find the ramps effectively entice slugs and snails to their death, but covered pubs seem less inviting to ground beetles. One slug pub is not enough; ideally, place one every stride or two about the vegetable plot, beds and borders, especially near susceptible plants.

### slug and snail natural controls

Parasitic eelworms (nematodes) are a simple but expensive solution. As long as the soil is moist and the temperature above 5°C (41°F), sprinkling on a solution of *Phasmarhabditis hermaphrodita*, a microscopic nematode, every six weeks or so will almost eradicate them. These nematodes are

ineffective in cold or drought because they swim in the water between soil particles looking for slugs, so are worth using only in late spring and early autumn. Parasitic eelworms are not so effective on snails, which are protected by their shells and by living out of the soil. However, nematodes may attack snails if watered onto the surfaces that the molluscs crawl across.

To get more nematodes per buck, search out dying slugs, some days after applying bought-in nematodes, put these to soak in warm water and water the solution onto the next area. The run-off from a snail composter, containing wastes from dying and dead snails, is bound to be nasty to the living and can be watered around susceptible plants. Keep it well away from salads and crops that are eaten raw – other, harmful pathogens may be present.

Ducks, especially Khaki Campbells and Indian Runners, love slugs and snails and do much less garden damage than hens, so are worth considering.

Nature's other helpers come for free.

Songbirds are especially useful and give so much pleasure. Do remember to leave a few big stones about to serve as anvils for thrushes to shatter snails' shells upon. Ponds and pools, particularly those with muddy edges and marginal areas, encourage marsh or sciarid flies, which attack slugs and snails. And those wet areas help frogs, newts and toads, which all keep down the mollusc population. Many ground beetles eat the odd slug or snail, but more importantly destroy their eggs. And of course in the UK hedgehogs are well known for their nightly foraging of all sorts of pests.

Woodlice do a lot of harm – unseen at night!

As do earwigs.

While ants farm pests for the exudates.

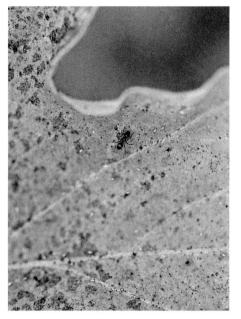

## woodlice and earwigs

Like slugs and snails, these pests leave trails of destruction behind them. However, they have different and smaller mouthparts and chew at the edges of leaves and petals and through and around small stems. They are often the real culprits instead of slugs and snails. Coming out mostly at night *en masse*, they do considerable damage – I've seen a pack of woodlice chewing down a potato plant. They also predate smaller pests and their eggs, process dead material such as decaying wood and are useful snacks for larger creatures, so have a part to play in garden ecology.

Woodlice (a.k.a. slaters, pill bugs, sow bugs, pea bugs) are easiest caught with a portable vacuum cleaner since they're too quick to catch by hand. Trap them under bits of decaying old wood or bark, in hollowed-out potatoes or roots and in stacks of tiles, bricks or saucers. Earwigs like hiding in straw-stuffed pots on top of canes, and in little tubes, such as bamboo. Winding corrugated cardboard

around a cane or stick makes an excellent trap, and one that's more easily emptied.

## ants

These milk, farm, protect, over-winter and increase the numbers of aphids and other pests on our plants. Black ants move aphids to better feeding on more tender shoots, and they keep almost all predators away from their 'flocks'. Ants like the sweet, partly digested sap excreted by aphids and encourage them to release it by stroking them. Ants may farm other pests such as scale insects, mealy bugs and whiteflies. They may however predate other pests; the Chinese used them to control caterpillars and other pests. When I gave a colony ample sugary foods, they stopped farming the pests, most of which disappeared. Ants do undermine the roots of seedlings and even bigger plants with their burrowing, and coat surrounding stems with the pulverised soil they excavate. This stuff may be an important nutrient source for other plants,

especially since it contains fine particles.

Ants can be stopped from climbing stems and trunks with bands of cotton wool and non-setting glues, by rings of fine powders such as lime or by creating moats in double saucers around plants in pots. You could also stand big pots on feet or bricks in trays of water or oil. It's said that strewing mint, especially spearmint or pennyroyal, repels ants. Growing mint or tansy near their nests or watering on the herbal teas discourages them, as does regularly hosing out their nests with soapy water. To find the nests, put out white sugar, watch where they go with it and mark the entrance. Then pour in boiling water until it stops bubbling.

A parasitic nematode, *Steinernema feltiae*, may be watered onto the nest, if the soil is moist and above 10–12°C (10–54°F). You can farm ants: put tin cans or pots on the tops of known nest sites and the ants will fill them with soil and move in the 'eggs' or cocoons to warm every afternoon. You come along mid-afternoon and empty soil, eggs and ants into a bucket of water; the soil and stones sink and the eggs, cocoons and ants float; pour through a sieve to catch them and give these nutritious goodies to chickens, wild birds or fish; add the mud to your compost heap. The ants do learn to avoid the tins after a time but it works for long enough to weaken the colonies.

## aphids

What you spot first are twisted or curled shoots and leaves. On trees and shrubs, this aphid damage, especially of tip growths, has much the same effect as proper summer pruning and may even be of benefit. Although they transmit diseases, moderate aphid attacks take relatively few nutrients and do not affect growth much of established plants; heavy infestations may prevent flowering or ripening. Seedlings and young plants are more badly affected by even just a few aphids and need immediate treatment. There are many different aphids (a.k.a. blackfly, greenfly, dolphin, plant lice); some are specific to a few species while others can live on many different garden plants.

They do not actually suck sap but allow sap to be pumped by pressure into them, taking what they need and excreting the excess sticky, sweet sap. The honeydew sticks to lower leaves and fruits where it feeds sooty mould, blocks light and clogs pores. Any sap falling on the ground, along with dead aphid skins and bodies, adds fertility to the soil and encourages soil micro-organisms – so the plant can bear an even bigger load of aphids next time, I guess. Unfortunately, it may ruin the grass on the way. Jets of water can dislodge aphids off shoots and rosebuds. Commercial soft-soap sprays work really well, but do not use washing-up liquid, detergent or shampoo because these may burn foliage – as may soft soap, or even water, in very hot sun.

## ants

Use cotton wool as a barrier to stop ants climbing...

... Or petroleum jelly.

Lifting the pot exposes the eggs and cocoons to the birds.

The pot lured them to fill it with the soil, eggs and cocoons, now exposed to birds.

Jetting pests off pineapples into the pool stops them climbing back.

Golden aphid, parasitised – moving this into the greenhouse will control aphids there.

Dusts, from cornstarch to wood ashes, make it difficult for them to move around and may even kill them. In the greenhouse, polytunnel or conservatory, it's possible to use specific diseases, parasites and predators to control aphids. You open the packets and they do the job for us.

The parasitic midge *Aphidoletes aphidimyza* and a minute wasp (*Aphidius* spp.) are the usual controls for aphids under cover and work if the temperature is at least 10°C (50°F). Ladybirds and lacewings are also commercially supplied. Lacewing larvae may be sprinkled on infested plants outdoors also and are very good hunters. I catch garden ladybirds to bring under cover and use a naturally occurring parasite to control aphids. Among my hedge I planted some Sweet Briar rose (*Rosa rubiginosa*): this carries early aphid attacks that do little harm; among them I can spot swollen, 'golden' aphids. These are

## methods against aphids

parasitised and, in a week or two, a hole appears in each through which the parasite quits to infect more aphids. I collect these leaves and move them to other plants that have aphids.

French marigolds (*Tagetes patula*) traditionally repel whitefly from tomatoes and may deter aphids. Growing basil under them is said to keep off aphids. Mind you, maybe that's because they seem only too happy on the basil. Mass plantings of chives, lavender and most aromatic herbs can disguise plants hidden among them from aphids, which hunt by smell. It's thought nasturtiums and French beans keep brassicas among them cleaner. Natural predators such as blue tits, wrens, wasps, ladybirds, lacewings and hoverflies are the best aphid controls, so fill your borders with attractant companion plants, and have more bird boxes. Hanging a fat ball among roses or fruit bushes in winter gets them cleaned of aphid eggs by birds waiting their turn on the fat ball.

Very similar in almost every way to aphids, except often smaller, are psyllids and leafhoppers; these are controlled by the same measures (see also Thrips, page 107). Root aphids are exactly that, sometimes they live top and bottom, like woolly aphids. These are hard to get at; on plants such as lettuce the roots can be inspected when transplanting them.

Dusting with anything to ensure cover.

Pull the leaf back to ensure the dusting gets on the undersides.

Soap spray also needs to be on the undersides.

Letting out the metaphycus, a minute wasp, which controls scale pests.

## scale insects and mealy bugs

Sometimes scales are really hard to spot, and then you suddenly see them everywhere. They look like small, helmet-shaped bumps on stems, a bit like buds or indeed scales, and when squished, may exude white powder (eggs). Smaller ones look like bran on the back of leaves and stems. Hard scales are tougher, found on many garden plants, variable in shape and specific to the host plant, so are unlikely to infect different plants around. Mussel scale is a hard scale shaped like a mussel that builds up in masses. Soft scales are slightly less armored, usually dome-shaped and spread about more widely; they are mostly a problem under cover. In their huge numbers, they yellow and kill foliage, shrivel flowers, fruits and buds and provide a breeding ground for sooty moulds with their excreta. Very similar are mealy bugs; sometimes more mobile, they are pinkish- or greyish-white and covered in cottony wax and fluff. Both pests plague perennial plants under cover and some garden specimens, especially evergreens such as bay; they may move onto annuals, especially mealy bugs. Ants often farm scales and increase the problem.

Traditionally, both pests were washed or brushed off by hand with soapy water or dabbed with neat or very strong alcohol to

Scale on citrus.

poison them. In winter, cowpat poultices were applied to stems and trunks to choke them, very effectively. We can use emulsions of vegetable oil in the same way. Mealy bugs may be lured onto 'trap plants' of sprouting potatoes, tomatoes or cucurbits and disposed of. Scales do not oblige so easily. If it is above 14°C (57°F) under cover, use a nematode (*Steinernema* spp.) against soft scale or a wasp (*Metaphycus helvolus*) at a minimum of

Scale eggs.

22°C (72°F) to parasitise the scales. The shaggy white larvae of *Cryptolaemus montrouzieri*, a ladybird, control mealy bugs, if the temperature is at least 20°C (68°F). Both pests may be controlled by lacewings or, on low-growing plants, by the *Hypoaspis* mite.

## capsid bugs and cuckoo spit

These beetles are usually greenish and about the size of a fat aphid or small ladybird, but

**Red spider mite controls placed on an infected leaf.**

**Mealy bug masses on tomatoes.**

**Painting mealy bug with alcohol.**

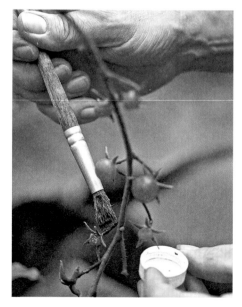

Ladybirds control many different pests and should be encouraged or even captured and brought into the greenhouse.

Cuckoo spit looks much worse than it is.

you rarely spot them, although you may come across the similar froghopper, which sits in its own froth of cuckoo spit. The latter is rarely a problem except perhaps on lavender and a few other plants where it may cause the shoots to wilt; it can be washed off with soft soap solutions. Infestations of capsid and the related tarnished bugs often cause damage to leaves, shoots and fruits, which doesn't often show until long after the pest has gone. Early attacks may be thwarted by shaking or jetting infested trees or bushes so the capsids fall off; they may be gathered on a sheet or prevented from regaining their places by sticky bands around trunks and stems. Other than good hygiene and encouraging natural predators, there is little else you can do.

## vine weevils

Two things occur, apparently independently. Pencil-sized holes appear clipped out of the leaf edges and some plants weaken and suddenly die. These are both due to several species of small, beetle-like weevils. Adults chew the leaves, doing little harm, but in the soil their larvae, whitish grubs about fingernail length, with dark heads, destroy the roots and corms of plants. (Especially attacked are begonias, cyclamen, fuchsias, grapevines, primulas, strawberries and evergreen ornamentals.)

If you surround a suspected plant with newspaper and visit it at night, you can shake off any beetles present. They hide in dry cracks between pot and soil and can be

trapped in bundles of rolled-up corrugated cardboard. Chickens or ducks control them although these are suitable only in areas such as vineyards or fruit cages. Adult weevils can be kept away from pot plants by rings of non-setting glue or by standing the pots in double saucers with a moat between of oil or preferably salty water. Large tubs can be stood on feet in trays and treated similarly. Any suspect plants in pots should be evicted and inspected. In open ground, the grubs are obviously harder to find, but disinter all dead plants and inspect the soil.

When the soil is moist and over 12°C (54°F), water on a solution of the microscopic nematodes *Heterorhabditis megidis* or *Steinernema* species; these swim in the soil

A plastic tube cloche (old bottle) keeps off many pests, diseases, problems and the weather.

water, searching out vine-weevil grubs to parasitise. Nematodes are also most effective in pots and the greenhouse border.

There are many other weevils that are far less serious than vine weevils and usually much smaller. Generally, they are more of an annoyance than a threat, except to seedlings. Trap them in hollow reeds or canes and blow them out into salty water.

## swift-moth caterpillars

The swift-moth's root-eating caterpillars cause similar damage to vine weevil larvae and are whitish with a red head. They may be found eating the roots of almost any herbaceous or bulbous plants. Lure them onto chips of potato and carrot pushed into holes alongside infested plants and cull them regularly.

## cutworms

Cutworms are dingy brown, soil-living caterpillars that often decimate young seedlings. They do most damage from mid- to late summer and into autumn. As they visit the soil surface at night, they are easy to spot with a torch.

## chafers, wireworms and leatherjackets (bots)

These pests attack mostly grasses. However, attacks on other plants may be frequent in the first years after converting turfed areas to a vegetable bed or flower border, and also in beds weedy with grasses. The symptoms are sick, weak plants and poor patches of yellowing growth in turf, which birds, foxes and badgers tear up to get at the grubs. Chafers are whitish grubs with brown heads and six small legs that destroy roots and tubers. They may be about the same size or up to three times larger than vine weevil grubs, which they roughly resemble. The lustrous chafer beetles may also seriously damage foliage and flowers.

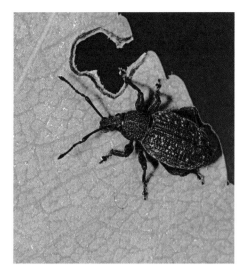

Vine weevil.

Wireworm.

Symphalids.

Wireworms are long, thin, hard, yellowish grubs, with three pairs of tiny legs too small to notice. Rather difficult to squish, these are the larvae of the click beetle. (The adult, if placed on its back, springs upright emitting a click.) Wireworms are pests of grass roots but long-lived and, after their first year, may move off the grass to eat roots of plants nearby for the next four or five years! Digging in green manures of mustard should get rid of this pest. Or trap them as for swift-moth caterpillars.

Leatherjackets are violently wriggling, pointed grey grubs, similar to cutworms but with no legs and a tad bigger than the wireworms. The adult is the crane fly or daddy-long-legs, a fearsome-looking but harmless giant 'mosquito'. The grubs do horrendous damage to lawns and other plants; unlike most pests, they eat throughout winter too.

All of these pests like damp and dark and can be brought to the surface for the birds or chickens by laying carpet, cardboard or opaque plastic sheet over well-soaked ground; roll it back first thing in the morning. They can also be baited onto chips of potato and carrot, germinating grain, bran and even bread hidden under pieces of bark, wet newspaper or cardboard. You can water parasitic nematodes onto wet soil – *Heterorhabditis megidis* for chafers when the soil is warmer than 12°C (54°F) and *Steinernema feltiae* for leatherjackets when the soil is over 10–12°C (50–54°F).

## millipedes

Holes in roots and stems and general damage at ground level are likely to involve millipedes, which if they did not start the damage soon move in. They are thin and rounded, long and dark or black, with many legs underneath and when discovered often curl up. They eat some pests but also attack roots, seedlings and fruits. (Centipedes are flattened and long, often rusty-brown, with legs sticking out sideways and are useful predators.) Millipedes are best trapped with hollowed-out potatoes, turnips or swedes.

## eelworms or nematodes

Afflicted plants sicken and do badly for no obvious reason, especially where the same sort of plant that has been grown for years in the same soil. Although we use some parasitic nematodes to control pests, many others are serious pests – especially to potatoes and tomatoes, and begonias, chrysanthemums, coleus, delphiniums, gloxinias, irises, tulips, narcissus, orchids and salvias. Onion and leek leaves swell and distort, and their bulbs crack and rot. Other bulbs show softening, and leaf and stem shortening. With chrysanthemums, ferns, phlox and sweet Williams, eelworms swim up wet surfaces to penetrate the leaves and stems, causing browning, splitting, stunting or whippiness. Root knot eelworms cause galls, from tiny spots to huge lumps on the roots as big as plums, and ruin crops such

as beans, cucumbers, lettuces and tomatoes with little remedy; they are worst in light, warm soils. It is claimed that powdered leaves of the Madagascar periwinkle, *Catharanthus roseus*, reduce their populations.

Eelworms survive in the soil for a long time and there is no cure for infected plants, which should be burnt straightaway. The old boys found that bulbs and roots of plants such as chrysanthemums, phlox, strawberries and tulips may be cleaned by heating their roots in a water bath at 43°C (110°F) for twenty minutes or so and chilling them. Eelworms sometimes are on bought-in plants but are not noticed and only become a problem once they have built up to damaging levels. Then you just cannot grow some types of bedding or crops there any more. Applying large quantities of garden compost helps, as may digging in green manures of *Tagetes* and possibly of mustard. However, eelworms are very hard to eradicate and it's easier to stop growing susceptible plants or grow them in pots of sterile compost as long as possible before planting in infected ground.

## symphalids

These small, white, slender grubs are often confused with eelworms, but are in fact much bigger, up to as long as your fingernail. Prevalent in soils rich in organic matter, these can be a pest of beans, cucumbers, lettuce, tomatoes and other greenhouse crops. They often attack

Hardly anyone doesn't know this problem.

at ground level at night, leaving exposed roots looking corky and gnarled, and then rots get in. They are best thinned out by planting sacrificial crops of the plants listed above, which you dig up to get at symphalids feeding on their roots, or replace your soil or potting compost with fresh. Spread infested compost onto a plastic sheet for birds to scratch up the pests.

## flatworms

All these revolting, slimy, unpleasantly large flatworms eat other useful worms and so destroy garden drainage and fertility. Most are confined to the more acid-soiled, damper regions where they are serious pests. They may be trapped under slabs and between stacks of saucers, tiles and so on. Do not handle them – they could cause a skin reaction. Scissors are very satisfying.

## caterpillars, maggots and 'worms'

These all do much the same damage, taking bits out of leaves, shoots and fruits. Although the majority are pests, a few are useful like the lacewing larvae, a revolting grub but valuable predator. Some caterpillars are beautiful, and many of the butterflies and moths they become are even more so, yet most are pests. Many plants are attacked by their own, often quite small, sawfly caterpillars: a common identifying characteristic is that they rear up from the stem or leaf edge or drop off when shaken or disturbed.

Common offenders are the tortrix moth family; the grubs wriggle backwards if tapped on the head and tie leaf tips together to make 'tents'. The angle-shades moth looks like a crumpled leaf and devastates most plants; its small, olive-brown or greenish caterpillars are often found eating flowers or leaves near flower buds. Both these may be hand picked, and the smallest killed with soft-soap sprays or choked

Non-setting glue bands stop many pests climbing stems.

Corrugated cardboard bands wound round a stem or trunk traps many pests.

with dusts such as wood ashes. Loopers are so-called because they move their front and back ends separately, forming a bridge or loop as they go. The adult moths have delightful names like green pug, March, mottled umber, pepper and salt and winter, but their offspring damage many fruits and ornamentals.

There are some biological controls available, which you merely water or sprinkle on your cabbages. *Bacillus thuringiensis* for brassica caterpillars is currently unavailable to amateur gardeners in the UK, but may be licensed again in the future; it is still available in some countries. Most caterpillar, maggot, worm and grub attacks may be avoided by growing crops under nets or fleeces to exclude the flying adults. Under cover, fit ventilation and doors with mesh screens. A few species have non-flying adults; these may be easily excluded with non-setting sticky bands on the trunks.

We think of caterpillars as leaf eaters, but other maggots, 'worms' and various grubs usually live inside fruits and storage organs such as bulbs which makes them harder to tackle. Good hygiene, regular inspection, removal and disposal are your main weapons to prevent attacks from increasing year on year. Some pests have specific predators and parasites that catch them at different stages and companion plants will encourage these.

True worms do little damage. The casts of big lugworms may cause problems on the turf – but the extra drainage and aeration is a greater benefit. But worms also drag over onion and shallot sets and leek plants by their leaves. The sets need their dead bits of leaf to be removed before they are put out. Cut away enough of the longer leaf tips of leeks so the remainder stands proud and does not drag on the soil. Onion and shallot sets may be held firmly in place with a small, surrounding mound of fine soil or sharp sand that may be brushed away later.

Releasing lace wing larvae to control many pests.

Flea beetle damage.

## thrips, sciarid flies and flea beetles

Little tiny black things jumping about indoors are probably thrips, especially if they are on African violets (*Saintpaulia*) or chrysanthemums. They cause all sorts of problems considering their small size; mottling, distortion, leaf blistering, loss of growing points and damaged flowers. Look for small, whitish areas of damage surrounded by black dots. Thrips are worst in hot, dry years. Syringing plants regularly can wash off thrips; adding soft soap may help. They can be caught on sticky adhesive floor coverings under the plants, where they fall if disturbed, or you can release predatory mites (*Amblyseius* spp.) in temperatures over 18°C (64°F).

Very similar to thrips are sciarid or compost flies; these tend to indicate sour, wet, acid compost and are not usually pests, but eat the roots of some young bedding, notably Busy Lizzies (*Impatiens*). Improving the compost's drainage, adding lime if possible and vacuum cleaning the area will help. Releasing the predatory mite *Hypoaspis* in temperatures above 11°C (52°F) will control them as well as thrips. On a few crops such as brassicas and on seedlings outdoors, more often the little, black, jumping things will be flea beetles. These destroy small seedlings and leave a multitude of tiny holes in many others; they are especially fond of brassicas and related plants. Discouraged by wet and by dusting with lime or wood ashes, thrips and especially flea beetles may be trapped by waving sticky flypaper close above them (they jump if disturbed, and stick). Flea beetles may be repelled by the smell of tomato foliage so discarded sideshoots keep them away from seedbeds.

## psyllids and leafhoppers

Psyllids are like aphids (see page 99–101), but these and the similar leafhoppers are tiny, yellowish, active insects that attack leaves, leaving bleached areas, and dropping honey-dew. Both are treated much the same as thrips.

# methods against mites

Red spider mite – serious infection on watermelon.

Sometimes the predators come in coarse bran or cocoa shell, which needs depositing on the leaves.

Syringing helps.

## spider mites and other mites

These mites, especially red spider mites, are not spiders (which are useful predators) and cause a great deal of damage. They also carry diseases. Red spider mites are not red, but greyish-green with a couple of brown blobs, and become rusty brown in autumn when they disappear to hide over winter. The mites are just visible as tiny specks; more often we notice the gossamer webbing that covers younger shoots and tips. The leaves turn yellow and desiccated with tens of thousands of tiny pinpricks. The undersides of leaves become bronzed; older leaves become withered or crisp. The fine webbing protects these pests from many predators, sprays and dusts.

Red spider mites may attack soft fruits outdoors in hot weather, and are a common and serious problem on plants under cover and on dry walls. The predatory mites *Phytoseiulus persimilis* are just bigger than the spider mites and control them very well if introduced early enough in the season, at 16–20°C (61–68°F) or warmer. Otherwise keeping the air humid and spraying water on the undersides of leaves discourages them, and seaweed and soft soap solutions more so. Attracting them onto melon or broad bean plants in pots that are then taken away and composted may thin the pests out.

## whiteflies

These are really tiny white moths. Under cover, you rarely go long before whiteflies appear, often in clouds. The flying adults lay their eggs on the undersides of leaves, and their attacks soon weaken plants. Thin them out with a vacuum cleaner or introduce sweet tobacco (*Nicotiana*) plants in pots and remove them once the whiteflies have settled on them (hold them in place with sugar syrup or hair spray). They can be choked with soft-soap sprays; yellow sticky traps are not effective traps but good indicators of the pests' numbers.

The biological control is *Encarsia formosa*, small, parasitic wasps that have been phenomenally effective since the 1920s. They reduce whitefly populations, in temperatures above 18°C (64°F), by attacking the whitish scales (immature nymphs), which turn black once parasitised. Under warm cover with year-round plantings, I find plants such as *Lippia dulcis* and *Salvia coccinea* act as bankers, always carrying some whitefly but also some parasites, so the pest is permanently under control without new introductions. Outdoors, there is a different creature entirely, a moth-like fly with powdery wings, that very closely resembles the glasshouse whitefly; it is found on brassicas and can also be controlled with a vacuum cleaner or soft soap or excluded with fine mesh netting.

## methods against whiteflies

See the fly – not long before a spider gets it. The spider is hiding under the tube fastened under the horizontal rail.

Whiteflies are attracted to tobacco, even getting stuck on sticky ones such as *Nicotiana sylvestris*.

Sucking up whitefly works!

Yellow sticky traps are more indicators than traps.

## leaf miners

Early attacks of leaf miners, which bother only a few plants anyway and are usually specific to that genus, are due to various grubs and larvae that tunnel inside and eat the leaf. They leave the transparent leaf surfaces intact to protect themselves. Initially these may appear as small spots in the leaf that soon turn into patterns, revealing the tunnels. These insects may be squished or needled with a sharp pin.

# methods against flies

Flies spread pests and diseases and damage fruits.

Fly and wasp trap of a bottle of sweet liquid.

UV light, effective against mozzies and night creatures.

Sundews don't catch many, but help.

## wasps

From early spring, true wasps slaughter plant pests to feed their young and are our greatest allies, but come midsummer and they start on our fruits. They suck all the juice out of berries, leaving withered skins, hollow out top fruit and bother us when we eat *al fresco*. I leave them alone. However, if you must destroy them do so only when they are on your fruit. Catch some wasps in a jammy jar, towards dusk dust them with flour, release them one at a time and follow them home. When you find the nest, employ a professional to clear it – you do not want to try yourself, believe me.

Alternatively, protect individual fruits, whole branches or pot-grown bushes with muslin or fine netting bags and use wasp traps. These are bottles or jars that are half filled with water mixed with jam; the sweet, fruity smell attracts wasps, which fly in, can't land, slip and drown. Make traps more effective by reducing the entrances to one or two pencil-sized holes in aluminium foil wrapped over the mouth. Killing the first scouts often prevents bigger-scale attacks. Never use honey as bait because it attracts bees as well.

## flies

These spread disease by vomiting on food as well as walking on it, which is why we need to wash fruit and so on, especially if there are animal faeces or dead bodies about. Plagues of flies indicate that something died and are a blessing in disguise – the smell of a decaying rat is much worse than the flies. Flies also add to existing damage on fruit. Fine mesh on windows and doors keeps them out. Flypapers are excellent. Wasp traps work well for flies too. UV traps seem to work only on the occasional fly and are better for attracting night-flying critters, such as mozzies.

Netting bags keep off wasps and flies.

## mosquitoes and gnats

These pose not so much a problem to the garden as to gardeners and their pets and children, especially if you live by water. There is little you can do but you can prevent local breeding in water butts. Pour a little cooking oil onto the surface of the water to suffocate the larvae or keep a goldfish or two in every butt – I've done this for years and the water comes pre-fertilised with fish poo. (In two decades, the butts have occasionally frozen half solid and the fish always survived; however a kingfisher has had many.)

## galls

One of the oddest things people ever see is the rose bedeguar gall, or Robin's pincushion. Reddish or greenish, spiky, lumpy golf balls appear on the stems of roses and can be rather pretty. Each is caused by a small insect that lives in the gall, a swelling produced by the rose in response to the insect's saliva. Similar galls occur on other plants, especially brambles. Other galls, of countless shapes and sizes, from little rubbery stars and fingers to odd excrescences, appear on all sorts of plants. Few ever do much actual harm.

# larger common pests

## birds

Your seeds stolen, seedlings razored off, fruit and foliage damaged and missing? Who is to blame? A dead giveaway is the beak-shaped, triangular nature of the damage. One of the commonest problems for most gardeners is birds. They also peck out buds and pull off petals, flowers and labels. Birds are curious and destructive; try a parrot if you don't believe me. They dust-bathe in seedbeds and kick mulches all over the place. Large birds such as wood pigeons can tackle nuts and trample or even pull up plants. Of course many birds do much good, but others cause much loss.

Birds can either be frightened away or physically excluded (some such as wood pigeons are considered agricultural pests and may be shot in season). A scarecrow will not work on local garden birds, but may deter the odd flock, but if it does not move soon it will not even frighten them. Indeed all bird-scaring devices work much better if they are replaced with different ones frequently. So hanging a few tin lids or old CDs to act as glitter bangs only works for the first day or so. Change them for balloons, then ribbons, or flags and back to CDs every other day or so. This keeps up the bird paranoia and works especially well if you also 'fly', or suspend, some lifelike, fake hawks; even remarkably un-lifelike ones work, with a V-silhouette. I've had amazing success with a potato and a few feathers, paper kites and even plastic model aircraft blown along fishing lines. This is real psychological warfare!

Add to their doubts with a colony of regularly moved, fake cats made from old fur coats, fake snakes made from bits of hose-pipe and, best of all, fake spiders. Even if the local spiders are not bird-eating ones, birds are so scared of them that even a lacy, holey piece

of worn-out cloth laid over a fruit bush to look like a spider's web can be almost as effective as a proper net. Fake spiders' webs can be bought but are fiddly to use. Huge fairground spiders scare well, and are fun. Black cotton tied from twig to twig or around short canes over a seedbed or just above flowers works in a similar way. The birds are unhappy about anything touching their legs or wings as they move about, especially if it is thread-like. Humming flashing tape can be bought and works for a while, but don't use old cassette tapes; their coating falls off and pollutes. Shouting is traditional; hanging a bell and a string in the tree is less effort and an electric one with a flashing light even better. A sprinkler on the end of a hose may shock birds the first few times. A real cat certainly keeps birds on their toes. But best of all is secure netting.

## birds and fruit cages

A fruit cage is a must. You can net individual bushes and smaller trees, but economies of scale make a cage the best option. And the bigger, the better. I never got a cherry for twenty years until I grew new trees in a huge cage, which leaves plenty of space underneath for all the soft fruits. It is made from a recycled polytunnel, with the plastic sheet replaced by plastic netting. Along the base is wire netting since most damage and wear occurs at ground level. Whatever the size of cage, it makes sense to mulch heavily throughout to keep weeds down and this suits the majority of plants in it because they are mostly denizens of the woodland edge.

Don't get too small a cage or, more importantly, too low a cage; height is important for comfort and for many fruits. Birds have all day, every day, to break in so patch any hole;

Netting is the best bird preventative. Be careful they don't get in at the bottom.

look out for holes at ground level made by hedgehogs, cats and rats since these are the ones the birds spot soonest. Ensure that the gate shuts closely and especially that there is no gap at the bottom. If you live in a snow-prone area, remove snow from the roof before it gets weighed down. And do let birds have access in winter so they can clean up hibernating pests, waste fruits and fallen seeds.

Birds often enter greenhouses and polytunnels, especially to steal fruits such as ripening tomatoes. Fitting doors, windows and vents with plastic netting is worthwhile. In the seedbed, birds can be kept off with wire netting laid flat or over supports or wire guards (which I make from recycled fridge and cooker shelves bent around my knee). Most important are individual plastic 'cloches' cut from drinks bottles. These allow the seedling or transplant full light and air while keeping off the birds completely. Do make and use them neatly, otherwise they look awful.

**Wire trays stop birds evicting the contents.**

Cats are a mixed blessing. They can be trained to do anything, even chase grey squirrels.

## moles

These are hated by gardeners due to the damage to lawns and borders. Molehills are useful for adding to potting composts. Moles do eat some soil pests, but generally they are unwelcome. They are usually quiet in mid-summer and most busy in spring and autumn. You may pour overpowering unwanted celebrity perfumes or other foul things down their runs, push in twiggy, thorny pieces, flood them, gas them with car exhaust or drive them mad with plastic windmills and whistling bottles – but you will only discourage them for a while or drive them to the neighbours.

Companion plants rumoured to repel moles, such as castor oil plants (*Ricinus communis*), euphorbias and *Incarvillea*, have never proved to work consistently. An alternative is to lift all the turf and replace it over painted, galvanised chicken mesh so that the moles cannot come up. The same works in greenhouses where mesh may

**Care is needed. Human smell stops traps working.**

be set under the borders and fixed to the frame. Individual plants and newly sown rows may be protected by inserting huge pins, made from wire coat hangers or bicycle spokes. Ultrasonic and other hi-tech devices have so far failed to impress me. Trapping and shooting are surer. Professional mole catchers are worth their fee!

## cats

As well as leaving gifts of flesh or fowl about the place, cats do real damage. Chewing leaves and stems, particularly of houseplants, scratching trunks, rolling on top of treasured plants. Leaves they merely pierce later appear with an odd series of holes as the leaf expands. Many contrivances to keep birds off seedbeds work for cats, but, more quickly than birds, cats work out which are the real threats. Cats dislike noise, strong smells and harassment, so a couple of yappy dogs work really well. They especially dislike wet, so automatic sprinklers, soggy seedbeds and borders, dripping ground cover and no place to shelter will keep your patch safer. Appearing with a hose or water pistol works well. I like cats so provide them with sunny corners to bask in and beds of catnip to roll on. Cat biscuits are hidden in molehills, and when a mole, squirrel or rodent is caught all the cats get their favourite junk food. They've not yet brought back a deer...

## dogs and foxes

Dead patches in lawns as if poison was poured there are sure signs that a bitch has urinated on them. If possible, water any spots immediately to reduce the effect or, honestly, feed the bitch tomato purée every day; apparently it makes the urine less toxic to grass. Trees or shrubs, even roses, doing unexpectedly well then suddenly dying may be signs of marking points. Several dogs' sprayings initially fertilise the plant, then over-fertilise it and soon kill it off. Dogs also dig holes, pull up and chew up and scratch plants and rubbish bags, if not trained. Exclude visiting dogs unless accompanied by adults. It makes sense to get good gates and fences. Foxes do very similar damage to dogs but cannot be kept out as easily since they can climb. Well known for stealing poultry, they also make off with wee Tiddles and the contents of your rubbish bins. Foxes are loved by many suburbanites despite their unhealthy habits, so discreet legal trapping and disposal is your only recourse; sadly more will soon arrive.

## badgers

Your lawn looks like it has undergone mine-field clearance. Your vegetable plot has been plundered and the fences battered down. Treasured plants are chewed up and both the King Charles spaniel and Tiddles are

Good fencing stops rabbits. Nasty but effective, mouse trap right hand, mole traps left hand.

mysteriously missing. I exaggerate, but to listen to some folk you'd think these creatures were worse than the neighbours from hell. Especially since they have a regular route they follow every night, as did their ancestors. These are protected species in the UK and you are not allowed to interfere in any way so 'you're \*\*\*\*\*\*\*'. Learn to live with them or sell viewing rights… If local or national laws permit, you may be able to keep them out with unclimbable fencing of at least head height with an overhanging, anti-scale lip.

## squirrels

All your nuts are gone and nut seedlings appear in every border and pot. Tree saplings are chewed up and bark destroyed high above ground level, and songbirds' eggs and young go missing. Grey squirrels are rats with fluffy tails. Trapping can reduce numbers. Trees may be fitted with giant rat guards, inverted funnel-shaped skirts, or slippery plastic coverings that stop squirrels climbing. This works only where all trees with adjoining canopies are protected or on isolated trees.

## deer

Browsed foliage is usually not a problem, but browsed bark is; it can kill or severely set back a tree and allow in disease and pests. Usually damaged bark above knee height is done by deer. Fortunately, they can be kept out with good fencing (at least 2.5m tall to allow for snow) and are fairly easily frightened away. It is said that human hair, preferably whiffy, stuck on shrubs deters them. Small, yappy dogs are probably more effective.

## rabbits and hares

I have planted allegedly rabbit-proof plants to find them nibbled to a cushion by the next day. Hungry bunnies chew everything; given time, they turn your garden into a short sward,

perforated with burrows and liberally fertilised with piles of pellets. You need very secure fencing set into the ground or bent out across a foot or more on the outside and pegged down, and a plank on the inside to let out any rabbits that manage to jump in. Make sure that the gate fits securely at the bottom since they sneak through small gaps. Individual tree guards are sensible for valuable specimens.

Hares are much scarcer than rabbits, but can be a problem in winter when they bark trees; they are particularly fond of parsley plants. Both rabbits and hares walk on top of snow, so can do damage higher up that is later mistaken for a sign of deer. All these animals leave teeth marks, whereas dogs, foxes, badgers and cats leave longer, vertical scratches and rarely teeth marks. Small, yappy dogs will not work so well with rabbits as with hares and deer because the bunnies sneak back as soon as the dogs give up.

## mice, rats and voles

Not only do they eat seeds, fruits and other stores, they nibble and destroy clothes, rubber boots and even structures. Rats in particular do serious damage to buildings and undermine the foundations. Voles and mice nibble off flowerheads and may do weird things such as stacking up little piles of strawberries with the seeds

chewed off. You can tell if you have mice, a problem, or rats, a big problem, by the size of any hole (smaller than a golf ball, it's only mice), the droppings (those of mice are rice-sized, of rats are raisins) and the teeth marks – mice's are tiny, while rats' teeth leave broad scrapes. Traps, bait, cats, all are required to control these rodents before they do untold damage. Do not be squeamish: you must deal with rats and mice; do it now.

## two-legged rats

Traditionally small children scrumped fruit, but vandalism is now a problem. Do not attract attention from the street; keep your front areas well hedged or fenced and gated and do not put bait such as choice fruits in view! Allotment growers may find fleece or netting used to exclude pests also works against self-service shoppers. Ensure sheds and other outbuildings have secure locks and hinges. All valuable garden furniture and equipment are less likely to go walkabout if inscribed with your initials and postcode. If you paint your tools a fluorescent colour as well, they are much easier to find and unlikely to disappear. Small, yappy dogs are the most effective deterrent to idle thieves, but even guard dogs have been bribed with sausages. Plant your choice of prickly shrubs and few will want to wander about your garden in the dark.

# the commonest diseases

### what to do about them

As with plant pests, indeed more so, we may combat most diseases, common and specific, with good hygiene and cultural practice. Good growing conditions make plants almost immune to many problems and regular inspection allows any initial infections to be dealt with before they spread. Close investigation of all bought- or brought-in plants, where these are known to harbour diseases, may stop some rarer problems arriving. However, most common diseases have spores and infective agents blowing in the wind. So it is important to ensure that your plants are sturdy and vigorous, not soft and vulnerable.

## mildews

These come in two types: downy and powdery. Both can cause whitish coatings on almost any part of almost any plant. On leaves and flowers, they may cause distortion and discoloration; the more matted and greyer downy mildew usually does worse damage, with tissue beneath the patches darkened and scarred. Fruits and berries usually split if they swell after their skins have been hardened by mildews. Almost all mildew attacks are initiated by stress, especially water stress, usually in damp and occasionally by very dry conditions. Particularly at risk are wet spots on foliage or other parts when the roots are dry. These wet spots allow spores to grow, while the plant finds it hard to resist invasion.

Under cover, extra care has to be given to good ventilation but beware: sudden chilling can result in attacks. A classic mistake is to leave the greenhouse, cold frame or conservatory closed so that it heats up and the plants cook, then, to make matters worse, to open it up in a hurry, chilling the plants in a draught. Attacks of mildew have also been traced back to where they started near a gutter that held a pool of water and thus a damp atmosphere.

Mildews mostly come from water stress. Clematis, grapes and other climbers are most at risk because of the huge leaf areas.

### controlling mildews

Keeping congestion down, using open pruning and maintaining a good airflow, both indoors and out, all help to reduce mildew attacks. There is little point in picking off infected parts, although in bad cases a drastic cutting back may be called for. Picking up and destroying infected leaves by burying or by fire, or heavily mulching after leaf fall, may help but may not be sufficient if the disease persists on parts above ground. Keeping plants moister at the roots and drier overhead can reduce attacks; sprinkling and misting

Bordeaux mixture is very effective, if old fashioned. It looks ghastly but is barely poisonous.

may be risky, so it's safer to water at the roots. Mulches help considerably to keep soil moist and cool. Dressings of wood ashes which are naturally high in potash, seaweed meal, well made garden compost or well rotted manure all help improve plants' natural resistance, as may underplanting with alliums like chives or garlic, stinging nettles or chamomile.

You may also increase plant resistance or control mildew with drenches or sprays of seaweed solution. Horsetail (*Equisetum*) tea and garlic extracts are effective against powdery mildew on cucumbers. Milk, mustard flour and stinging nettle sprays are thought to make plants more resistant. And a use for a pernicious weed – extract of the leaf of Japanese knotweed (*Fallopia japonica*) – has been shown to control powdery mildew. These sprays should be used with care (if current local and national legislation permit their use), and never in hot, bright conditions when scorch may occur.

For those wishing for a traditional but relatively safe fungicide, laws permitting, there is Bordeaux mixture, a dust or spray. Discovered accidentally by vine growers wishing to discourage children from stealing grapes, this bluish solution when sprayed on foliage and fruits looks ghastly, but amazingly is very

effective at preventing most mildews, tomato and potato blight, peach leaf curl, and many other fungal diseases – if it does not wash off. It is a fine suspension of a relatively insoluble copper compound with garden lime so is a chemical, but it's allowed under organic standards because it's not especially harmful to the soil life or us. Even so, it should be

used only as a last resort. It is a preventative, not a cure, so must be applied before any attack has spread widely.

Sodium bicarbonate powder and solution has also been used as a fungicide and to improve the storage life of fruits; the solution was particularly useful against gooseberry mildew. Unfortunately, it is not allowed under current UK legislation, but may be permitted elsewhere. It is also even more difficult than Bordeaux mixture to keep stuck on plants in wet conditions.

Sulphur is a pure element and has long been used either puffed as dust or sprayed as an emulsion. It is allowed under organic standards for controlling powdery mildews on flowers, fruit and vegetables. Sulphur dust is also good for stopping rots in damaged or cut bulbs and tubers. I find it extremely efficacious in stopping mildew on grapevines. Beware of using sulphur on all fruit trees and bushes; some cultivars are sulphur-shy and suffer if treated – these are usually listed on the packaging.

Sulphur dust – any dust needs to be plied uniformly. (Where's your mask, Bob?)

Grey mould, a big problem in humid conditions.

under cover at the beginning and end of the growing season, these are hard to avoid. Improving conditions is important: aim for drier air. Some of the treatments for mildews (see pages 116–7) may help. Oddly, it has been found that a mist of fresh urine may stop grey mould – hardly likely to become popular, is it? Some control on French beans has been reported from extracts made from parsley and parsnip seed. Other plants have been given some protection by coating them with yeasts. A grey-black, sticky mould that occurs mostly on uppermost surfaces, and is not fluffy, is sooty mould. It is a collection of organisms and detritus that lives on the sap (honeydew) ejected by aphids, scale or similar pests on leaves and shoots higher up. This mould may be carefully washed off with warm, slightly soapy water and a sponge.

## coral spot

Once seen never forgotten, the pink, pinhead-sized pimples are symptoms worthy of the name. This is a common disease, appearing on dead wood on roses, shrubs, hedges and trees. It rarely attacks conifers. Coral spot can

## rusts

Very much like mildews, rusts appear when conditions stress the plants. Their name is exact – they look like rusty patches, scabs, streaks or craters. Rusts are closely related to, and can be treated in much the same way as, mildews (see pages 116–7). Although they may attack several hosts, in practice they rarely move from one garden species to another, although it may look like they do. It is just that they all appear at the same, stressful times. However, good hygiene and picking off all the infected bits and dead leaves does help, as will ruthless extermination of infected individuals before the rust

spreads. You may choose to use Bordeaux mixture or sulphur on them as well. Be careful when watering not to splash the foliage and spread the disease.

Smuts are very similar to rusts and mildews in many ways, although they do not usually have the red coloration of the former and cause more physical disruption to plant tissue than the latter.

## grey moulds

Fluffy, grey moulds (usually *Botrytis cinerea*) on foliage and fruits are nearly always due to poor growing conditions: low light, cold and damp or stagnant air. Especially prevalent

Coral spot – lives up to its name.

Fireblight, rarely a problem as all the susceptible plants are already dead and gone.

Black spot on roses – really annoying, but usually not very serious.

move from the dead into the live wood and may even eventually kill the whole plant. Prune out infected wood, paint wounds with sealant, collect any infected wood lying around and burn it. Give the wood ashes back to the plants, together with more ash if available, mulch with compost and spray with seaweed solution.

## fireblight

This bacterial infection looks like its name too; the tree or shrub looks as if a scorching flame has hit it. It gets in through the flowers, leaving them hanging along with the dead leaves, all of which go brown and nasty.

Cankers appear at bases of dead shoots and reddish-brown discoloration appears inside. Cut out diseased wood well below affected tissues. Disinfect pruning tools after use and burn the trash to try to save the plant, or at least others. Some plants are now only lightly attacked, as most of the cultivars left alive are partially resistant. Most badly affected is the rose family: amelanchiers, apples, coton-easters, hawthorns, pears, pyracanthas and quinces.

## leaf spots

All sorts of diseases cause spots on, in or through the leaves of many plants. Very few are very serious and a cause for worry, although some may also bronze and curl the leaves. Sometimes small holes, especially on houseplants, are caused by cats piercing leaves before they unfurl. Exhaust-fume condensates, aircraft-fuel droplets, window-cleaning fluids and many other harmful chemicals can fall onto foliage and flowers, causing spotting, holes and similar reactions. Holes are just a symptom; look for other signs.

## rots, moulds and wilts

Stored roots, bulbs, corms and tubers, seeds too if you're careless, all may rot and mould. There are many diseases that cause rot and mould, but basically dampness is the main initiator so keeping these things better dried and aerated often prevents attacks. Damaged tissues often provide a point of entry and so more care needs to be taken when handling them. Wood ashes, sodium bicarbonate powder (unfortunately, not allowed in the UK) and sulphur dust, along with better storage, may help prevent most of these rots, but cannot affect any that come from inside, such as potato-tuber blight.

With many plants, it is an unidentified root rot, wilt or phytophthora that gets them. All cause unexpected sudden deaths; when a seedling or small plant just dies away, it's probably suffered a soil- or water-borne wilt attack. With shoots, you may see a dark green to brown core on cutting them through. Phytophtora is more likely to attack ornamental cherries and related (*Prunus*) species, conifers and rhododendrons, which suffer yellowing and wilting of individual stems and branches before the whole plant expires. Using sterile sowing and potting composts, clean, fresh water and commercially produced seeds and plants should avoid future outbreaks. Gardens prone to such root rots and sudden root death may have soils that are sour and lacking in lime or are poorly drained.

Rots and mouldy patches on stems, leaves and fruits are often difficult to identify and usually secondary to some other damage, such as bruising or animal attack. Although there are many specific diseases, any damaged and exposed tissue is likely to get infected, rot and maybe take the rest of the plant with it. Damage caused by a hoe or trimmer close to the soil surface is often unnoticed until a sudden death. The collar of a plant – where

the top-growth meets the root at the site of the old seed – is especially vulnerable and many soil pathogens gain entrance here.

When dealing with wounds on trunks and branches of trees and shrubs, I reckon that cleaning them, treating them with a blowtorch or alcohol, and then painting them with a proprietary sealant may at least stop some diseases getting in. It seems sensible to do the same with roots if they are damaged during transplanting.

## viruses

These often weaken and distort growth; the leaves may curl, lose their colour, become mottled, sometimes in a mosaic pattern, often yellow, and flowers and crops may fail to form properly. Viruses may attack any plants but many ornamental plants, especially those usually propagated by cuttings or buds such as carnations, chrysanthemums, dahlias and roses, are particularly at risk. Courgettes and their kin (cucurbits) are often infected by the widespread cucumber mosaic virus, which is spread by aphids and dirty water. Tobacco mosaic virus can move from a tobacco smoker's hands to damage tomato plants in the greenhouse – honest. Pests such as aphids can spread viruses, so controlling these insects can help to reduce cross-infection; raspberries and blackcurrants succumb to such viruses. Dirty knives, secateurs and saws should be cleaned and dowsed in spirit alcohol before being used on each new victim. Needless to say, virus-infected plants should be ruthlessly destroyed before they infect others. Buying clean, certified plants ensures less chance of bringing in new viruses.

## cankers

Cankers are like ulcers where the living bark is being eaten away. They leave weak points where other rots and pests may gain entry and, if they encircle a branch or trunk, may kill all the growth above. Often they are fungal, and the mycelium blocks up the plant's plumbing; sometimes they are bacterial; they are often secondary to other damage. Many cankers are symptomatic of poor growth and damp, stagnant conditions. Correct pruning, treating individual wounds, generally good hygiene, top dressings of compost and well rotted manure with separate dressings of wood ashes, and possibly for the stone fruits some lime, may be of help. Seaweed sprays can boost resistance.

## mushrooms and worse

Little panics gardeners more than the sight of mushrooms and toadstools appearing. Although there are those such as the dreaded honey fungus, which threaten whole gardens of plants (especially the rose family), fortunately most toadstools and mushrooms are just harmless bits of nature and appear on wood that is already dead. Many trees and shrubs can endure fungi living on their roots to no detriment; a few even have them inside and on the living wood. But generally when you see toadstools it is too late to do anything – the real fungus has grown its 'root' system (mycelium) unseen and the bit that is now appearing is effectively the 'fruit', which will spread spores if left. Real mushrooms may develop from mushroom waste that has been used as mulch, but are best ignored for safety. For mushroom rings, see pages 146–47.

Honey fungus itself is noticeable as a mesh of black, flattish 'bootlaces' passing through the soil onto living trees and shrubs and getting under the bark. Another way to identify it is to look under the bark near the roots: there may be fresh, white patches (mycelium) that smell strongly of mushroom. Its masses of small, honey-coloured toadstools are easily confused with countless other toadstools. There also seem to be vicious and weak strains of honey fungus. It is best to dig out stumps of live wood because these encourage it and, when planting, try to cause minimal root injuries since these are where it may gain access. Plant smaller specimens than usual and surround them in clean, bought-in compost so that their roots can heal before coming into contact with infected soil.

Honey fungus – can be deadly, usually is, but by this stage it's too late to do anything anyway.

# which problem in what place

Particular problems on specific plants ● Annual, patio and bedding plants ● Beds and borders: herbaceous plants, bulbs, climbers, shrubs, roses ● Ornamental trees ● Water features ● The lawn and areas of turf ● Hedges ● The herb garden: perennial and annual herbs

- The vegetable garden outdoors ● Crops under cover ● Indoor and conservatory plants
- Crops in the greenhouse or polytunnel ● Fruit-cage crops: strawberries, cane fruits and vines
- Trained and orchard fruit trees ● Garden DIY: paths and driveways, gutters, pipes and water tanks

# particular problems and specific plants

## troublesome tendencies

Whereas the great majority of challenges come from just the few commonest cultural, pest and disease problems, described in the previous chapter, every plant suffers its own unique trials – some more than others. Indeed, the more widely grown plants such as roses, tomatoes and apples have a shed-load of specialised pests and diseases designed to plague them, as well as most of the usual woes. One way of avoiding many threats is to grow unusual plants; these often escape their specific pests and diseases and may be less troubled by commoner ones, which may not 'recognise' them. Also, most of the various ornamentals that we grow have been introduced relatively unimproved from the wild form and show more vigour and resistance than plants, such as roses, that have been selected and bred over many generations. By 'improving' a cultivar in the pursuit of size, colour and so on we have often lost, inadvertently, its natural, defensive genes.

I cannot emphasise enough that browsing this chapter is similar to perusing a medical dictionary – don't become a hypochondriac! The vast majority of these problems are never going to occur in most gardens. In some ways, we should consider many of these afflictions as curiosities of nature, perhaps as indicators that not all is well and that something in our garden needs adjustment rather than as enemies to be dealt with.

## signals for action

In the following pages, I have indicated the likely degree of seriousness involved by the way I refer to each problem. Where a plant is rather more prone than most to a common problem, which is described in the previous chapter, or has a minor problem, which is interesting but rarely needs action, the problem is named only in the text.

Where the problem is more serious and you may need to take action, the problem will be described in the text and listed at the end of the text on that plant, for example RED SPIDER MITE.

You may then wish to refer back to the previous chapter on the commonest pests and diseases to learn more.

Finally, where the problem is usually a serious one and you are likely to have to take urgent action, as well as being described in the text, it will be listed, with a cross-reference to more details, at the end of the text on that plant, for example RED SPIDER MITE (P.108).

*Aster novi-belgii* (Michaelmas daisy).

# annual, patio and bedding plants

## temporary troubles

The commonest problems are of course cultural: over-watering, under-watering, failure to harden off, poor compost and so on. Replanting the same bed for decades, with similar combinations of plants, often gives rise to eelworm and other soil-borne problems. The inclusion of marigolds (*Tagetes*) in almost every scheme may be an unconscious effort to correct this. Many popular and colourful plants are now sterile or set little seed; others, mostly species, set seed then stop flowering so deadheading is important in getting continuity of bloom. Most plants treated as annuals are in fact biennial or perennial; some are tender, such as lobelia and pelargoniums, so can't make it through winter or become scrappy after the first season, such as wallflowers (*Erysimum*) and sweet William (*Dianthus barbatus*), so are barely worth retaining. The very brevity of their lives makes many problems transitory and there is little sense in expending a great deal of time and effort to save a display that will be gone anyway in another few weeks. Fortunately, the vast majority rarely suffer any troubles other than attacks by the commonest offenders.

### *Arabis* (Rock cress)

These sometimes get a touch of shiny patches of white rust, or brownish- or greyish-white, powdery ones of grey mould. Good hygiene and sulphur dust control these.

### *Dianthus* (Pinks, carnations and sweet William)

These are not long-lived and need regular regeneration from 'pipings': non-flowering shoots pulled off the plant to use as softwood cuttings. Do this otherwise the plants will be lost, as birds pull them to bits as they get old and loose. Most need lime in the soil and loathe waterlogging – they simply fall to bits, although technically suffering from dieback or wilt. These need instant action to clean up infected material, as does any leaf spotting. Rust often appears, as reddish-brown spots or yellow-brown cushions: treat with Bordeaux mixture or wholesale destruction. Be careful when watering not to splash foliage. Carnations when under glass are also rather prone to red spider mites (looking yellow-brown and dusty); aphids (yellow-mottled leaves); and tortrix moth (leaves rolled together, need hand picking). Thrips show as pale, yellowed leaves covered in minute, black flecks and distorted or speckled flowers.
APHIDS, RED SPIDER MITE, RUST, THRIPS

### *Erysimum* (Wallflowers), *Matthiola* (Stocks), and *Tropaeolum* (Nasturtiums)

These can suffer from most of the problems besetting brassicas (see page 157) but, with the exception of caterpillars devouring the nasturtiums, aphids and slugs as always, flea beetles decimating the stocks and wallflowers, and pigeons mashing up the lot, they get away unscathed. Yellow sawfly caterpillars may also eat the leaves from beneath; jet them off or use soft soap.
APHIDS, CATERPILLARS, FLEA BEETLE, SLUGS, WOOD PIGEONS, CLUBROOT

### *Helianthus annuus* (Sunflowers)

Birds rob ripening seed heads unless they are netted. Plants can suffer severe rust attacks, with brown patches leading to withered leaves and plants. It is often worst from collected seed, which can carry the disease, so buy fresh, clean seed! Burn affected plants. Sunflowers grow well with cucurbits and nasturtiums beneath, but not so well near potatoes, runner beans or any grasses.
RUST

Sweet William
Matthiola (Stocks).

ABOVE *Lathyrus odoratus* (sweet peas).
MIDDLE Petunia.
BELOW *Primula* (Polyanthus Group).

### Lathyrus odoratus *(Sweet peas)*

Lack of flowering may signal drought at the roots or seedpods setting. Sweet peas must be deadheaded regularly because any seed forming will stop flowering. These plants may get earwig and aphid attacks, but neither do much harm. Symphalids may attack the roots of plants started under glass. They sometimes get a stem rot or grey mould at ground level in wet conditions, causing leaves to yellow and the plant to wilt and die; sowing in pots of sterile compost before planting out gets round both. Yellow mottling or brown streaking on stems and discoloured foliage suggest virus, or 'streak'; if the plant does not respond fairly quickly to seaweed-solution sprays and wood ashes, burn it.
SYMPHALIDS

### Lobularia maritima *(Sweet alyssum)*

Numerous small holes in leaves and whole seed (cotyledon) leaves missing at seedling stage and early on are signs of a flea beetle attack, but this rarely hurts the plants much as they grow on.

### Pelargonium

Rarely do these die of drought, so any symptoms are more likely signs of over-watering, especially in winter. Damp conditions allow in grey mould. Do not spray or mist unless it is a drying day. Watch out for grey mould on dead leaves and flowers and especially on the discarded bud covers in spring. Clean up any infected material and improve the airflow and it will go. Wet roots may get black leg, where whole seedlings and young stems and plants turn black from the bases up. If symptoms persist or the leaves turn sickly yellow, or if pale spots appear on the stems, promptly burn all affected plants – it is the more contagious stem rot. In either case, burn or dispose of all affected plants and the soil about the stem bases. Several sorts of leaf spots are worst in stagnant air; pick and destroy infected leaves and use Bordeaux mixture if necessary. Angle-shades-moth caterpillars may be hand picked.
BLACK LEG, GREY MOULD, STEM ROT

### Petunia

In recent years, some of the very popular Surfinia Series have been propagated with a virus that causes them to weaken and do badly, so be careful to use only really healthy stocks for propagation.

### Primula, Auricula primulas *and* Polyanthus Group *(Primroses)*

Sudden or slow death is often due to vine weevil grubs (see page 103); be worried by leaf notches cut by vine weevils since these are likely to wipe out your colony. Look out for whitish-green root aphids. Wash the roots clean in soapy, warm water and rinse and repot in good compost. Treat yellowish patches of leaf spot with Bordeaux mixture. These are unhappy plants in hot, dry conditions and prefer cool, moist, light shade. Occasionally these may suffer from angle-shades-moth caterpillars; hand pick them.
ANGLE SHADES MOTH, ROOT APHIDS, VINE WEEVIL (P.103)

### Sempervivum *(Houseleeks)*

These simply die away in shade or wet. They also may get rust, giving their leaves yellowish-brown spots. Pull up and burn affected ones before it spreads. Birds rip colonies to pieces looking for bugs. Wire or – better – fine, black plastic netting keeps them off.

### Senecio cineraria *(Cinerarias)*

Caterpillars of the angle-shades moth may attack the foliage. These plants also suffer from the same leaf miner as sow thistles (*Sonchus* spp.) and chrysanthemums.
ANGLE-SHADES MOTH

# beds and borders: herbaceous plants

## general care

Such plants are usually best grown in their own bed or border; they are difficult to combine with trees or shrubs because they suffer from the competition. Bulbs and small subshrubs are usually regarded as herbaceous. Tidy the plants in late autumn: wait until the stems have withered and all the nutrients are absorbed, then cut them off, not close, but ankle high. The old stem bases then trap leaves and soil and support and protect the young shoots as they emerge. Apply a thick, weed-free mulch after tidying to seal down weed seeds and disease spores, as well as protect the crowns. Sharp-sand mulches over dormant crowns seriously reduce slug damage and weeds and mark the spots for safer stepping and hoeing.

*Aquilegia* (Columbines).

### *Alcea rosea (Hollyhock)*

These suffer badly from rust (see page 118), with much orange spottiness, but they can flower prolifically regardless if in rich, moist soil. Growing them as biennials with careful hygiene gives considerable control, but rust will continually recur. Bordeaux mixture offers some relief. Some such as the fig-leafed sorts are partly resistant. Hollyhocks are sometimes attacked by caterpillars that bore down the stems, causing wilting; prune out the stems and burn them.

RUST (P.118)

### *Antirrhinum (Snapdragons)*

Greenish-brown angle-shades-moth caterpillars sometimes attack and need picking off. A leaf spot sometimes causes brownish or whitish spots, but rarely troubles much. Rust is more serious and only the newer, more resistant cultivars are worth growing. Good drainage and airflow help to reduce attacks, as do sulphur dusts; prompt hygienic action is needed.

ANGLE-SHADES MOTH, RUST

### *Aquilegia (Columbines)*

Stalk and bulb rot, a disease that more often attacks bulbs, sometimes causes these plants to fail; a damaged spot at the base of the stem causes the shoot above to wither and die away. They also often get leaf spots, but rarely badly enough to need treatment.

### *Aster novi-belgii (Michaelmas daisy)*

These asters reliably provide late flowers, but suffer from a wilt that causes shoots to weaken and die away, with yellow mottled leaves at the bottom and browning off. A similar-looking stem rot also turns the bottom of the shoot black. In both cases, dig up the infected plant, roots and all, and burn it. Several viral diseases have reduced this once-popular plant to a memory of the best cultivars and a pleasingly common weed of railway cuttings. They share an aphid with plums so should not be grown near each other.

STEM ROT WILT

### *Campanula (Bellflowers)*

A stem and root rot similar to that on aquilegias may affect these plants. Promptly and hygienically dispose of affected plants and move survivors to another spot.

### *Chrysanthemum*

Caterpillars of tortrix moth and angle-shades moth may eat the leaves. You may even get attacks of gothic-moth, cabbage-moth and turnip-moth caterpillars. The plants are more prone to aphid and capsid-bug attacks, which twist and distort leaves, dwarf and deform

Delphinium.

*Digitalis* (foxgloves).

Helenium.

flowers and cause galls on stems; treat both with the usual remedies. Leaf miners tunnelling whitish-yellow lines in the leaves can be an especial problem, with little cure save squishing or accurate needling. The same species attacks cinerarias and sow thistles, so control the weed. Ironically, the flowers of chrysanthemums now known as *Tanacetum cinerariifolium* and *Tanacetum coccineum* have been powdered for thousands of years for use as an insecticide, which is now called pyrethrum and has a low toxicity to mammals.

Chrysanthemums sometimes get a touch of mildew and a leaf spot, but rarely are they a problem, although rust may be. Rust appears on the undersides of leaves, often in dry years and first on overfed plants. Prompt, hygienic action is needed (see page 118). Earwigs can get in the flowers and damage shoots. An eel-worm that attacks chrysanthemums may also infest asters, dahlias, delphiniums, rudbeckias and verbenas, so beware of planting these nearby or before or after chrysanthemums.
ANGLE-SHADES MOTH, APHIDS, CAPSID BUG, LEAF MINERS (P.109), TORTRIX MOTH

### *Convallaria majalis* (Lily-of-the-valley)
This plant hates being transplanted and needs a moist, rich soil, but then romps and spreads. Never underplant or follow peonies with *Convallaria*; they share a common rot (*Botrytis*) that browns their leaves so they drop off.
BOTRYTIS

### *Delphinium*
These are often really bothered by slugs! Weak or sickly plants may have an eelworm infestation or white, swift-moth caterpillars eating the roots.
SLUGS

### *Digitalis* (Foxgloves)
Some species die after flowering, so do not be surprised, although prompt deadheading may save the plant. Sometimes caterpillars bore down the stems causing wilting; just prune these stems out and burn them.

### Ferns
Apart from suffering from drying out or too arid a site, ferns get mealy bugs and thrips; a fern mite that causes distortion, swelling, and tiny brown spots on the fronds; and eelworms. Fascinatingly, the old boys found that these pests can all be removed with hot-water treatment of the plants – immersing them at 43°C (110°F) for twenty minutes before cooling and repotting. Ferns can be killed rather easily by excess soil fertility.
EELWORMS, FERN MITE, MEALY BUG, THRIPS

### Geranium
Generally tough, these plants sometimes get eaten by caterpillars of the angle-shades moth. Aphids and leafhoppers may do some small damage.
ANGLE-SHADES MOTH

### *Geum* (Avens)
Often this plant is prey to froghoppers and their cuckoo spit; they are easily got rid of with soft-soap sprays.

### *Helenium*
Leaves may be stuck together by tortrix-moth caterpillars, which need squishing.
TORTRIX MOTH

### *Helleborus* (Hellebores)
Christmas and Lent roses are poisonous, but rarely cause problems. I find they resent being moved once they are large. They some-times suffer from mildew, with pale patches on top and a white, powdery patch under the leaves. A leaf spot may cause black and yellow patches. Pick and burn affected leaves and mulch heavily afterwards.

### *Hosta*
The plant is known for its foliage's susceptibility to slugs (see pages 94–7) rather than its scent, so 'Royal Standard' may surprise you. Vine weevils (see page 103) cause a slow death.
SLUGS (PP.94–7) VINE WEEVIL (P.103)

### *Kniphofia* (Red hot pokers)
These prefer it hot and wet in summer and cold and dry in winter, otherwise they are prone to rot away. They are not happy in heavy winter rains; put them in a dry site and water well in summer.

*Lupinus* (lupins).

### *Lupinus* (Lupins)

Aphids on these are almost worth barbecuing – you'll see what I mean; they're huge! However, if the first flower heads are trimmed back together with the topmost leaves, you can often remove most of a colony and gain a second flush of flower. Deadheading also stops the plants exhausting themselves. Small, grey weevils eating crescent-shaped pieces from the leaves are usually a curiosity – except to seedlings. Luckily, they are not the same beetles as the more serious vine weevils. White, swift-moth caterpillars eat the roots until the plant dies. Sudden death may be due to root rot where the roots turn black with white fungus marks; this may be worse on lime-rich soils. Lupin foliage traps dew for insects so is especially beneficial; the plants are also said to suppress germination of seeds near them. Divide them every third year or so to stop them fading away. They are leguminous and may become overly lush and problem-prone if heavily fed with nitrogenous fertilisers.
ROOT ROT

### *Melissa officinalis* (Lemon balm)

The gold-splashed form continually reverts to the green unless regularly policed, so cut out all green bits promptly. Both forms also seed prolifically and need deadheading.

Ferns are good for shady, damp places.

*Viola* (pansy, violets).

## Nepeta *(Catmints)*

The catnip *Nepeta cataria* is loved to death by feline herbivores; the less loved *Nepeta* x *faassenii* is bigger, with more pointed leaves. These and valerian are nibbled to the ground, rolled on and shredded by cats. Plant them underneath empty wire baskets to allow them to grow; cats can nibble what sticks out.

## Oenothera biennis *(Evening primrose)*

Be warned: these are self-seeding weeds and rather prone to the same eelworm problem as phlox, so keep the two apart.

## Paeonia *(Peonies)*

Ants are often seen on the flower heads, but do little harm unless they're farming aphids. Sometimes the plants get rot (*Botrytis*), with browning and wilting leaves and shoots well above ground level; pick off what you can and treat the rest with Bordeaux mixture. In winter, cut and burn stems and mulch heavily. Peonies suffer a rust in common with lily of-the-valley, so don't plant the two near each other. Tree peonies must not be pruned since they rarely resprout. Ordinary peonies need a lot of water, sulk if moved and may not flower for several years.

APHIDS, BOTRYTIS

## Phlox

Occasionally, tortrix-moth caterpillars attack phlox. Cuckoo spit from froghoppers may be troublesome in hot, dry years, which phlox detests – it likes cool, moist summers. It is prone to nematode attacks – these unusually live in the stem, not the roots, so take care when propagating.

CUCKOO SPIT, TORTRIX MOTH

## Polygonatum *(Solomon's seal)*

Greyish Solomon's seal sawfly, or sawfly slug worms, can strip this plant bare almost overnight. Plants in the shade often escape attack. The larvae are best vacuumed off since birds do not like them; they can also be dusted with wood ashes to hinder their movements and choke them.

SOLOMON'S SEAL SAWFLY

## Rudbeckia *(Coneflowers)*

Sometimes these and related echinaceas get attacked by tortrix moth on the leaves and white, swift-moth caterpillars at their roots.

TORTRIX MOTH

## Sedum spectabile *(Ice plants)*

Sudden weakening and death is caused by vine weevil at the roots (see page 103).

VINE WEEVIL (P.103)

## Solidago *(Golden rod)*

Tortrix-moth caterpillars sometimes do minor damage to the leaves; cuckoo spit on the stems may be hosed off.

TORTRIX MOTH

## Viola *(Pansy, Violets)*

In hot, dry sites and under cover, red spider mite massacres these plants, curling and puckering the foliage; wetter conditions discourage it. Angle-shades-moth caterpillars attack violets under cover. The plants can get all sorts of minor infections of leaf spots, rusts and smut, but usually a bit of tidying will control them.

ANGLE-SHADES MOTH, RED SPIDER MITE

# beds and borders: bulbs

## general care

These are least trouble grown as herbaceous plants in clumps in borders; although most may be naturalised in grass, it is then difficult to cut the grass early in the year as neatness requires. Bulbs are thus better in drifts around trees and along the bases of hedges where the grass can be left to grow long with little detriment. Do not cut or tie up the leaves before they have started to wither because it reduces the bulbs' vigour and flowering. Often, they get congested with age and clumps need digging and splitting. Others, such as agapanthus, do well only when congested. Always check the exact planting depth – which begins from the top of the bulb. When planting, for safety, err on the deep side and, in heavy or wet soils, give the bulbs a bedding and topping of sharp sand or potting compost. Be sure to store bulbs that need it in perfectly appropriate conditions or be sure to lose them.

### Allium

The ornamental onions are tough, reliable bloomers – of balls or globes on sticks – although somewhat invasive and prone to many of the same woes as the vegetable onions (see page 163). P.S. For impressive, cheap displays, buy shop leeks: stick them in like any other bulbs, keep them moist and you'll have a fantastic show.

### Anemone

These can get a stalk and bulb rot that rots and withers the stem and a stem rot that attacks the bulbs, making them waxy. Examine taller-growing specimens for small spots and cluster cup fungi forming red or orange, cup-shaped blotches on the stems. With all three infections, dig up and burn affected plants. Olive-brown or greenish caterpillars on the Saint Bridgid Group of anemones are probably of angle-shades moth and best hand picked.
ANGLE-SHADES MOTH, CLUSTER CUP FUNGI, STALK AND BULB ROT, STEM ROT

### Crocus

Often grown through grass, they soon die out if the leaves are removed too soon by early cutting. Traditionally, one of the first jobs of the year is to put up black cotton tied to sticks to stop birds damaging the flowers. The bulbs disappear because rodents and voles have eaten them.
BIRDS

### Cyclamen

Almost certainly any poor performance indicates that vine weevil grubs are on the roots and need evicting (see page 103). In the wild, cyclamen are eaten by wild pigs. Pot-grown houseplants need a rest in summer.
VINE WEEVIL (P.103)

### Dahlia

These plants are very prone to earwig attacks; trap them to avoid damage, especially to flowers. Olive-green caterpillars eating the leaves are probably of angle-shades moth and need hand picking. The tubers may be damaged by swift-moth caterpillars, which are hard to deal with except by digging or de-potting and physically extracting the grubs. Eelworms can build up in the soil if dahlias are grown there for long without rotation. Be careful not to encourage leaf spot (yellowish-green spots

ABOVE **Bulbs.**
MIDDLE **Anemone.**
BELOW **Allium.**

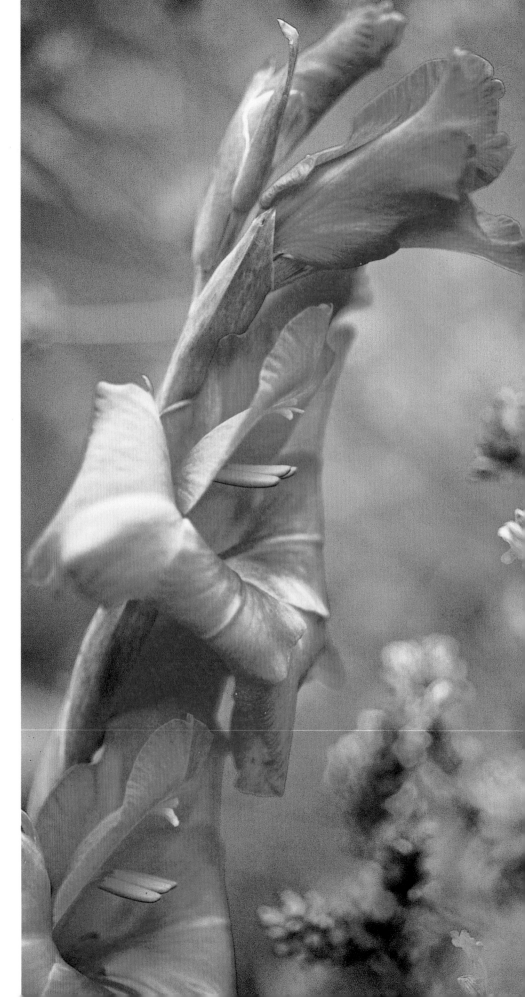

Gladiolus.

turning greyish-brown) by storing any dead leaves or twigs with the tubers. Watch out for any mottled or distorted plants that may have a virus and any suddenly flagging plants, which may have wilt. Both need prompt, hygienic disposal. Quickly destroy plants if cauliflower-like growths appear among the roots at the base, this is crown gall and it's best to move your dahlia bed to another part of the garden. ANGLE-SHADES MOTH, CROWN GALL, EARWIGS, EELWORM, LEAF SPOT, VIRUS, WILT

### *Fritillaria imperialis* (*Crown imperial*)
The stinky lily of early spring is yellow or orange; both colours never do equally well on the same sites. The bulbs tend to push themselves to the surface and may need replanting.

### *Galanthus* (*Snowdrops*)
These are happiest if moved or bought while green (in leaf) because the dried bulbs are prone to wither away. Lack of flowering, called 'blindness', may be due to excess nitrogen, but more likely to crowding. Divide and spread them out thinly; they soon multiply and flower profusely. Rotting bulbs may have a grey mould – the bulbs and the soil around them should be dug up and burnt. If they are naturalised, never cut the grass they grow in until their leaves have withered.

### *Gladiolus*
Overly wet conditions or a very heavy soil may encourage basal rot (also called base decay): rust-like spots on the leaves become black and eventually the leaves and stems rot off. Use raised beds, lighten and drain the soil or grow plants in containers to avoid this problem. Three other diseases may rarely attack; hard rot, dry rot and smut, which all arrive or multiply on infected corms. Do not plant any corms with any blemishes, like spots or sunken patches. With hard rot, the

Iris.

Narcissus (daffodils).

leaves get yellow patches turning brown; with dry rot, all the leaves yellow and then brown and the plant may rot off at the stem base. With smut, black raised spots appear on all parts. In every case, destroy affected plants and corms. Gladioli may also be subject to various penicillium and fusarium rots; shown as leaves fading, weakening and wilting, corms and roots withering and rotting, especially in wet conditions – again, burn infected plants. Tulips and gladioli share a grey bulb rot so make bad companions, in joint or consecutive plantings. Flagging plants and eaten corms are probably signs of swift-moth grubs on the roots; dig them up and burn them. Occasionally angle-shades-moth caterpillars develop a taste for the tops; hand pick to clear them.
ANGLE-SHADES MOTH, BASAL ROT, DRY ROT, HARD ROT, SMUT

## Hyacinthus (Hyacinths)
Bulbs that had been forced for indoor use are often planted out and after a few years can't be found – they degenerate to resemble blue-bells, although they are different species and not really desirable. (Bluebells prefer moist, light shade and are rarely offered for sale.)

## Iris
If yellow or brown streaks or spots appear in autumn, it may be iris leaf spot: it is easiest treated by good hygiene if caught early; sulphur dust may help. Irises also suffer leaf spots if

short of lime – the remedy is obvious. If the roots show any sign of softness or rot, rhizome rot is likely and confirmed by its evil smell. Hygienically dispose of infected plants and the surrounding soil; do not grow irises in wet sites since that promotes the rot. Flagging leaves and eaten-out rhizomes are probably down to swift-moth grubs on the roots. When replanting rhizomatous irises, place them on the surface, cover the feeding roots, and support the top growth, with a brick on each side, water, and they should establish well. Bury the rhizomes and they may rot.
RHIZOME ROT

## Lilium (Lilies)
Unlike some genera, these have widely varying needs, according to the species. However they all need well drained soils rich in leaf mould, but some need acid conditions. Some prefer full sun, others part shade; some need shallow planting and some deep – check the labels! The lily beetle, a bright red-orange, rather smart beastie, has a grub that looks like a bird dropping and destroys the leaves. Hand picking, although distasteful, works; dusting seriously handicaps them. Aphids do so little apparent harm that they're too often ignored, but need controlling since they spread viruses. Lilies are very susceptible to viruses, especially mosaic viruses – destroy any plants with mottled, variegated or distorted leaves immediately. Madonna lilies (Lilium candidum) and their

hybrids are especially prone to leaf spot in stagnant sites and poor conditions; it starts as red-brown leaf spots, dries up the stems and distorts surviving flowers. Bordeaux mixture works well, but spoils the plant's appearance because it must be applied so often.
APHIDS, LEAF SPOT, LILY BEETLE, MOSAIC VIRUSES

## Narcissus (Daffodils)
Sometimes bulbs die away from grey bulb rot; more often, greyish narcissus fly grubs eat the centres, causing leaves to yellow first. The adults somewhat resemble small bumblebees, but have only one pair of wings. The flies make a distinct drone when flying from late spring into early summer and may be easily caught in a butterfly net, especially when trying to lay their eggs near narcissus bases. Any plants with yellow stripes or mottling probably have a virus infection (see page 120). In all cases, dig up and burn affected bulbs; never plant soft bulbs. Do not cut the grass around naturalised narcissi until their leaves wither, otherwise they will flower poorly the next year. Since the bulbs are very prone to stop flowering from old, congested clumps, they need splitting and replanting regularly.
NARCISSUS FLY, VIRUS (P.120)

## Tulipa
Aphids may make a mess of these plants occasionally, but can be jetted off outdoors. Sometimes a virus causes them to break and perform badly, with small flowers; hygienic destruction is important before aphids spread it about. Fire disease looks like a rust but is a rot (Botrytis) and causes scorched spots of brownish-grey on every part, especially in wet conditions. Tulips may be naturalised in rough grass, but do not cut it until their leaves wither, otherwise flowering will suffer. Voles and other rodents eat the bulbs.
FIRE DISEASE

# beds and borders: climbers

FAR RIGHT *Passiflora* (passion flowers).
RIGHT Clematis.

## be forward thinking

That wee slip you are planting will soon have as large an area of foliage as a sail on a ship. Climbers get big and catch the wind so, for all except the self-clingers on walls, make your supports strong, durable and, most importantly, renewable. Most climbers are happiest left to ramble, say in trees, rather than enduring too much pruning and training.

BELOW *Lonicera* (honeysuckle).

### Clematis

These need their roots in cool, moist shade and their heads in full sun to flourish and most like limy soil. Clematis wilt often causes sudden death and there is little one can do after the event. It is not good to replant another on the same spot but, if planting another nearby, avert the risk by planting deeper than is normal for most plants. Woodlice and slug damage girdling new shoots on a young plant can also cause the stem above to wither. Large-flowered forms can be hard to establish – they're highly bred and may not take. They may wither away anyway, so just try again. Pruning is not complicated for most – leave them well alone or cut nearly to the ground, in winter, for almost all except the earlier-flowering ones. Many species do best with pruning only every ten years or so.
CLEMATIS WILT, SLUGS, WOODLICE

### Fremontodendron

The tiny hairs of this sun-loving American irritate everybody, get up their noses and in their eyes and can cause serious reactions, so be warned.

### Hedera helix (Common ivy)

Ivies are often thought of as problem plants, but their roots do not damage trees – only the loss of light and the weight. Ivy does not damage modern walls although it can get in through ventilation holes and block vents. However, if kept trimmed, it is a good, cheap plant for covering large areas, and as ground cover. If you want it to flower, be sure to get plants grown from flowering forms. Large-leaved, variegated ivies are not very hardy and easily suffer wind and frost damage. On hot, dry walls, they can get red spider mite.
RED SPIDER MITE

### Hydrangea anomala ssp. petiolaris
### (Climbing hydrangea)

Like the rest of its genus, this hydrangea is very thirsty and thus slow to establish and a poor performer on most walls. If it gets plenty of water, it becomes too vigorous and a problem plant.

### Jasminum (Jasmines)

*Jasmine nudiflorum* is hardly a climber and usually flowers poorly because it needs cutting almost to the ground immediately after flowering. Try this and see. *Jasmine officinale* is better left unpruned and allowed to find the sun if you want flowers.

### Lonicera (Honeysuckles)

These climbers are tough and easy to grow. They are prone to attract massive aphid attacks (see page 99–101), especially if overfed but less in light shade. Leave them unpruned to ramble as long as possible. They are prone to several viruses, so miffy plants should be destroyed.
APHID (P.99–101), VIRUSES

### Parthenocissus

*Parthenocissus quinquefolia* (Virginia creeper) and *P. tricuspidata* (Boston ivy) are both too vigorous for most places and are poor choices. They may even suffer the same problems as their relatives, the grapevines (see page 182).

### Passiflora *(Passion flowers)*

The hardy *Passiflora caerulea* often suffers from a virus that causes poor growth and distortion and mottling of the leaves. Eradication is the only option. To eliminate damage from hormonal weedkiller or something similar, cut the plant back hard in autumn, feed it in spring and hope: if growth is normal, it's not the virus. I find *Passiflora c. racemosa* to be more resistant. And yes, the fruit pulp is edible, but don't bother – it's miniscule and barely palatable.
VIRUS

### Vitis *(Grapevines)*

Ornamental species may fruit badly or have poor fruits. They also suffer the same problems as the fruiting vines (see page 182).

### Wisteria *(Wisterias)*

Wisteria has no problems, except they are slow at coming into flower. Pruning both summer and winter to leave moderately short stems on a main framework can encourage flowering; otherwise just wait until they bloom naturally.

# beds and borders: shrubs

## general pruning

Shrubs, and trees, that are grafted cultivars are prone to revert to the original rootstock or to the un-sported parent. Reverted shoots have different foliage: prune them out at the point they originate. Be especially careful with green shoots on cultivars with variegated or coloured foliage – the green leaves are generally so much more vigorous that they will soon replace the choicer foliage entirely. Many shrubs, fruit and ornamental trees have hosts of suckers coming from the base; these need removing, as low down as possible close to the rootstock, or they can be bent over and held down under a dense mulch to die in the dark.

Evergreen shrubs are never dormant so are best planted in spring and kept well watered until established. Choosing dwarfing, compact forms, not seedlings, reduces the need for pruning. Most shrubs respond best to simple pruning or shearing back immediately after flowering, but not all, so do check. Evergreens should rarely be pruned heavily but, if they must be, then it is better done in spring after the worst frosts are over. Those with larger leaves should not be cut with shears, otherwise the leaves brown. Prune hollow-stemmed shrubs such as *Buddleja*, *Leycesterias* and bamboos only in spring – water in the pruning 'holes' rots them down.

### Bamboos

This plant is very invasive and is a bad choice by ponds with plastic liners, which will soon leak. Bamboos are best placed in the middle of a grassed area so that straying shoots get cut with the grass. Every so many years, all bamboos of a given variety flower, seed and die together, everywhere – it just happens.

### Brachyglottis *(Dunedin Group) 'Sunshine'*

Yellow, waxy patches on the undersides of the leaves are caused by a rust. This shrub used to be called *Senecio greyi* and is related to groundsel (*Senecio vulgaris*) and ragwort (*Senecio jacobaea*), weeds which also carry this disease and should be eradicated.
RUST

### Buddleja *(Butterfly bushes)*

Cuttings root very readily, but larger established plants resent moving, so start a new one *in situ* by putting in three slips, or cuttings, and later choosing the best. Then you can eliminate the parent. If the flower trusses are small, prune hard. This plant ought to be pruned much harder and more often, so do so.

### Choisya ternata *(Mexican orange blossom)*

This shrub needs shelter from searing winds to protect its aromatic, evergreen foliage from burning, especially the yellow form which scorches in full sun.

### Cotoneaster

Various caterpillars sometimes attack these shrubs, usually ones that web leaves together: just cut out and burn affected parts.

### Crataegus *(Hawthorns)*

This may get attacked by various caterpillars webbing the leaves together; just cut out and burn affected parts.

### Cytisus *(Brooms)*

The brooms like hot, dry positions and sulk in wet or shade. They are generally short-lived and often die away suddenly anyway, as it is their habit.

### Daphne

The whole genus resents any pruning, is poisonous and miffy, but has exquisitely scented flowers. They are often difficult to establish, needing well drained, humus-rich soil; the most

LEFT
TOP Bamboos.
MIDDLE *Choisya ternata* (Mexican orange blossom).
BELOW *Daphne odora*.
RIGHT *Lavendula* (lavenders).

reliable is *Daphne odora* 'Aureomarginata'. Aphids are an insidious problem since they go unnoticed but spread many viruses. Virus problems often show as distorted or mottled leaves. Daphnes suffer sudden death syndrome, just failing after one year or ten. *D. mezereum*, a deciduous one with gorgeous scent, is especially prone to virus and dying off, loathes pruning even more than the others and is best grown from seed *in situ* to avoid misery.
APHIDS, SUDDEN DEATH, VIRUSES

### Elaeagnus

Although tough, these mostly evergreen shrubs are remarkably prone to sudden death syndrome. Do not be surprised, it just happens. Some fungus may then come in, or may be the cause, but there is no remedy other than replacement with something unrelated; do not replant another elaeagnus on the site.
SUDDEN DEATH

### Erica *(Heaths)*

Winter-flowering heathers are more tolerant of slightly limy soils than summer-flowering ones, but no heather will grow on chalk, no matter how much peat you add. Once they get old and scraggy, earth each plant up with a big mound of sharp, gritty, lime-free compost, leaving just the stem ends sticking out. A year later, you have dozens of new plants.

### Fuchsia

Some are much hardier than most imagine, if the roots are well protected, but vine weevils can devastate them (see page 103). Under glass, they become prey to all the usual woes, especially aphids, whiteflies and red spider mites.
APHIDS, RED SPIDER MITE, VINE WEEVIL (P103), WHITEFLY

### Hamamelis *(Witch hazels)*

These will not be very happy planted on dry or chalky soils because they need moist, rich soil to do well.

### Hydrangea

If your soil pH is too alkaline the flowers turn the wrong (pinkish) colour instead of bluish. Tealeaf mulches are a traditional way of 'blueing' them. Frosts may damage flower buds; leaving on deadheads can protect them.

### Ilex *(Hollies)*

As well as a tree (see page 143), this is grown as an ornamental shrub in many forms. You need male and female plants to get berries. For some bizarre reason, some male forms of *Ilex aquifolium* are named 'Golden Queen' and 'Silver Queen' and a female form of *I.* x *altaclerensis* as 'Golden King'!

### Juniperus *(Junipers)*

Occasionally, this gets eaten by various caterpillars that web the leaves together: just cut out and burn affected parts.

### Laburnum

If whole leaves brown in blotches and die, look for earlier damage caused by spring and summer leaf miners. Hand pick the leaves before the miners emerge, to control them.

### Lavendula *(Lavenders)*

This is often short-lived, more so in shade or wet, heavy soil or damp conditions. In full sun on a dryish soil, this is never a problem – as long as you trim it hard each year. However, replace the plants every decade or so because they get leggy. Froghoppers and their cuckoo spit may be a trouble in some years but can

be hosed off. For lasting perfume, pick the flowers as soon as they start opening.
CUCKOO SPIT

### Ligustrum *(Privets)*
Often the leaves are tunnelled by leaf miners. Hand pick the leaves and cocoons before they emerge, to control them.

### Magnolia
These can get too big, especially the evergreen *Magnolia grandiflora*, but they resent pruning and are best left alone. They also resent moving, so should be planted small, and need moist, loamy, low or lime-free soil otherwise they will be yellowed and chlorotic.

### Philadelphus *(Mock oranges)*
The golden form may lose its colour in shade and easily scorches in full sun. The shrubs are often subject to fierce aphid attacks, but usually get over it.
APHID

### Pieris
This is a plant needing lime-free soil and often not getting it, so showing chlorotic leaf markings (yellowing) and poor growth. It likes part shade and is not a front-of-border plant.

### Prunus laurocerasus *(Cherry laurel)*
This laurel is a tough evergreen and makes a big, thick screen anywhere; it should not be sheared but trimmed shoot by shoot, with secateurs, because cut leaves die and look awful. Be careful not to breathe in the burning leaves' smoke – it is reckoned to be poisonous.

### Pyracantha *(Firethorns)*
I detest firethorns; true, they have masses of flowers and fruit for bees and birds, but those mean thorns always irritate and infect, so be

Rhododendron.

Skimmia.

careful. They currently experience attacks from a leaf miner that does just that – I wish it all the best and a long and healthy career. Pulling out and burning the bush is a good option.
LEAF MINER

*Rhododendron (Azaleas, Rhododendrons)*
Well known for needing lime-free soil, these shrubs often suffer from vine weevil (see page 103). Large-leafed forms generally prefer shade, the smaller full sun. Bud blast can cause the buds to fall off; confirm it by looking for little black dots (fungal bodies ready to re-infect) on the buds and pick them up and compost or burn them. Otherwise bud drop is often due to drought, scorch or frost. Leaf miners can cause azaleas to drop their leaves after they turn brown: look for oval burrows near the midribs; leaves may be folded around cocoons, which need picking and burning. Whitefly may cause leaves to go pale; the scales may be seen under the leaves. It is best controlled with the parasitic

wasp *Encarsia formosa* (only possible under cover). Thrips may cause the leaves to go pale or even brown; telltale signs are little, blackish specks on the undersides. Dry conditions aggravate thrips on azaleas, so keep them misted and watered. The plants are often grown in pots and containers; they have fibrous rootballs and are obliging about confinement, but this does make them prone to all the problems of drought, drainage and feeding and so on. Slow death may well be due to cultural conditions.
BUD BLAST, DRAINAGE PROBLEMS, DROUGHT, FEEDING PROBLEMS, LEAF MINER, THRIPS, VINE WEEVIL (P.103), WHITEFLY

*Skimmia*
These shrubs are very prone to chlorotic (yellowing) leaves and poor growth in sun in dry, limey soils; they need moister, shadier, or leaf-mould-rich soil to do well. A lack of berries in some species is because you need both separate male and female plants.

*Syringa (Lilac)*
There are many excellent, smaller-growing lilacs than the common purple and whites, such as the Persian (*Syringa* x *persica*), the Korean (*S. meyeri* 'Palibin') and the Canadian Preston hybrids. If these set seed, the next year's flowering is reduced so it pays to deadhead them. And they are very prone to suckering! Often the leaves are tunnelled by leaf miners. Hand pick mined leaves and spun cocoons in rolled-up leaves before they emerge, to control them.

*Viburnum*
There are many attractive scented cultivars, yet the almost scentless *Viburnum tinus* 'Eve Price' and *V. opulus* (guelder rose) are most common. Choose the more compact *V.* x *juddii*, *V. carlcephalum* or *V. carlesii*. Viburnums, being commonly grafted, are very prone to suckering! The tiny hairs on a few varieties such as *V. rhytidophyllum* can cause adverse reactions, so be warned.

# beds and borders: roses

## pointless to pamper

Grown worldwide, roses are host to a multitude of woes but still give a good show most of the time. Heavy feeding makes roses disease- and pest-prone and over-pruning weakens them and reduces flowering – unless they are well fed, watered and mulched. Underplantings of alliums, especially chives (*Allium schoenoprasum*) and garlic (*A. sativum*), are thought to improve the rose's resistance to disease while lavenders are thought to deter aphids. Their roots prefer a rich, heavy, moist soil with their heads up in the sun and breeze, as if they've just climbed out from a tree or shrub. So they are unhappy on thin, poor soil or against hot, dry walls and then suffer from powdery mildew (see below).

## fungal diseases

Powdery mildew coats the leaves and even the whole plant as if it has been washed in milk. Badly affected leaves curl, wither and or go slightly purplish. Keeping the plants moist at the roots in dry summers is the best approach; do not overfeed roses with nitrogenous fertilisers. Mulches are doubly useful because they also seal down disease spores after leaf fall; mulch heavily on top of, or remove and compost, fallen leaves. On thin soils, wood ashes can improve resistance, as may seaweed sprays or, in desperation, Bordeaux mixture and sulphur dusts. Cultivars with glossy foliage seem to be most disease-resistant, while yellow-flowered sorts are more prone to weak growth and also to black spot ('Allgold' is an exception).

Black spot is as it sounds: purplish blotches, mostly on leaves but also on stems – irksome, although rarely fatal. Picking leaves off is pointless but, since most black spot survives winter on shoots, hard pruning is useful. Of course spraying with seaweed solution for vigour and Bordeaux mixture as a preventative helps those of a compulsive nature.

Orange spots and patches are signs of rust (see page 118). I rather like this on roses when it is in the first stages, often in leaf joints; it is rather pretty. But then it moves to coat the backs of the leaves with little, rusty pustules, which become craters and the leaves drop very soon after. It is worth picking these up for composting or burning. Prompt hygiene, soil moisture, mulches and no overfeeding all help. The cultivar 'The Queen Elizabeth' rarely suffers.

## sap-feeding pests

Aphids are always present but really a major problem only when they festoon shoots and on the flower buds, which they may even prevent from opening. Jetting them off with a hosepipe is especially effective; try other measures (see page 101). Scale insect may be a problem on roses by walls and in old beds. Look for small, round, flat, whitish discs stuck to the stems, prune hard in winter and brush off any that are left with soft soap or alcohol. On hot, dry walls, check for red spider mite attacks (see page 108).

## caterpillars and the rest

If the leaves are skeletonised, or scraped transparent, it is probably one of several sawfly slugworms attacking; spraying soft-soap solution should see them off, if done early enough. Occasionally the leaf-rolling sawfly may do exactly that, although it may be tortrix-moth caterpillars if the leaves are drawn together just at the tips. Various other caterpillars web leaves together; just cut out and burn affected parts.

The rose leafhopper causes a white mottling on the leaves, but is difficult to catch. Leaf-cutting bees eat odd, often semi-circular, pieces to make their nests out of the edges of rose leaves, which may look tattered as a result, although it is seldom enough to harm the plant – the bees are a rare curiosity of nature. Likewise the hairy rose bedeguar gall is very weird but beautiful and does no apparent harm to the rose (see page 111). Clay-coloured weevils may eat the lower buds, lower leaves and bark, even girdling stems of young plants. Luckily, these are not vine weevils and do little other harm. Late at night, lay newspaper quietly over the ground under the rose and shake the bush while shining a bright light; the weevils will jump off and may be brushed up. Alternatively, trap them in hollow reeds or canes and blow them into salty water.

APHIDS (PP.99–101), BLACK SPOT, MILDEW, RED SPIDER MITE (P.108), RUST (P.118)

# ornamental trees

## coping with damage

Trees suffer the same problems as shrubs save that they have a single stem or trunk, which if damaged risks everything. If cut to the base most trees die, particularly conifers. However, some survive serious damage by sprouting lower down, although this may spoil the tree. In some cases, a suitable leading stem may be selected and tied to a cane to replace the trunk and all other stems removed. Trees are often too big to treat, so there is rarely much the gardener can do, other than to improve soil conditions, water and nutrition. Leave most serious cutting and especially saw work, other than light pruning of trained forms, to insured professionals. As trees get bigger and older, they may lose branches, develop hollow trunks, become wizened and yet still have decades of attractive use, but in these days of public liability you must investigate any possible danger. Tree surgeons may err on the side of caution, and of profitable work, so get several surveys and quotations before confirming any contract.

### container-grown trees

A common problem with trees in recent years has been the result of container-grown plants. Containers enable trees to be sold year round rather than just when dormant. It is better to buy bare-rooted stock, which is sold from autumn until spring; plant it carefully with the roots spaced out and a stake to support the trunk until the roots grip. Anyway, sold year round, the trees have been planted year round – not always to their benefit. The container rootball causes three problems in trees that do not seem as troublesome with container-grown herbaceous plants or smaller shrubs.

● Firstly, the small rootball size requires only a small hole to be dug, so the roots have a tougher task growing into the surrounding hard-packed soil.
● Secondly, the roots find it harder to get out of the circling web that they formed inside the container. The roots really need teasing out and planting in soft soil that is well firmed (teasing out is easier in a bath of water).
● Thirdly, the doomed rootball is often jammed sufficiently tight into the planting hole for no stake to be deemed necessary. This results in very poor root formation and likely failure in the first summer. Even if rooting is successful, the tree may break off at the grafting point since a stake is needed to protect that too.

Back to the point – poor planting of a container-grown tree results in a badly connected root system and these symptoms: the tree comes into leaf and flowers well in spring, looks good until dry weather comes, drops most of its fruit, then lots of leaves, suffers its autumn in summer and does better only in very wet summers. Growth is stunted and any fruits tiny. Often if you get hold of it when still small and give a good yank, you can pull up such a tree. There is no cure, other than uprooting and replanting and this is not as difficult as you may imagine if done in late autumn – even if a tree has been in a long time! I moved one pear tree that had done badly for fourteen years; on its new site, it flourished and has cropped magnificently for twenty-four summers since. (For problems of fruit trees and related ornamentals, see pages 188–201.)

*Ilex* (holly).

### Acer pseudoplatanus (Sycamore)

Often these trees get a black spot (fungal) attack on the leaves, but unfortunately it rarely does more than weaken them. They are remarkably prone to funny little bits dangling under their leaves like tiny fingers; these are galls of a tiny insect and again do little harm.

### Aesculus hippocastaneum (Horse chestnut)

As I write, these trees in the UK are suffering a terrible plague of oozing cankers that lead to the death of whole limbs and eventually the tree. Although these can be cut out individually when small, the apparent country-wide scale of the attack makes control nearly impossible. I fear for their loss, going the same way as so recently the elms.
CANKER

### Betula (Birches)

Birch species are not long-lived, but very frost-resistant. They often get the fly agaric (*Agaricus muscarius*), the archetypal magic

I've allowed these elms to grow out of my hedge, but fear they will soon succumb to Dutch elm disease.

mushroom that has a crimson cap with white flecks, coming up at their bases. This mushroom used to be soaked in milk to make a very effective bait and poison for flies (sadly, their poisonous properties make this too dangerous to do today).

### Eucalyptus (Gum trees)
These get too big, fast. They lose their attractive, juvenile foliage as the growths get older. Cut back regularly to regrow the juvenile leaves. Large limbs are prone to whiplash and can shatter in strong winds.

### Ilex (Hollies)
If waterlogged for even a shortest while, holly is prone to leaf browning. If the leaves drop off, the tree may recover but if they stay on it's probably too far-gone. It is prey to a leaf miner, but there is little effective control other than squishing or accurate needling. Beyond a certain height, the foliage often loses its spines because the plant 'knows' that no giraffes are about in cool climates. (See also Ilex in Shrubs, page 137.)

### Salix (Willows)
Anthracnose (a fungal disease) has been attacking willows, causing red blistering and showers of damaged leaves and twigs. It is probably aggravated by droughts so you can try feeding and watering the tree to help it recover.

### Sambucus nigra (Common elder)
Often a shrubby big bush, this and its cultivars may be shaped into a pleasing small tree. It often suffers from horrendous aphid attacks on the tips and coating whole stems – which is odd, since for years the leaves were boiled with soft soap as an aphicide that apparently also worked on root-fly maggots and other pests.

### Ulmus (Elms)
Many elms have fallen to Dutch elm disease, but new saplings still follow the cycle: they get to a certain size; then the elm bark beetle arrives and does some burrowing, along with the fungus, which blocks the sap pathways; leaves on small branches yellow, then brown out; more die and so on until the whole tree has died. There has been some success with injecting Trichoderma virides, a parasitic fungus that is also used to control silver leaf disease on plums.
DUTCH ELM DISEASE

# water features

ABOVE Waterlilies exclude light from the water, preventing blanket weed and other algae growths.

BELOW Pond weed will 'wind out' on a revolving cane.

## pond creatures

Gnat and mosquito larvae are a common annoyance and, in anything bigger than a birdbath, are easily cured by introducing goldfish or preferably golden orfe. These fish control most insect pests, but may also eat frog, toad and newt eggs and tadpoles unless they are given a fish-free refuge at one end. It is unwise to put fish into shallow pools that may freeze solid and harm them. All stocked pools need a hole made through thick ice, to let out the gases given off by decomposition on the muddy bottom. A floating ball helps to keep a hole open in ice. Rather than hack at the ice, stand a tin can full of hot water on it; as it cools, replace the hot water until it melts a hole. Few problems are found with most aquatic plants, other than invasiveness.

## water quality

In summer, algal blooms may turn the water green; they are tiny plants growing on dissolved nutrients and may be avoided by sinking barley straw stuffed into weighted stockings to absorb surplus nutrients. Do not add tap water or allow fertiliser of any kind to get into the water or more blooms may result. Be careful of adding too much fertiliser to the potting compost of any water plants you put in. Stagnant, foul water is often the result of too many leaves going rank on the bottom; clear these out and introduce some oxygenating plants. These may themselves be invasive and cause problems; in particular Canadian pondweed (*Elodia canadensis*), with blue-green whirls of needle-like leaves. This weed may also be seen as a source of good composting material to be dragged out.

Blanket weed, a fine, hair-like mass, may be dragged out with a standard rake (with blunt points!) and floating duckweed skimmed off the top with a lawn rake. These last two weeds are surprisingly useful if laid up in layers, pressed gently and then dried to make mulch mats and basket liners. A cane turned slowly will pick up either weed in huge amounts. Watch carefully as you work: you may otherwise drag out many small creatures too.

ALGAL BLOOMS, BLANKET WEED, CANADIAN PONDWEED, DUCKWEED

### Gunnera manicata

This alien rhubarb is a moisture-loving plant that can easily get bigger than a house. Although interesting, architectural and indeed beautiful it is too big for most gardens! A bad choice and a problem plant.

### Lobelia cardinalis

A choice plant, this is often recommended as a marginal because it can provide a spike of brilliant-red flowers; what isn't mentioned is that, unless cunningly protected or surrounded completely by water, Slugs always make the plant disappear before it blooms.
SLUGS

### Nymphaea (Waterlilies)

If planted at the wrong depth for their type, or in too cold water, these plants may be hard to establish. Preferring still pools of calm water and slow-flowing rivers, waterlilies rarely thrive in fast-moving water or under fountains. A brown beetle and its brown-backed, yellow-bellied larvae may strip the waterlily leaves and flowers; it's best controlled by jetting the pests into the water – and keeping goldfish. Leaves are also eaten from beneath by caddis flies – caterpillars living in their own mandible-crafted, tubular homes of litter – that are also cleaned up by goldfish. A greenish-brown caterpillar, of the brown china-mark moth, eats the leaves from above, but may be hosed off. Droplets of wind-born herbicide, paints or cleaning fluids may cause spots. Sometimes infections, most common in rank, stagnant water, cause holes to drop out of the leaves. Good pond hygiene and changing the water will help.

This ornamental pool keeps the atmosphere moist and humid for the tropical plants around it.

# the lawn and turf

## general care

If the lawn is in otherwise good health, diseases are rarely troublesome. Most important is to use grass species that are suited to your soil. We are often sold expensive, fine grass seed that is more suited to bowling greens than recreational lawns; fine grasses are not strong growing and need acid conditions so are easily swamped by weeds and do poorly on many soils. Most soils have lime and, unless ericaceous plants are nearby, lime may be spread on grassed areas to great advantage. Cheaper, more vigorous grasses love lime and squeeze out weeds and mosses so over-sowing with suitable seed and lime soon builds a strong sward. (For lawn-cutting regimes, see pages 42–45.)

If you do not want dead patches, stay off frozen grass and do not treat the drive or paths with weedkiller, then walk across your lawn – as stupid as it seems, it's been done rather often. Do not patch bare, worn bits; replace them with stepping stones, otherwise they will wear again. If you need to repair a missing spot, use bits of chopped up turf from the edges; this will blend in and soon take if kept watered.

## lawn weeds

Many lawn weeds such as buttercups (*Ranunculus repens*) prefer acid conditions so liming handicaps most of them, especially the otherwise difficult-to-control speedwells (*Veronica* spp.). Daisies (*Bellis perennis*) are a sure sign the grass is being cut too closely and the soil is short of lime; they disappear if the cut height is raised and lime is added generously. Thistles of several species, plantains (*Plantago* spp.) and other rosette-forming weeds are best grubbed out with a sharp knife or better still a daisy grubber – a tool with a wee fork, rotating as a lever about a ball foot, that pulls up weeds, roots and all. Offering children piece rates for weeding can work out cheaper than herbicides, is safer and keeps them occupied! Dressings of maize meal suppress annual weeds like clover (*Trifolium* spp.) and dandelions (*Taraxacum officinale*) but stimulate grass. Milk has a similar effect, if applied diluted.

Moss is best defeated by serious scarifying, removing and composting the moss and grass thatch, then liming and feeding the soil with dressings of lime, seaweed meal or blood, fish and bone meal. Raising the cut height also discourages moss by removing its light. Shady, damp lawns are invariably mossy; open up the growth about them to let in air and light to the grass. If bothered by green patches of clover in the lawn when it browns out in a drought, try adding clovers everywhere else, to provide free nitrogen (fixed on their roots), which keeps grasses growing strongly in dry weather.

## fungal diseases

Fairy rings attacks annoys with its green rings, created as the fungus moves outwards. The greenness of the grass is from extra nutrients released by the fungal breakdown of old roots. If you dress the turf with nitrogenous feeds inside and outside the circle, the ring will almost disappear. It is possible to remove the fungal growth and repair the area, but few achieve satisfactory results. The mushrooms may be simply brushed off with a stiff broom.

More serious is damping off, a fungal attack of all sorts of species resulting in patches yellowing or reddening and wilting, then dying back. It is most prevalent in damp, humid conditions, often where growth is poor due to low light or poor soil conditions. In warmer weather, especially in

Use stepping stones or slabs where the path gets worn for a permanent fix.

Small beds and inserted plants make mowing the lawn more difficult.

late summer, fusarium patch, or snow mould, causes yellowish-brown, burnt-out patches that are sometimes huge, become slimy and then covered in whitish or pinkish 'cotton' and die. It is aggravated by heavy feeding and close mowing, but lessened by spring sprinklings of seaweed solution to increase the grass's resistance and by liming, if suited to the grass species and surrounding plants.

If there is a sticky redness to the grass, which looks bleached but does not waste away, then it could be red thread. A lens will reveal red, spiky outgrowths from the tips. Treat it by making the grass more resistant with seaweed sprays, feeding with garden compost and diluted urine (if permitted under local codes), and cutting with a sharper mower blade (the disease gets in through wounds). Do not leave clippings on the turf.

Very rarely, little, white mycelia show on burnt-out spots which are more brownish-yellow than bleached; this is dollar spot. Little black dots at the stem bases shows ophiobolus patch. Both are treated much the same as red thread. A general, dirty yellowness and a fine powder is mildew, but this rarely does more than look bad for a while. Feed the soil and water well, preferably with seaweed solution.

## turf pests

Leatherjackets (and the very similar bibio grubs), chafer grubs, cutworms and a few other beetles such as wireworms all live on grass roots (see pages 104–5). Birds, badgers or foxes tearing up the sward are probably trying to get at these bugs. Although most bugs are curable by watering on parasitic nematodes, it is expensive. It is simpler to cover well-wetted areas with an old carpet or plastic sheet. After a few days (before the grass yellows and dies!), roll back the cover early in the morning and birds will eat the grubs that have come up onto the surface. A scattering of rolled oats under the cover brings more of them up. Very rarely, minute, yellowish grubs of the hessian fly may cause poor growth since they sap the leaf bases, but it is not often a serious pest.

Many used to consider worms a lawn pest because their casts were alleged to encourage weeds and damage mower blades, so worms were killed deliberately or inadvertently by overuse of acid fertilisers and moss-killers. Worms are in fact essential for soil aeration and drainage and should be encouraged by dressings of lime, seaweed meal or blood, fish and bone meal.

CHAFER GRUBS (P.104), CUTWORM (P.104), DAMPING OFF, FAIRY RING, FUSARIUM PATCH, LEATHERJACKETS, RED THREAD, WIREWORMS (P.105)

# hedges

## pruning hedges

Often in a small garden a fence is more sensible; hedges need regular trimming and impoverish the surrounding soil for other plants. Of course they are good for shelter and wildlife and last longer than fences, but cutting them can be hard work. Put down a sheet first so picking up the trimmings is easier. Cut the sides of the hedge first, then the top; it will be denser and stand better if the sides taper slightly towards the top. Remember that a hedge slowly gets larger – unless you are vicious when you trim. Also it is far better to do several light cuts each year than one heavy one. Winter trimming encourages regrowth; summer trimming discourages it, so in the early years winter-trim, but when the required size is attained go over to summer trimming. Another mistake in the early years is to not cut heavily enough (after the year of planting), thereby getting a sparse hedge.

## plugging the gaps

If planting a hedge to exclude stock, plant a staggered double row, ideally with the plants laid in at an angle, and in opposite directions in each row. This gives the densest, most animal-proof hedge. A single row of upright plants is cheaper and quicker for privacy, but is nearly always gappy at the base. Never plant seedlings, which can be variable, but raise or buy rooted cuttings so that the hedge is more uniform. If the odd plant dies early on, by all means, replace it, with extra feeding and watering until it establishes. In a mature hedge, it is very difficult to get a new plant of the same species to establish, unless an inordinate amount of soil is removed and replaced.

Many hedges such as beech (*Fagus sylvatica*), haw- or quickthorn (*Crataegus monogyna*), privet (*Ligustrum* spp.), yew (*Taxus baccata*), and sometimes holly (*Ilex* spp.) and laurel (*Prunus* spp.), may be cut very hard, almost to the roots, and will recover to make a new hedge. Almost all conifers never sprout from bare wood so never, ever, trim, shear or prune them back beyond green shoots. Otherwise you will have a bare spot. Another option is laying a plant: half-cutting through the stems and bending them nearly horizontal, so that they sprout from their sideshoots. They thicken up into an excellent hedge – if well done – and can bridge quite large gaps. If an old hedge has to be patched, fill the gaps with plants such as holly or yew that grow well in dappled shade.

## pests and diseases

If several gaps occur, it may be an invasive disease such as honey fungus (see page 121). Most hedges occasionally suffer aphid attacks and some get mildew; jetting down with a hose and watering the base alleviate these problems. Mushrooms often appear at the bases of old hedges because they can be rich in leaf mould, but the fungi are rarely a problem. Watch out for coral spot (see page 118).

HONEY FUNGUS (P.121) CORAL SPOT (P.118)

**Check for bird's nests before cutting a hedge – you wouldn't want to disturb them, and besides it's illegal!**

# garden DIY

## paths and driveways

Paths crumble and crack: before they become unsafe, fill any crack or crevice with cement or sand to stop leaf mould and soil filling it instead, or use a sterile sowing compost mixed with seed of prostrate plants such as thymes (*Thymus*). Slippery paths are made safer, especially in frosts, by sprinkling them regularly with sharp sand; it may carry on shoes into the house, but does at least give sure footing and rubs off any algae on the path. Lift rocking stones or slabs, remove the soil from underneath and re-bed them on sharp sand or concrete. Watch the edges of poured concrete paths; these often get undercut and, if not reinforced, will break away.

It is best if solid paths and stepping-stones are exactly level with the grass so they do not interfere with mowing. Paths or slabs below grass level will gradually be covered by encroaching grass. Proud ones blunt blades! Loose gravel paths must be raised above surrounding beds, with a retaining board or edge to stop soil getting on the path and encouraging weeds. It is then easy to add more gravel to the path and mix trespassed gravel into the bed soil. Bark mulches are softer than gravel and well suited to some plants and themes, but get kicked everywhere by birds so they are better informal with no, or very high, fixed edges, for instance so they merge into bark-mulched beds and plants. Seeds just love to germinate in a stone-, gravel- or bark-mulched path so regularly deadhead all plants nearby, especially weeds. And do not skimp; shallow layers or, worse, muddy bits let the worms bring soil up and there will be a weedy mess that is hard to control. Thick layers stay cleaner and may be raked.

A simple error is to make pathways that follow geometric lines for aesthetics or convenience, ignoring our habit of cutting corners. If there is a short cut off the path, it will be taken, causing wear and damage in the wrong places. If the path doesn't follow an easy route, use informal hedges or even prickly shrubs to enforce compliance.

## gutters, pipes and tanks

It is essential for all of us to save as much water as possible, by guttering every roof and providing sufficient tanks and butts to store it in. Gutters and pipes should be of as big a bore as possible and feed into butts that eventually lead to a soakaway. The gutters should have an adequate fall towards the downpipes or they will soon flow over. Never allow butts to overflow because water running down the side undercuts the edge and makes it sink. Overrunning water is detrimental to any wall nearby and must be rectified. Most rain falls in winter so it is sensible to empty and clean butts and gutters in autumn; it is best done in dry weather when the 'mud' and leaves may be vacuumed out of gutters. Put the sediment from both on the compost heap. Fitting downpipes with old-sock filters keeps out much of the muck and a lid on the tank will stop kids and birds falling in. When placing a new butt, remember that if you want to use a spigot and tap you need to place the butt on blocks high enough to get a watering can underneath! I prefer to dip it in the top as it's quicker – I've even sawn the ends off a pair of watering cans to speed up watering.

It is foolish to have trees overhanging or climbers rampant on your roof; the gutters soon block and vermin run up to your attic and roof space. I love the cool in summer, the birds nearby and the cottage-garden look, but it causes too many extra chores. Evergreens usually drop leaves continually so plant shade trees, if you are lucky enough to need them, that are deciduous; their leaves will fall and may be cleared at the same time – shade is not needed in winter anyway.

If it's been a long dry spell, make sure your gutters and pipes still join up.

# the herb garden

## perennial herbs

Most of these are remarkably tough, problem-free plants. They generally need a hot, dry site on well drained, poor soil in full sun and live for years. Even so, they do need renewing; usually cuttings or layering are easy. A few have specific problems.

### Aloysia triphylla (Lemon verbena)

The true lemon verbena has a gorgeous lemon scent, kept by dried leaves for many years. It is probably one of the most pest-prone plants I know – loved by aphids and red spider mite. It is not very hardy and does not survive hard frosts unless planted against a warm wall. Since it is easily grown from cuttings, it is a good idea to have back-ups in a pot under cover or as houseplants.
APHIDS, RED SPIDER MITE

### Artemisia dracunculus (Tarragon)

If you are lucky and have the true French tarragon, be careful not to lose it. It is propagated only by root division, which must be done every third year or so, otherwise it will die away. The herb needs a warm spot with extra protection in the coldest, dampest winters. Never be fobbed off with the miserable Russian tarragon, which is frequently sold as the French because it is cheap and easy to propagate. Taste it: if it's the French it will be sweet and piquant, not rank and sour.

### Laurus nobilis (Bay)

Not a very hardy shrub, this may suffer leaf burn from harsh winds while small and so is easily lost, especially if in a tub where the roots get frosted. Once established, bay is a tough, medium-sized tree that can be cut to the ground and yet recover. It can be taken under cover in winter, but becomes prone to pests, especially red spider mite and scale insect, which bother it indoors and out. Scale insect (see page 102) is invariably a problem if ants are farming it.
SCALE INSECT (P.102)

### Mentha (Mints)

The exception to the rule – these perennial herbs love cool, wet sites and suffer on dry ones. They may get rust (see page 118), with yellow pustules that turn brown. Rust requires religious hygiene: trim and bin, bury or properly compost the stems, then mulch the soil with sterile compost. The old boys found they could clean rust spores off roots for forcing or transplanting by heating them in water for ten minutes at 44.5°C (112°F). Contain these invasive herbs in tubs or big pots, in a pot that is buried in the soil with the rim proud, or in beds surrounded by regularly cut grass. Gold- and silver-variegated and scented forms are less vigorous and die out or revert to plainer forms, unless regularly divided and replanted. Mint allegedly benefits cabbage and tomatoes though choking them. Spearmint (Mentha spicata) suppresses aphid attacks by putting off the ants. Dried mint may be used to repel rodents, clothes moths, fleas and flea beetles.
RUST (P.118)

### Origanum majorana (Oregano, Sweet marjoram)

There are many cultivars, all similar to the oregano that is essential for Italian cuisine. The problem is that the best-flavoured ones are not hardy and do not like being under cover either. Common marjoram (Origanum vulgare) has a passably good flavour and is the only one that easily survives in a pot under cover for winter use. True oreganos may survive on a dry, bright, frost-free windowsill; just hope the moulds don't get them.

LEFT
TOP *Aloysia triphylla* (lemon verbena).
MIDDLE *Artemisia dracunculus* (tarragon).
BELOW *Laurus nobilis* (bay).
RIGHT *Salvia officinalis* (common sage).

### *Rosmarinus officinalis* *(Rosemary)*

Not very hardy, rosemary can be lost in hard frosts, especially if in a container when the roots get frozen. It may be taken in a pot under cover, but is likely to suffer red spider mite and other pests. A new pest is killing off rosemary in the UK. Stems die back, and eventually the whole plant. On examination, a small pupa, or more, from a small moth or similar insect is usually found low down in some frass and webbing; prune out affected parts and burn them.

RED SPIDER MITE

### *Salvia officinalis* *(Common sage)*

This dies out as it gets straggly but resents pruning and needs replacing every few years. It may be earthed up and the rooted stems then cut off as new plants. Multicoloured sages, and especially the decorative summer salvias, are not very hardy and cannot be expected to survive winter frosts. Clary sage (*Salvia sclarea*) is another easily lost herb; it is normally a biennial and dies after seeding.

### *Thymus* *(Thymes)*

These need replenishing every few years since they die away naturally, but until then, they should be vigorous. Thymes suffer in shade or damp and resent wet soils.

*Anethum graveolens* (dill).

## *Allium schoenoprasum* (Chive)

Chives may suffer from rust and need replacing (see page 118). Ironically, these alliums are probably mostly used for keeping fungal diseases off other plants. They have been used against black spot on roses, scab on apples, aphids on chrysanthemums, sunflowers and tomatoes, and allegedly benefit carrots if planted *en masse* underneath. Chive sprays have been used against downy and powdery mildew on cucumbers and gooseberries. Old clumps decline; divide them every few years and increase them to use as edgings. Left to flower, they self-seed and the leaves become poor; cut them back hard every so often on alternate plants to stagger their regrowth.
RUST (P.118)

## *Anethum graveolens* (Dill)

This is prone to mould off more than most herbs in early and late sowings, unless kept warmer and drier. It's not liked nearby carrots, but is said to benefit cabbages, lettuce, onions, sweetcorn and cucumber by repelling aphids and red spider mites.

## *Angelica archangelica* (Angelica)

This is a tough but short-lived, often biennial, herbaceous plant – not a perennial! It likes shady, rich, moist soil and becomes bitter and unpleasant in hot, dry sites.

## *Claytonia perfoliata* (Miner's lettuce, Winter purslane)

This is really a weed because it self-seeds exuberantly and does awfully well in shady, moist, rich conditions, even growing in midwinter under cover. It is remarkably problem-free, except for slugs that eat the roots. Pull any plants that are becoming orangey-yellow and stunted and, if they come away easily, examine the rooting site closely for all sorts but especially

## saladings and annual herbs

Whereas perennial herbs like dry sun and poor soil, annual herbs prefer moister sites. We gather the younger shoots and tender leaves, and most of these are more palatable and succulent in rich soil – although too much muck may spoil their flavour. Since they are prone to bolting if over-crowded or dry, most saladings and annual herbs are safest sown shallowly *in situ* from mid-spring. For most, there is no need to sow or thin to one plant per site, as long as they are not congested. Most resent transplanting, but are easier to manage if they are started in small pots or cells, potted up as needed, hardened off and planted out after the last frost. With most, the flavour is coarsened once flowering commences, although some may be cut back for a new flush. Generally, small successive sowings are a better idea. All suffer every now and then from the usual culprits, such as slug and snail damage, but generally have few real problems.

*Allium schoenoprasum* (chive).

*Angelica archangelica* (angelica).

*Petroselinum crispum* (parsley).

black keel slugs. I find this herb also makes an excellent green manure for winter.
SLUGS

### Eruca vesicaria *(Rocket)*
Probably the most useful salad crop, this will grow year round under cover. It gets too peppery if hot, dry or too mature. Although old plants that are approaching flowering may be cut down for a new flush of leaf, it is far better to sow seeds every week or so. It is prone to flea beetle (see page 107).
FLEA BEETLE (P.107)

### Ocimum basilicum *(Basil)*
Without warmth this will not germinate or grow. It is one of the tastiest herbs in the garden and needs more warmth and wind protection than it usually gets. Give it a cloche or grow it indoors. It is very difficult to keep this going through the darker days, even under cover, because mould will always get it. Basil is a trap plant for aphids so is often planted under tomatoes.

### Petroselinum crispum *(Parsley)*
If the plants begin to yellow, they are probably under attack by the carrot root fly (see page

160). The seed is often hard to germinate, but if you leave parsley to self-seed it will become a weed in moist soils. Sow fresh, pre-soaked seed (half an hour, no more) on the surface of soil that you have previously scalded with boiling water, then barely cover the seed with sowing compost and tamp down gently. Parsley freezes and dries well and plants may be dug up, potted and moved under cover or cloches for winter use.
CARROT ROOT FLY (P.160)

### Portulaca oleracea *(Summer purslane)*
Suddenly, after years of obscurity, this is much in demand as one of the richest vegetable sources of omega-3 fatty acids. It is an infuriating crop because it's difficult to get bought seed to germinate but self-seeds happily. Let it self-seed onto a sterile area of soil or compost, and then it will come up ever after.

### Raphanus sativa *(Radish)*
If these are hot and tough, they were not grown quickly enough in rich, moist conditions. If allowed to flower, they produce pods that are tasty and nutritious while small and tender, and are far better eating than tough roots. Black Spanish and Japanese radishes bolt

unless sown after midsummer, need to be treated more like turnips than radishes and are hot anyway. Although radish may be attacked by all the usual brassica pests (see page 158) and by scab (which also afflicts brassica roots, beetroot and potatoes), the commonest problem, which is always worse in dry conditions, is flea beetle (see page 107).
FLEA BEETLE (P.107)

### Tropaeolum majus *(Nasturtium)*
These are very prone to the same caterpillars that attack brassicas (see page 158). The plants are seldom grown as a salad, but are edible in all parts; the flowers and young leaves add a unique, peppery flavour and the seeds are excellent pickled. Blackfly (aphids) may attack them; do not overfeed, otherwise there will be few flowers.
CABBAGE WHITE BUTTERFLY (P.158), CABBAGE MOTH (P.158)

### Valerianella locusta *(Corn salad, Lamb's lettuce)*
This tends to hide slugs and often has dirty leaves, so is best grown under cover. Pick leaves rather than the whole plant. I find this makes an excellent green manure for winter.

# the vegetable bed

These are a unique bunch, as unlike most plants as Olympic athletes are to most of us! They have been selected and bred to be able to perform far beyond their wild ancestor's capabilities. But this means they are more demanding, needing better aerated and drained, moister, richer, soil conditions, and with more sun and good airflow than is needed by many ornamental plants. If not given their near optimum conditions not only do they perform poorly but they quickly become prone to all sorts of pests and diseases. However, there are solutions to almost all of these, provided that cultural conditions are first ensured adequate.

RIGHT You can eat asparagus raw, when freshly picked. FAR RIGHT Broad beans are so nutritious and one of the earliest crops to harvest.

## Asparagus (Asparagus officinalis)

This crop often disappoints: it takes patience because the crowns need to grow strong enough to throw out plenty of thick spears; it is at least three years usually before they become productive, and premature cutting stunts growth. Over-cutting also reduces crops; never cut after the last day of spring. Likewise do not clear away the ferny foliage until it has dried up in autumn. Cramping the plants gives poor yields: crowns need to be wide apart for the best crops, but spacings vary in practice, the closest being for short-term beds and the widest for the longer term.

Sow in situ in a well prepared bed or get one-year-old crowns to plant as early as possible in spring. Do not divide or move old crowns, nor ever buy crowns older than one year. If possible, buy pot-grown plantlets and wash their roots out under water to separate them for planting. Damage to these fleshy roots may lose the crown, so spread them gently over a mound in the base of a trench and cover firmly with good soil so that the buds on the crown are just under the surface. Mark the spot with a thin mulch of sharp sand, which will deter slugs.

Purple and green asparagus has more flavour than the whiter, blanched spears that some are used to. If it's bitter, though, it may not be fresh; it becomes bitter as it ages and even faster if it is stood in water to stop it withering. Crops are late in shady or dry positions. Do not mulch asparagus if you want early spears; regularly shallow-hoed soil that is darkened with soot gives best results. Asparagus really grows best on its own, although it has long been grown with grapevines in Beaujolais. It dislikes alliums, but sharing a bed with tomatoes helps to hide it from the asparagus beetle, while a nematode (Trichodorus) that attacks tomato roots is hindered by a secretion from the asparagus roots.

### asparagus pests

Slugs may take seedlings, sometimes they graze a spear on the side, causing it to bend and rot. Frost may also bend or distort spears or kill them entirely. In wet soils, the roots may rot. The asparagus beetle can be troublesome; it comes and goes over the years. What you notice is the ferny foliage turning into dead sticks and, on close inspection, you see many small, slug-like larvae devouring the fern. Attacks can be stopped with frequent soft-soap sprays or by dusting with fine dusts such as wood ashes or lime in the early morning. The treatments hurt the fern, but choke the pests. Leaving one plant in every dozen uncut in spring lures the pests to lay their eggs on it. The plant can then be cut and burnt to destroy the eggs and later generations. Do not trim the fern early but when you do, bundle it up and leave it lying among the stumps. Leave the stumps – I know the books say otherwise, but do not cut them close. In the middle of winter, cut off the stumps and burn them with the adult beetles hiding in them and then shake out the fern, to save ladybirds and friendly beetles, and burn the rest with the fern.

### asparagus diseases

Like many of the lily family, this suffers from a rust. Red-orange blisters on the stems and leaves browning before autumn are the signs; scrupulous clearance of all infected material followed by mulching is required. Grow resistant cultivars such as 'Mary Washington'.

(An orange-rusty streak on young shoots is a minor blemish and not rust.) A rusty, brownish or purplish colour to the roots and crown indicate violet root rot, which is nasty and requires extirpation and burning all infected material since it also attacks most root crops. Fortunately, it's rare.
ASPARAGUS BEETLE, RUST, VIOLET ROOT ROT

## Beans, broad or field (Vicia faba)

Beans are said to grow well mixed among brassicas, carrots, celery and cucurbits, and are good with main-crop potatoes, but do not get on very well near garlic and onions.

Blackfly (aphids) trouble these beans on the tips, so nip out the soft tips of the plants once a crop of flowers has set to get control. These aphids overwinter on Euonymous trees and shrubs, so don't grow them nearby. Summer (Satureja hortensis) and winter savory (Satureja montana) planted nearby may help. Beans also suffer from thrips in dry summers. Small, greyish-brown weevils eating the leaf edges do little harm; you may trap them in hollow canes or reeds and blow them into salty water. The bean seed fly attacks germinating seeds if conditions are poor and the seed slow to move. Douse a clean, firm seedbed with seaweed solution to hide the smell of the beans and use cloches or fleece to exclude the flies and encourage speedy germination. Various bean and pea beetles eat holes in the stored seeds, but are easily eliminated by not sowing infected seed.

French beans rarely suffer much from pests or diseases, though they hate the cold.

Sometimes beans get the aptly named chocolate spot on their pods, leaves and stems, but it's rarely bad enough to defoliate the plant. Other leaf spots, mosaic viruses and rusts are rare and it is usually enough to pull and burn any oddly marked plants. Good hygiene avoids most of these.
CHOCOLATE SPOT

### Beans, French (Phaseolus vulgaris)
The only real problem is getting these beans out of the ground in cold, wet springs. Mostly, low yields are caused by overcrowding and failing to keep the plants picked clean! French beans are said to grow best with celery, cucurbits, potatoes, strawberries and sweetcorn, but not very well near garlic and onions.

French beans do not crop well in dry soils; they may get red spider mite in hot years and under cover. A root knot eelworm can cause galls on the roots (see page 105). These beans suffer from anthracnose, a fungal disease that causes dark speckling on every part, which mostly worsens into sunken, brownish and then whitish patches and eventually shrivels. Sowing clean (not spotty) or bought-in seed in pots and planting out the seedlings gives better results. Another seed-borne problem is halo blight, where the plants wilt and have small, angular lesions surrounded by yellowish haloes. Wet weather can aggravate halo blight so that the leaves brown and wilt, then blister. Pull and burn infected plants before the blister stage and dispose of them. Leaf spots, mosaic virus and rusts are rare; it is usually enough to pull and burn any oddly marked plants.
RED SPIDER MITE

### Beans, runner (Phaseolus coccineus)
Not difficult to crop if you can get the seedlings going – the seeds do not like germinating nor do seedlings like emerging in cold conditions. Often they do better if sown late or pot-grown

Runner beans, if warm and wet enough, are almost immune to problems.

Beetroot may bolt if dry or overcrowded, but rarely suffers other problems.

Chard is too easy and has few problems if well-spaced.

indoors and planted out later. The plants are happier on canes and wire netting than on string or plastic netting (unless these are stretched taut). Water shortages reduce crops and cause flowers to drop. The first blooms often abort anyway. Adding more water usually cures a lack of crop setting and spraying the blooms can help. Pollinators may be rare; attract them by mixing in a few sweet peas (*Lathyrus odoratus*) with the beans. Runner beans are said to grow best with sweetcorn and summer savory – but do not get on very well near beetroot, chards or kohlrabi.

In hot, dry summers, red spider mite may attack, browning the leaves, as do aphids occasionally. Any leaf spots, mosaic virus and rusts are rare and it is usually enough to pull and burn any oddly marked plants.
RED SPIDER MITE

### Beetroot and chards (*Beta vulgaris* and *Beta vulgaris* ssp. *cicla* var. *flavescens*)
Beets and chards are said to grow best planted among brassicas, garlic, kohlrabi, onions, parsnips, swedes and most beans, but do not get on very well near runner beans.

The biggest problem is bird damage! Seed

is often thought poor when in fact it had germinated, emerged and was eaten before you ever noticed it. These crops may bolt if sown too closely or when it is too hot and dry. The usual suspects sometimes attack the roots. Very occasionally they are attacked by blackfly (aphids), flea beetles and even more rarely by the root knot eelworm that attacks peas, but not very badly. Small, whitish grubs of the mangold fly may tunnel and blister the undersides of the leaves, so that they eventually fall. The grubs pupate in the soil and three generations may occur in one summer. Remove all affected foliage and rake the soil beneath to enable birds to get at the pupae. You could also use soft soap.

Leaf spots can cause blistering similar to that of mangold fly, but in this case the spots become small holes. On heavily limed land and in dry summers, the leaves turn black and die, first at the crown, then the outer leaves die, then the root rots – a condition known as heart rot; good hygiene and more compost control it. If the root turned black and died first, it was black leg; this is seed-borne, so do not use your own seed. Rough patches are just common scab – similar but

different to the one that attacks potatoes. However, both are aggravated by excess lime and ameliorated by more humus and fresh grass clippings or green manures in the soil.

Virus yellows is a disease spread by aphids that does what it says – yellowed patches later turn reddish and brittle; there is no cure and affected plants must be destroyed. Grow the crop under fleece to keep the aphids off. Very rarely beets and chards may be attacked by the violet root rot that kills asparagus, so they are bad neighbours.
BIRDS, MANGOLD FLY, VIOLET ROOT ROT

### Brassicas, Cabbage family (*Brassica oleracea* Groups)
These vegetables, and their ornamental cousins, are happier on heavy, moist, limey soil and are prone to loose heads (especially sprouts) and bolting if hot, dry, loosely planted or in light, loose soil. Cauliflowers (*Brassica oleracea* Botrytis Group) are prone to making tiny heads if stressed, checked, overcrowded or just unhappy. Often these and the broccolis (*Brassica oleracea* Italica Group) are better sown direct and thinned rather than transplanted from a seedbed or modules. On acid

ABOVE  Slugs, caterpillars and wood pigeons
are the cabbage's enemies.
MIDDLE  Brussels sprouts are tough and
often stand out all winter.
BELOW  Purple-sprouting broccoli is
valuable as a late winter and spring crop.

soil, brassicas do badly: lime vegetable beds every fourth year after growing legumes (peas and beans) the year before; it will just do to mix in finely ground lime on planting. Brassicas also need a lot of nitrogen and may do badly if it is lacking, although too much makes them soft. If your cabbages (*Brassica oleracea* Capitata Group) smell rank on cooking, cut back on fertiliser and compost any manures for longer before applying them. Cauliflowers go over quickly – stop the curd from yellowing by bending or placing leaves over it to keep off the sun. Most brassicas may be made to stand longer, by bending them over in the ground away from the sun, or longer still by pulling and hanging them upside-down in a cool place. Brassicas are said to grow best with beetroot and chards, celery, dill, garlic, nasturtiums, onions, peas and potatoes, but do not get on well near runner beans or strawberries.

## brassica pests

These suffer a wide range of pests – birds especially. Wood pigeons decimate crops and must be kept out with netting. All the usual suspects may cause problems, particularly slugs – keep them from ruining cabbage heads by surrounding the stem with a foil cylinder that is coated in petroleum jelly and dusted with salt. Control flea beetles that eat away the seedling leaves with regular wettings (see page 107). Bluish-grey, mealy aphids crowd the undersides of leaves and cause distortion. They are often controlled by a parasitic chalcid wasp (*Aphidius*), whose grub leaves the brown, dead, aphid body through a wee hole. Soft soap cures aphids rapidly. Aphid numbers are also reduced if the brassicas are grown through an underplanting of French beans, clover, bird's foot trefoil or other legumes. Cabbage whitefly, actually a wee moth, can reach epidemic numbers, but is treatable with soft-soap sprays (after a good vacuum-clean).

Caterpillars: the green and black ones of the cabbage white butterfly, strip the leaves, and the dingier brown ones of the cabbage moth, ruin the hearts. Clusters of yellow eggs of the first can be found on the backs of leaves and picked or squished, but the moth's eggs are laid singly and hard to spot. Both the caterpillars may be hand picked. *Bacillus thuringiensis*, a naturally occurring disease, is currently unavailable to amateur gardeners in the UK, but may be licensed again in the future; it is still available in some countries. The old boys would sprinkle heavily infected soil onto the caterpillars to infect them naturally. Attacks of diamond-back moth caterpillars have become commoner; the green caterpillars eat away the undersides of the leaves to leave transparent skins. All the many caterpillars may be averted by excluding the adults from the crop with fine mesh netting.

Another common pest is the cabbage root fly. This attacks inside the roots of small plants, causing them to discolour and fail. The adult must lay its eggs against the base of the stem by the roots in the soil, so covering these with a mat of cardboard or felt for each plant works – if it fits closely about the stem and flat to the ground. Other deterrents are collars of soot or wood ashes or fine mesh netting over the entire crop. Less common is the turnip gall weevil, which also causes plants to stunt and flag, but the maggots cause galls on the roots that look like club root. Hygienic destruction of the plant should clear it up. The swede midge maggot is tiny, but may be the cause of any brassica going blind; always cut the tip open to check – the plant will be useless anyway.

## brassica diseases

The worst problem is club root: also known as clubfoot, clubbing or anbury, it is a slime fungus that ruins yields. Although it may occur in different strains and affect some plants more

Red cabbage grows well protected by the nasturtium from caterpillars, and pickles well with the seeds.

than others, it is always serious, particularly since it persists in the soil for decades. It exists in many old gardens and especially allotments and is worst in acid or poorly limed soils. The plants fail and have swollen roots, which if opened will be full of putrid matter (a root maggot causes similar damage). There is no cure, although starting plants off in pots of clean compost and planting them out in pits lined with lime-enriched, clean soil can produce a crop. Resistant cultivars of cabbage, cauliflower and kale (*Brassica oleracea* Acephala Group) are now available. Putting rhubarb in the planting holes apparently gives slight protection, and extracts of peppermint, summer savoury and thyme a bit more.

If the leaves are thin and narrow and the plant goes blind in acid soil, it is probably whiptail caused by a deficiency of the mineral molybdenum; the soil needs large doses of lime and seaweed solution or seaweed meal and calcified seaweed, applied regularly in future. Brassicas may get mosaic viruses and must be destroyed. Worse, rare and unlikely is a black rot, which is aggravated by hot, humid conditions: the leaves yellow, the veins blacken and the plant is killed or stunted. Dispose of any affected plants, roots and soil hygienically.

An ordinary leaf spot, a ring spot that can be especially bad on broccoli and has brown spots surrounded by green rings may attack. White blister, a fungus evident as gleaming white pustules that damage the leaves, is aggravated by overcrowding, damp and stagnant air; eradicate its host plants – cruciferous weeds such as shepherd's purse (*Capsella bursa-pastoris*). Otherwise, like grey mould and downy mildew, it rarely gets bad enough to need treating. Black leg or canker causes a brown rot at the stem base.
CABBAGE MOTH, CABBAGE ROOT FLY, CABBAGE WHITE BUTTERFLY, CABBAGE WHITEFLY, CLUB ROOT, NITROGEN DEFICIENCY, SLUGS, WHIPTAIL, WOOD PIGEONS

The flavour of carrots is stronger in sunny dry conditions and better with regular sprayings of seaweed solution.

*Celery and celeriac* (*Apium graveolens* var. *dulce* and *Apium graveolens* var. *rapaceum*)
Most choice sorts of celery need blanching – self-blanching types are inferior. If you want only celery flavour from the leaves, sow it *in situ* and thickly, like chervil or parsley. Celeriac is similar, but easier to grow, and gives a swollen root for soups and grating. If it fails to swell, remove the oldest leaves. Celery grows best of all with leeks, does well with beans and tomatoes and benefits brassicas by deterring cabbage white butterflies. Celery is not an easy crop, especially if you do not have a rich, moist soil. If it is ever checked or dries out, it will bolt.

This crop suffers much from slug damage, sometimes from aphids and even from carrot root fly. Celery fly lays eggs on the undersides of the leaves and the maggots feed inside blisters; other than good hygiene and squishing, there is little control. Watering with nettle tea may help and a high-nitrogen liquid feed may carry plants through an attack. Celery may suffer a root rot, causing worst-case plants to fall off at ground level; this is seed-borne, so sow new seed on fresh ground. Soft rot sometimes gets in through damaged tissue and the inside moulds away. Rust and leaf spot disease on celery are serious and once introduced (often on seed) are hard to eradicate, but attention to hygiene helps. The tiny spots become larger until the entire leaf is ruined. Bordeaux spray is permissible and these diseases may be discouraged with a tea made from stinging nettles and horsetail.
CELERY FLY, LEAF SPOT, RUST, SLUGS

## Cucurbits

These crops include cucumbers (*Cucumis sativus*), courgettes (*Cucurbita pepo*), marrows (*Cucurbita pepo*), melons (*Cucumis melo*), pumpkins and squashes (*Cucurbita* spp.). These are all thought to grow best with beans, nasturtiums, peas, tansy (*Tanacetum vulgare*) and sweetcorn but do not get on well near

## Carrots (*Daucus carota*)

Carrots are said to do best grown with chives, garlic, leeks, lettuce, onions, peas and tomatoes. There may be difficulties germinating the seed in cold years, cutworms and so on slaughter the seedlings, and several sorts of aphids may appear on the leaves. However the only major problem is the carrot root fly: its maggot makes brown tunnels around the carrots, destroying their appeal and even the whole crop in bad cases. A giveaway is foliage turning reddish-orange. Although there are some less vulnerable (I can hardly agree 'resistant') cultivars, it is possible to avoid any damage simply by covering the crop in fine-meshed fleece to exclude the flying adults. A low fence, to knee- or thigh-height, also excludes most adults because they fly close to the ground. Strong-smelling plants and herbs mask the scent of the carrots. When thinning or pulling carrots, take the foliage immediately to the compost heap and leave it on top so the flies will lay their eggs there! The carrot willow aphid transmits carrot motley dwarf virus, which turns the outer leaves red and gives yellow mottling on inner leaves; pull and eradicate any infected plants. Celery eelworm causes thickening of the leaf bases and weak growth; again destroy infected plants.
CARROT ROOT FLY

Pumpkins only need warmth and moisture to do well – and lots of space.

potatoes. They often do badly because they went out too soon, were too cold and then kept too dry! Cucumbers also make good partners for dill, in the garden and on the table.

Under cover and in hot summers, red spider mite can be a problem, especially if the plants were not sown *in situ* but planted out from an infected place such as an old greenhouse. Too high temperatures also cause only male (non-fruiting) flowers to be produced, especially if they are grown under cover. The plants get a mildew that requires hygienic disposal of infected plants but is nothing compared to the mottling and distortion caused by several viruses. These are often first noticed on the fruits, which become distorted, mottled and stunted. In every case, remove and burn or bury the infected plants. Cucurbits are prone to other diseases, but most modern cultivars are resistant. VIRUSES

Courgette flowers.

Artichokes conveniently can be squeezed in almost anywhere.

### Globe artichokes and cardoons (Cynara cardunculus Scolymus Group and C. cardunculus)

These two crops look much the same but artichokes are perennials, whereas cardoons must be grown annually from seed – the skill is to grow them in rich, moist soil without check or bolting to make a succulent heart for blanching. Globe artichokes may also be grown from seed instead of the usual offsets (thongs), but then give rather variable plants that need selection. Do not let artichokes flower, especially in their first year, because it weakens them: eat or just remove buds before they open. Slugs may damage seedlings and young shoots and geese grub out shoots and buds. Black and green aphids, and occasionally earwigs, get into artichoke heads, so soak them in salt water before cooking to get these pests out.
APHIDS, SLUGS

### Jerusalem artichokes (Helianthus tuberosus)

These are no close relation to globe artichokes, but the flavours are not dissimilar. Jerusalem artichokes suffer few problems save geese and rats, which grub up the tubers to eat them. Small tubers result from crowding – plant one rubber-booted foot apart in early spring. In windy areas, these tall plants need strong supports or to be tied onto tripods. The tubers store well only if left in the soil; cover the bed with a deep layer of soil or mulch in late autumn (plastic sheeting or insulating carpet materials encourage rodents). This stops frost freezing them hard in the ground, so you can dig them up when all else fails in a tough winter.

### Kohlrabi (Brassica oleracea Gongylodes Group)

A tough, disease-resistant crop much like a turnip, this will grow in relatively poor conditions and, unlike turnips, may be transplanted. Some sorts when fully grown will store for months. Kohlrabi can be grown with beets, onions, and ridge cucumbers, but not with brassicas, peppers, runner beans, strawberries or tomatoes.

### Leeks (Allium porrum)

These alliums are said to grow well with carrots, celery, and onions; I find leeks do best with celery. Leek moth drills the plants in the middle and ruins the crop; it is best kept off with fine-meshed netting. Leeks rarely suffer the same sort of problems as the other alliums, except rust that causes yellow or reddish spots and streaks. Resistant cultivars that crop well despite attacks are worth growing.
LEEK MOTH, RUST

### Lettuce and endives (Lactuca sativa and Cichorium endivia)

Overwintering lettuces need to be grown under cover, not so much for the warmth as for protection from the weather and hungry creatures, and need to be special cultivars. Lettuces will bolt if too crowded, too hot or too dry. They will be bitter if not grown quickly in moist soil and full sun. Endives are grown like lettuces, but must be tied up to blanch them, as must tall Cos lettuces, otherwise they are bitter. If it is hot, sow lettuce in shade; they will not germinate if the soil is too warm. Lettuces do best among carrots, chervil, cucumbers, radish and strawberries, but may not prosper near broccoli.

There are problems with birds – then slugs and most of the common suspects. Lettuce may suffer from leaf aphids early in the season and, worse, from root aphids later; growing chervil nearby may protect them. Root aphids overwinter as eggs on poplar trees, move on to the leaf stalks and cause galls, which split in midsummer when the aphids move on to lettuces. (Anthocorid bugs destroy these galls and reduce the pest numbers.) The old boys used a solution made from elderberry leaves boiled in soft soap to drench the roots and kill root aphids. In poor growing conditions, lettuces

ABOVE Kohlrabi never knows any problems.
MIDDLE Thick sown lettuce for cut and come again.
BELOW Onions are easier from sets than seed.

moulder and rot. In damp, downy mildew turns the leaves yellowish-brown and stunts the plants, while grey mould turns them grey and rotten. Ring spot kills in cold wet; brown spots on the leaves turn whitish and fall out, leaving white-margined holes. Improving ventilation, hygiene and adding wood ashes to the soil help. Symphalids may eat their roots at ground level (see page 105). The root knot eelworm can cause roots galls (see page 105); it is unlikely to occur, but can be serious and is difficult to treat.

BIRDS, DOWNY MILDEW, GREY MOULD, SLUGS, SYMPHALIDS (P.105) EELWORMS (P.105)

### Onions, shallots and garlic *(Allium cepa* and *Allium sativum)*

Do *not* press sets in place because this damages the basal plate; make a small pile of soil or sand over and around the set to hold it in place until it has rooted. Do *not* bend the necks down to 'help ripening'; it just lets in rots, particularly neck rot, which appears later especially when the crop is stored in stagnant conditions! Do not store onions unless you have dried them really well and not in plaited ropes, but as open and exposed to dry air as possible, as in wire-netting hammocks slung in roof spaces. Onions are said to grow best with beetroot and chards, lettuces, strawberries, summer savoury and tomatoes, but do not get on very well near beans or peas.

### Onion pests

Slugs can be a problem with seedlings, especially autumn-sown ones. I find mixing in seed of the cultivar 'Buffalo' expedient; slugs seem to prefer this one and, in eating it away, thin the plants for me, leaving the main cultivar relatively untouched. Birds and worms pull up the sets and scatter them so they need constant replanting. Hold the sets down temporarily with a handful of sharp sand, to be later brushed away.

Removing the dead leaf from each set helps.

The most serious pest is onion fly. This attacks seedlings, but sets are often too big and escape damage. The eggs are laid on the neck of the plant and the maggots eat the roots, causing flagging and yellowing; dig out and burn affected plants, together with the soil surrounding their roots. Just pulling the plant leaves the rotting roots and maggots in the soil. Growing onions under a fine-meshed net excludes the adult flies and strong-smelling herbs nearby confuse them. All alliums may suffer from an eelworm that makes the leaves swell and distort and the bulbs crack and rot; once infected, hygienic disposal is needed.

### Onion diseases

Onion smut starts with greyish-black spots and streaks on seedling leaves, which then twist and distort, and black spores ooze from under the bulb scales. Burn infected onions and the soil around them, and use only clean seed. Bright orange spots are signs of onion rust, which kills seedlings. It is commoner on other alliums and all need erad-icating to clear the disease. If leaves wilt, yellow and die back without obvious damage and come away when pulled, but there are no maggots eating the roots, look for white mould – the dreaded white rot. Once this is in the soil (do not use cheap or shop-bought shallots and garlic as sets), it is impossible to be rid of and the ground will need resting from all alliums for a decade. Burn infected plants along with the soil around them. In wet years, onion and shallot leaves yellow and die or simply look awful with a light greyish felt. This is downy mildew: little may be done once it's seen, although Bordeaux mixture helps and a dusting with wood ashes dries up mild attacks. Do not plant soft bulbs.

BIRDS, DOWNY MILDEW, NECK ROT, ONION FLY, ONION RUST, ONION SMUT, WHITE ROT, WORMS

Parsnips taste best once frosted a few times.

***Pak choi, leaf mustards and Chinese greens*** *(Brassica rapa* var. *chinensis* and *Brassica rapa* varieties)*
These can be tough, hot and unpleasant if grown hot and dry. They need to be raised fast in rich, moist soil, otherwise are poor, and all tend to bolt if sown before midsummer. Most make good autumn and winter crops if protected under cloches. Under cover, crops may be scorched and then rot; they suffer several soil-borne rots and are best watered at the base so the leaves are never wetted. Slugs and snails, flea beetles and caterpillars that attack brassicas (see page 158) may all cause problems. Healthy plants may be cut to leave the root and base to produce fresh heads.

***Parsnips*** *(Pastinaca sativa)*
If you get mostly roots that are too small, try increasing the spacing. In heavy or stony soils, make guide holes by plunging in a crowbar, fill them with sowing compost, sow three seeds in each hole, and later thin to the best seedling per site. Parsnips sometimes get attacked by carrot root fly (see page 160) and get occasional damage from all the usual suspects. The worst problem, now seen mostly with older cultivars, is canker, which causes the skins to ulcerate with a rusty brown rot that cracks the tissues and, in bad cases, makes them go rotten and black. Most modern cultivars are resistant and do not suffer badly. CANKER

***Peas*** *(Pisum sativum)*
Peas love cool, moist, rich soil and are said to grow best with beans, carrots, cucurbits, potatoes, sweetcorn and turnips, but do not get on very well near onions and garlic. These legumes have problems germinating in a cold, wet spring; use temporary cloches, sow in ridges and sow smaller batches in succession

These have been picked too late, been kept too long and look tough.

each week so that some will hit the best windows in the weather. Sow suitable cultivars; not all are recommended for spring sowing! Do not sow too deep and, if your soil is prone to capping, top off with a layer of good, sterile compost. Do not pre-soak early sowings because they will rot.

## pea pests

Slugs are often a problem. Mice steal the seed. Aphids seldom attack except young, sick and weak crops and those under cover; then the usual remedies apply. Pea moth is responsible for those annoying grubs in the peas. Early crops avoid it, as do the very latest. Fine mesh can keep it off and spraying with seaweed throughout flowering disguises the plants. Birds are a big problem since they love the seed and seedlings. If you don't use all the usual bird guards (see page 112), you may never see a crop. Seedlings appearing with their leaf edges nibbled in tiny, semi-circular notches indicate pea and bean weevils, which are best controlled by regular hoeing or dusting with lime about the bases of the stems, or even a brisk brushing of the surrounding soil on dry days. Hoeing and dusting, particularly with lime, also help to control thrips, which initially silver the peas' growths. Sometimes tiny, white pea midges infest the shoot tips and flowers, but rarely do as much damage as the black thrips. Thrips do other damage to peas; often they start at ground level on the stems, stunting seedlings, destroying growing points, distorting growth and turning pods brown. Very similar symptoms may occasionally be caused by a parasitic root knot eelworm (see page 105).

## pea diseases

In late summer, the later cultivars all suffer from pea mildew and little can be done because it comes so suddenly on the whole row. Mulching and watering before an attack may stave it off; some cultivars are resistant; sulphur dust may help. Pea wilt is rare, often seen at flowering time when the leaves go grey, then yellow and wilt, but is serious; burn the plants with the roots and grow no peas in the site for five years! Small crops are best improved with a good watering when the flowers appear. Soils that have never grown peas or beans may not contain beneficial bacteria and fungi that enable the plants' roots to take up food and water efficiently, so it may be necessary to import some soil from a friend's plot who does grow them. (Do make sure that there is no other problem such as club root present in their soil!)

BIRDS (SEE P.112), MICE, PEA MILDEW, PEA MOTH, PEA WILT, SLUGS, THRIPS

### Potatoes *(Solanum tuberosum)*

Potatoes seem to get on well with beans, especially broad beans, brassicas, peas and sweetcorn, nasturtiums, summer savory, celery and flax or linseed (*Linum usitatissimum*), and surprisingly well with asparagus. They are grown with horseradish (*Armoracia rusticana*) in China, but do not get on very well near sunflowers, cucurbits, raspberries and tomatoes.

Main-crop potatoes give a greater yield than 'earlies', but take longer to do so. For earlier crops, use 'earlies' and plant them early as well. For earlier still potatoes, start, or chit, the sets into early growth, under cover in a light, frost-free place. Stand the sets, rose end up, in egg trays or a tray. (The rose end is the one with more buds, often in a spiral, not the root end where a wee bit of root may still hang on.) Do not chit main-crop sets if you want big crops later in the season.

### potato planting

If your crops are poor, check that you are planting sets rose end up; if not, it will halve yields. For sets already sprouted, gently bed them in with soil all round the sprouts to lead them to the surface. If you plant sets from the warm into very cold soil, they go into shock and produce a few, wee tubers, then die. Warm up the soil before planting. If you want big tubers, use big sets, rub off all bar three 'eyes' or shoots and plant the sets far apart. If you want many small tubers, leave on all the eyes and plant closer. Be careful with home-saved sets. If you save the smaller spuds as sets and if any one plant produces mostly small tubers, with no effort, you will breed a mini-yielding cultivar in only a couple of years. Save seed potatoes only from healthy plants that crop well. If the yields are very light, good watering, especially at flowering time, achieves more of an increase than simply applying fertiliser. Digging in wood ashes, manure or compost, or

My seed potatoes drying off and greeening up so they will keep well.

green manuring beforehand, also repays with healthier, tastier, bigger crops. Remove the flowers and seed heads to divert the resources into tuber production.

Green potatoes result when light touches them. As the tubers expand, they often get forced out of the ground into the light, green up and become slightly poisonous. (They can be used as sets for next year.) Mulching before then with any loose mulch – grass clippings in thin layers are good – or earthing up with soil stops greening. Dig up tubers that you want to store on a dry day; leave them to dry in the sun and air for a few hours before packing in paper sacks and storing in a cool, dark place.

## potato pests

Yields are often appalling in dry years, and bigger but still appalling because of the slug holes, in wet years. Slugs, slugs and then more slugs are a major problem (see pages 94–7). Much often secondary damage comes from other soil pests such as millipedes, wireworms, and woodlice, with the usual remedies. Bait with slug pubs and sacrificial chips of old spuds, carrots or other roots as soon as you see flowers on the potato plants, to thin out many pests just as the new tubers are about to form.

Colorado beetle continually threatens, although it is not yet a problem in the UK. Both the yellow ladybird-like beetle with black stripes and reddish-orange grubs with six small legs destroy potato foliage. The beetles reproduce in a month and reach plague proportions quickly; they demand immediate action, notify authorities and individually eliminate by hand. Some eelworms (see page 105) seriously damage potatoes, causing poor crops. Symptoms are unhealthy growth, stunting, poor crops and tiny, bead-like nodules on the roots. These are hard to clear, although many partly resistant cultivars are available, such as 'Santé'.

## potato diseases

Common scab causes scabby patches, but are not serious. It is aggravated by dry soils that are short of organic matter: incorporate leaves and grass clippings when planting the sets and water and mulch in dry conditions. Lime is normally not needed in great amounts by potatoes; they get scabbier if lime, soot or ashes are applied at or just before planting. If the scab is rough and warty, it may be wart disease, which is serious and notifiable but very rare – most modern cultivars are immune but it may occur on old allotments with heritage cultivars. Leaf roll, crinkle and mosaic-viruses affect the leaves with symptoms typified by their names and are spread by aphids. Use only clean, certified sets for planting and rogue out any odd-looking plants immediately. Black leg comes in on the seed so occurs rarely. Here and there a failed plant will be found to have rotted from ground level up. The crop from this plant and those on either side should be eaten and not saved for sets.

Blight starts similarly on one or two plants, but here the symptoms appear first on leaf or stem surfaces; darker blotches appear and turn black or brown with a whitish mould. The foliage soon wilts and dies and the stain of the unpleasant-smelling rot runs down the stem. If the haulm is pulled or cut before the rot reaches the tubers, they can be saved – don't dig them up until a fortnight after the haulm was removed. (Blighted tubers have rusty red stains under the skin and will rot; until then, they are actually edible but unpalatable.) Bordeaux mixture is effective against blight. There are several semi-resistant and resistant cultivars. Blight tends to be most of a problem in warm, humid weather and attacks before early summer are unusual. Volunteer potatoes from undug crops, discards and wildlings can start a new epidemic, so must be eradicated by midsummer's day.

BLACK LEG, BLIGHT, COMMON SCAB, MILLIPEDES, POTATO CYST EELWORM (P.105), SLUGS (P96–7), VIRUSES, WART DISEASE, WIREWORMS, WOODLICE

Not all spinaches are true spinach but are best treated as spinach.

### Rhubarb *(Rheum x hybridum)*

This is rarely troubled, but aphids may sometimes occur on it. Remove the flower spikes to avoid wasting energy, give it a good mucking to keep up yields and replace it every decade or so. Crown rot although rare is serious: all the plant goes soft and rotten and is best destroyed; plant a new, virus-free clone on a fresh site. If your crop is not early enough, force it by covering it with a bottomless drum (a bucket is too small), filling the drum with very loose straw and blocking out the light with a lid. I use a stack of car tyres with their sides cut out.
APHIDS, CROWN ROT

### Spinach *(Spinacia oleracea)*

This bolts, okay. If it doesn't for you, carry on with whatever you are doing. For the rest of us it's a case of sowing in smaller batches more often, in moister, richer soil. It is a crop worth growing through synthetic fabric mulch to keep soil off the leaves as well as aid growth and isolate pests. Round-seeded spinaches do best in summer, but for winter and early spring sow prickly-seeded spinaches. New Zealand spinach *(Tetragonia tetragonioides)* is an alternative that is used and grown in the same way; it needs more space, but is far better in hot, dry conditions and more reluctant to bolt.

Protect the plants from birds with black cotton, use slug traps and never allow them or the plants to dry out. Spinach may occasionally get attacked by the mangold fly, which also attacks beetroot (see page 157). If the leaves have yellow spots and a violet or grey mould, it's downy mildew. This is worst in wet conditions and may be stopped with sulphur dust, but it is better to choose mildew-resistant cultivars. Although cloches can stop the weather shredding and muddying up the leaves, they encourage mildew and other moulds.
DOWNY MILDEW, MANGOLD FLY (P.157)

If you mix varieties, this is the sort of thing that may happen, but it's not really a problem.

Turnips are best grown quickly and eaten small.

### Swedes and turnips (Brassica napus Napobrassica Group and Brassica rapa Rapifera Group)

Turnips grow well among peas and winter tares (*Vicia sativa*), but are bad for peppers. Both may bolt if stressed by drought or overcrowding; swedes are even less tolerant of drier, sunnier weather than turnips. Being related to brassicas, these crops suffer from most of the same pests and diseases, but not as badly in rich, moist soil. Flea beetles will probably need to be controlled in any other than a rich, moist soil. Sometimes the turnip gall weevil makes lumpy swellings that conceal whitish, legless grubs; they are best controlled by good hygiene, successional sowing, regular hoeing and alternate misting and dusting. These crops might get club root (see page 159). Turnips may suffer a similar soft rot to celery if small pest damage allows the disease to rot the heart out. I find poor growth can be corrected by additional watering (the plants detest drought and get a mildew, see pages 116–17) or adding a little powdered bone meal to the soil.
CLUB ROOT (P.159), MILDEW (P.116–17)

### Sweetcorn (Zea mays)

This is a crop that responds well to extra water and feed, especially fish-based ones. It is said to grow best with beans, which can climb up it, and cucurbits rambling underneath, or with peas and potatoes. Sweetcorn is not a very tender plant, but is easily wind-chilled and needs warm, aerated soil; in cold, wet soil early in the year, it may turn pale and die away. The plant also resents being moved, so should be sown *in situ* or individually in small pots. Early, pot-grown plants should be kept drier and not too warm and be planted out before they get root-bound; this does not give as good a plant or as large a crop, but makes the crop earlier and more reliable despite the check of being moved. Lessen wind damage and aid stronger growth by earthing up the bases of the plants, when reaching knee- and again waist-height.

Better pollination and less misses can be had by pulling silky female tassles on young cobs alternately with male tassles on top. Sometimes, especially when grown under cover, the males flower before the females and miss so save some of the pollen in a paper bag until they arrive. Planting many cultivars near each other may result in cross-pollination; this rarely damages the eating quality, but may spoil the appearance or shelf life. Poor crops result from overcrowding (no closer than a foot) and very poor or worse, dry, soil. Smut is seen only in warm, wet years; large boils erupt anywhere on the plant, especially from the cobs, which ooze fungal growth. The disease can cause stunting; burn infected plants promptly.

# crops under cover

Notice plenty of ventilation being given, even in cool weather.

## conservatory plants

The majority of popular house- and conservatory plants are justly favoured because they are relatively trouble-free. These plants rarely have specific problems and if suffering they are almost certainly under attack from all the usual offenders – aphids, red spider mite, scale insects, mealy bugs, et al. Most of these problems are brought in since the natural ecology does not intrude much in the almost sealed system indoors. Scrutiny of every new plant and a quarantine period are good ideas. A gift of second-hand pots may seem safe, but may be full of starving hordes just waiting for a bit of greenery to infest. Even be careful of yourself and your clothing – do not wear the same outfit when visiting the pest-infested greenhouse of a friend as for tending your own plants. Seriously, mealy bugs, scale and red spider mites and others will hitch rides. Fortunately, there are effective, commercially available controls for all the common pests indoors although they are not cheap.

## soil-grown crops under cover

Unlike house- and conservatory plants, crop plants under cover suffer a large number of problems that are aggravated by the fact that so many of the plants are closely related (aubergines, peppers, potatoes and tomatoes, are all Solanaceae). Also, it is difficult to rotate plants in a small area when there are so few other crops with which to alternate them. Of course, some rotation may be worked out, extra lime and compost added in their turn, and green manures dug in. Consider replacing all the soil under cover every ten years or so if yields drop; replace it with turf rotted *in situ*, good topsoil or even garden or potting compost. Mind you, I am now in the twentieth year of cropping the same soil – with few problems! Sterilisation of the soil, fabric and accessories is simply not an effective alternative, although probably some help, but it is better to introduce controls.

## biological controls

If appropriate predators and parasites are introduced early enough (not so early that they starve to death first), almost all the usual offenders will pose no serious threat. The biological controls have proved their effectiveness on a large scale on commercial crops and, although expensive, are worthwhile to the amateur grower plagued by the same pests year after year. If you always suffer, say, red spider mite on your melons, order the predator beforehand; the suppliers should advise you and deliver the controls in several batches on appropriate days for your circumstances. Read the instructions. There are some for free: I collect ladybirds and release them on my aphid infestations. Spiders are good friends too and should be encouraged with plastic caps of water, nest sites of hollow tubes, and strings to help them build their webs in useful places. Newts, frogs and beetles may all be made welcome with a cool, damp corner and some ground cover plants in a larger greenhouse or tunnel (this will also encourage slugs, so take precautions). I even constructed mine abutting a pool, with the end replaced at the bottom with a rotten log wall that allows little critters to move in and out easily.

## rotating the cover

If you have the space, consider moving your polytunnel to a new site each time you re-cover it, to make a clean break with most problems. Better still, put up a new one and use the old site and frame as a fruit cage by simply covering it with net. The soil conditions suit soft fruit

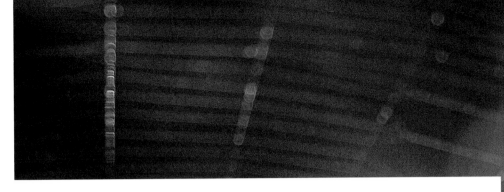

exceedingly well after a few years under cover, then in another five or ten years or so you could swap back. Two small tunnels and the intervening space between combine well with hens; they may run in the fruit cage after harvest right until the next fruits set. I have often run chicks underneath the greenhouse staging: it's a safe, warm, dry place and they sure keep pests down; their warmth and breath also keep the plants comfy at night. Mind you, to be fair, it did pong a bit and the dust was horrific! It is not impossible to move a greenhouse; in fact it's surprisingly quick and easy in most cases. Remember that the glass must be rigorously cleaned at least annually and twice yearly if plants are in it in winter.

### Aubergines (*Solanum melongena*)

Also known as eggplants, these need warmer conditions than peppers or tomatoes. Their main problems are aphids (see page 99–101) and red spider mites (see page 108), which they get really badly. Mealy bugs do relatively less damage. Plants need staking and supporting since their crops are heavy. Be careful handling the fruits – they have small spines on their stalks.

APHIDS (PP.99–101), RED SPIDER MITE (P.108)

### Bananas (*Musa acuminata* 'Dwarf Cavendish')

First of all, don't hope to eat fruits from seed-raised banana plants; they might flower and set fruits, but you won't want to eat them! If you want ornamental bananas, grow any sort (some are almost hardy) but if you want fruits to eat, the only one worth growing is this tender cultivar. It has distinctive but faint purplish markings on the young leaves. It reaches only ceiling height or so and may be squeezed into large greenhouses and conservatories.

Obviously space, light and warmth are crucial, but to get a good crop you must thin the number of shoots coming from the ground – too many sap the plant. You should leave three at the most: one just cropping to be cut down afterwards; one nearly full-grown to replace it; and a small one to come up next. Keep the flowers dry (they do not want pollination), otherwise they moulder and rot the fruits. After the fruits at the top start to swell, trim off the female flowers on a dry day and remove the male flower bud from the end of the fruit truss. This is considered a delicacy in many cuisines.

Spray the leaves daily top and bottom with tap water, but water the roots with rainwater. I have managed to crop one, with much feeding and watering, in a plastic garbage bin, which it burst. Larger containers or planting in the greenhouse border give better results.

With amateur cultivation in temperate climates, the main problems are frost or cold spells, which cause leaves to yellow, die and brown; cold may injure the flower bud within a shoot even if the leaves survive and cause loss, rot or distortion as it emerges later. Red spider mite may be a problem in very dry conditions, but bananas love being misted, so do this to control the mites and aid leaf emergence. Mealy bug can be a problem: jet them off and use soft soap or the commercially available predators.

### Cape gooseberries (*Physalis peruviana*)

Notably problem-free, these crops have only one difficulty: they take longer to crop than the season in temperate climates like that of the UK allows. So seed-raised plants crop poorly and too late. If you overwinter plants or cuttings anywhere frost-free, and start them off earlier in the year as greenhouse perennials, they crop magnificently and earlier in the summer. Puckering and distortion of the leaves with dew-like drops (guttation) may occur in very close, humid conditions; increase the ventilation and reduce watering to help the plant get rid of its excess water.

### Citrus (*Citrus*)

These fruits, including lemons and oranges, are very vulnerable to neglect. They must have rainwater because tap water can soon cause chlorosis (leaf yellowing and browning). The compost must be almost an ericaceous mix, with little lime, and really well drained; citrus will not tolerate waterlogging. Their roots hate being deeply buried or in plastic pots – they prefer terracotta or wooden containers. If you must use plastic tubs, drill dozens of air holes in the sides. Never let *Citrus* dry out, but be even more careful not to let them drown: they will not take standing in a saucer of water! In winter, definitely err on the side

Citrus – disease prone but excellent value and crop easily.

Little oranges greater oranges grow from.

Modern varieties are easier than you imagine.

of caution and keep them only just short of drought. Feel the fruits (which ripen in winter): if they are soft, the plant needs much more water, if hard, then not much. In summer the plants enjoy being misted and, in winter under cover, still like it occasionally on sunny days.

Citrus need heavy feeding during the growing season, with a high-nitrogen soil dressing and a liquid feed. The plants tend to over-crop so fruits need to be thinned when they first set, otherwise they will all be small. Although they must be kept frost-free, they prefer being outdoors and, after hardening off, should be out all through summer and early autumn. Commonly attacked by just about everything, especially aphids, scale insects, red spider mites (their own special variety), these are tough plants and endure and crop surprisingly well for years in small containers.
APHIDS, SCALE INSECTS, RED SPIDER MITE

### Cucumbers (Cucumis sativus)
Indoor cucumbers are bitter if allowed to be pollinated! Growing all-female cultivars now circumvents this classic error. If you grow older sorts, remove every male flower before it opens (male flower buds have no fruits behind them). Bright sun can scorch the plants, so give them shade when needed.

Indoor cucumbers are always under attack from red spider mite, so take precautions. They also suffer from root knot eelworm, which builds up in compost and equipment under cover and causes little galls on the roots. Remove all traces by replacing the compost and washing pots, trays and equipment.

In cold, wet compost, the plants easily canker or rot off at the neck, or collar, where stem meets root – especially so if the collar is wetted, injured or deeply buried. Modern cultivars rarely suffer from most diseases, although there are several that bother older cultivars. In cold soil, they may get verticillium wilt and, in warm soil, fusarium wilt; both result in wilting, yellowing and desiccation and verticillium often shows a stain in the cut

stem. The symptoms are similar to those of red spider mite and may be misdiagnosed either way. Leaf spot, with pale red or green spots, can be fatal, although improved humidity, temperature control and hygiene (remove infected material) can halt attacks. If the leaves mottle, pucker, wrinkle, distort or have yellow mottling, suspect a virus – the commonest is cucumber mosaic virus – and destroy the plants before the disease spreads. If powdery mildew covers younger growths with a powdery infection, it is best destroyed with the entire plant – although sulphur dust may give some protection; most modern cultivars are resistant.
CUCUMBER MOSAIC VIRUS, POWDERY MILDEW, RED SPIDER MITE

It's easy to grow green peppers as good as supermarket ones.

### Guavas *(Psidium guajava)*

This fruit should be grown in more conservatories for its perfume as much as for its eating. This shrubby tree is very thirsty and prone to mealy bug, but otherwise easy. The evergreen form, cherry or strawberry guava (*Psidium littorale* var. *longipes*), is even more decorative; it has a less well scented but more palatable fruit and is not plagued so much by mealy bug.

MEALY BUG

### Melons *(Cucumis melo)*

Germination of melon seed is thought to be aided by morning glory (*Ipomoea*) and to do well with peanuts (*Arachis hypogaea*), sweetcorn and sunflowers, but not potatoes. Melons have exactly the same problems and solutions as cucumbers (see page 173), although they do need pollinating to set the fruits. Reluctance to produce female flowers or set fruits may be due to rampant growth, so try stopping leading shoots (nip off the top bit). One fruit ripening ahead of others may cause them to stop or abort. Do not let the fruits hang unsupported because they drop off when ripe: put up netting bags to catch them. The support also helps the fruits to grow bigger. Melon plants are very prone to aphids, thrips and woodlice and much more plagued by red spider mite than cucumbers. Leafhoppers may bleach leaves (so does scorch), so look for little yellow pests underneath the leaves and soft soap them. Melons may get cucumber mosaic virus and powdery mildew, but not as seriously as on cucumbers.

LEAFHOPPERS, RED SPIDER MITE

### Passion fruits *(Passiflora)*

These do better if kept warm rather than just frost-free, since they are prone to root rots when cold and damp. Although plagued by mealy bug, they are not often bothered by much else – the usual suspects may hole the leaves. They are remarkably easy to grow, but sometimes not self-fertile so need cross-pollinating with another plant to set good crops.

MEALY BUG

### Peppers, sweet and chilli *(Capsicum annuum* and *Capsicum annuum* var. *annuum* Grossum Group)*

Sweet and chilli peppers both get attacked by aphids and whiteflies, but seldom badly; soft-soap sprays will control them. Slugs can ruin crops by making one small entrance hole in each fruit and messing up the inside. The roots do not like high temperatures and need shielding from direct sun, with a foil cover to the sides of the pot. Pepper roots are not strong and prone to rots, especially if waterlogged or badly drained, and do not like being transplanted. Sweet peppers carry very heavy crops so need staking and support – otherwise limbs break off. Other pests such as red spider mite do attack, but not often very badly. It's said that peppers grow best with basil, but do not get on very well near kohlrabi or radishes.

Surprisingly easy to flower and not difficult to fruit.

### Pineapples *(Ananas comosus)*

This is an easy plant to grow if kept frost-free. Provide some bottom heat (with soil-warming cables) and a large container, and superb fruits may be grown. They are prone to root rots and need to be kept dry from autumn until late winter and misted throughout the growing season. Bad soil aeration stunts them since they need gritty, well drained compost. Pale foliage may be corrected with soot water – half-fill a sock of soot and soak in a watering can overnight. Withhold watering as the fruit ripens. Watch out for mealy bug; paint it with soft soap solution.
MEALY BUG

### Tomatoes *(Lycopersicon esculentum)*

If your crop is not coming soon enough, you may be starting it too late, growing an unsuitably slow cultivar, keeping it too cold, too wet or too dry. But I'll bet it's because you are feeding them too much. Heavy feeding increases yields but delays the harvest significantly. Too hot and dry conditions also stop early tomatoes setting. Pollinating the first flowers by hand will help, especially to get the earliest crops. To get those first fruits to ripen, keep a ripe banana, or discarded skins, by the tomatoes (remove the banana before fruit flies multiply!). As soon as any tomatoes ripen, remove them, because they suppress further fruits. To get the most fruits, remove them as they colour and finish them on a windowsill.

If your crop is too light, you may be keeping them too dry, not removing the sideshoots or, just possibly, not feeding enough. I give tomato plants in pots a feed in their water of borage, comfrey and seaweed. Too little nitrogen and you get very pale leaves, too much and you get rank soft growth. Too little potash and they crop and taste poor, but too much and they get chlorotic. Tomatoes are best in a compost-enriched, moist soil and

The earliest tomatoes benefit from hand pollination.

sprayed often with seaweed solution to prevent a multitude of possible nutritional problems. Very rare nowadays, but once commoner, is hormone weedkiller contamination, which causes distortion and stunting of the plant and hollow, elongated, woody fruits.

Tomatoes are said to grow best with asparagus, carrots, brassicas, garlic, onions and parsley; they like basil and French marigolds underneath to keep off pests, but do not get on very well when near kohlrabi or potatoes.

## Tomato pests

Birds damage more fruit than they eat and some intrepid birds raid greenhouses, so you may need to net doors and vents to keep these thieves out. Slugs and snails can do a surprising amount of damage to seedlings, young plants and ripening fruits. The tomato-moth caterpillar sometimes eats the leaves at night; if disturbed it drops, onto waiting sheets if you're clever. Whitefly (see page 108), thrips (see page 107) and mealy bug (see

Don't let them rest on the ground – they can rot.

page 102) can be big problems under cover and move outdoors aboard hardened-off plants.

Potato eelworm may attack tomatoes and root knot eelworm can cause galls on the roots (see page 105). Springtails are tiny to small, brownish or whitish insects that jump or spring away when disturbed. They are most common in sour and damp conditions, especially in the greenhouse in poorly drained compost, where they attack the roots and cause plants to wilt. They may be trapped on sticky fly paper laid about the plants or are easily eliminated with soft soap. Symphalids (see page 105) are also commonest under glass and cause similar problems at the stem base. New and better compost is the answer.

## tomato diseases

It is diseases that really trouble tomatoes. The same blight that bothers potatoes gets tomatoes and makes brown, sunken spots on the fruits, as well as decimating the foliage. Blight may occur under cover but is kept at bay from midsummer on by maintaining dry air conditions with minimal influx of fresh air when the weather is damp and sultry. Outdoor crops may at least be given a plastic flysheet to keep the rain off. (It helps them establish in a cold spring as well.) Resistant cultivars are now available such as 'Ferline', 'Histon Cropper' and 'Legend'. Blight is often confused with leaf mould, which occurs more often under glass; the leaves get violet-grey patches underneath, turn yellow and purplish- or reddish-brown as they go brittle, and die. Careful hygiene and ventilation will control it.

Young seedlings and even big plants suffer from all sorts of root, foot and fruit rots, but a classic to avoid is blossom end rot, where the flower end of each fruit has a brown, inedible, scabby patch. This is invariably caused by water stress, and especially common in plants grown in bags of compost or tubs – I've rarely seen it on plants in the ground, indoors or out.

So don't grow tomatoes in limited quantities of compost, but in huge amounts, and keep them well watered. Hard, unripe, green patches, particularly around the necks of tomatoes, are common in greenhouse plants and result from heat stress; some cultivars are more prone, others almost immune. Tobacco mosaic virus causes serious losses – often an infection is carried in on the hands or tobacco of a smoker; commercial growers stopped almost all attacks when they banned smokers from the greenhouses. Watch out for viruses – showing as dark green mottling on leaves, brown streaking on stems and brittleness – and burn any affected plants.

Young seedlings may suffer wilt and bigger plants may get fusarium or verticillium wilts, but good hygiene and healthy conditions eliminate them. At the end of the season, grey mould (see page 118) becomes a serious issue; it is controlled only by hotter, drier conditions and artificial light to keep the plants growing strongly. Didymella stem rot occasionally affects large plants, which suddenly wilt because

of an ulcerating rot at the stem base: burn all affected plants and their supports. Bacterial canker may affect leaves: they brown on one side of the leaf stalks, which are streaked yellow-brown inside, and the fruits are spotted and streaked from the stalk ends. Burn all infected plants and supports and use clean seed. BLIGHT, BLOSSOM END ROT, EELWORM (P.105), GREY MOULD, LEAF MOULD, MEALY BUG (P.102), THRIPS (P.107), TOMATO MOTH, VIRUSES, WHITEFLY (P.108)

*Watermelons (Citrullus lanatus)*
These melons resemble cucumbers (see page 173) in many ways, but need even higher soil temperatures to survive; the old boys kept them at a minimum of 21°C (70°F). Gently lift the fruits when tiny and, without moving them, slip a piece of wooden board underneath; this stops them rotting where they touch the soil. Watermelons are subject to the same problems as cucumbers, but the only one that will bother most crops (other than cold soil and not enough sun) is red spider mite. RED SPIDER MITE

# fruit-cage crops

## the fruit cage

These are mostly short-lived crops that barely outlive their cage. Strawberries need replacing every three or four years, raspberries and blackcurrants every decade, gooseberries after a decade and a half; blackberry hybrids and red and white currants are poor after twenty years. There is little point saving old subjects since new ones will usually be more vigorous, heavier-cropping, better cultivars and often resistant to common diseases and pests. Indeed, almost all the problems described here are actually quite rare on most modern cultivars. It is often not even worth bothering too much if a plant does die since it will be cheap and quick to replace it.

**Blueberries are nutritious, productive, easy and, without a net, a way to feed your local birds.**

### Bilberries, blueberries, cranberries and cowberries *(Vaccinium myrtillus, Vaccinium corymbosum, Vaccinium macrocarpon and Vaccinium vitis-idaea)*
Other than drought, lime in their water and birds, these suffer few problems. They crop much more heavily if several cultivars are near each other for pollination.
BIRDS, DROUGHT

### Blackberries and other brambles *(Rubus fruticosus)*
Bramble hybrid, raspberry-like berries include the loganberry (*Rubus* x *loganobaccus*), boysenberry (*Rubus* 'Boysenberry, Thornless' and tayberry (Rubus Tayberry Group). They are remarkably vigorous and remain productive for longer than some other soft fruits – true blackberries more than their hybrids. Blackberries also sometimes crop on side-shoots on old wood, which hybrids rarely do. Thornless cultivars rarely perform as well as thorny forms. Corky and dried up parts to the fruits and little, white maggots are signs of the raspberry beetle (see page 183), which commonly does more harm to the fruits of loganberries and similar hybrids than to raspberries. Capsid bugs and aphids may also do damage, (see page 103). The caterpillar of the bramble shoot moth is first whitish then brownish-red with a black head and sometimes webs the leaves together; cut out and burn the leaves as soon as seen in early summer. Very un-even ripening of the fruits with odd shapes and reddish appearance could be symptoms of a redberry mite attack. Prune hard immediately after harvest and cut out not just the old, but the spindly and poor, stems; burn them along with their unripe fruits, then mulch thickly.

Blackberries sometimes get bedeguar galls, like a golf-ball-sized pincushion on their stems, caused by small grubs inside but do little other harm. Very rarely, the leaves distort with a mosaic mottling and the stems proliferate, but remain stunted. These are signs of a viral disease (reversion) or dwarfing and hygienic eradication is needed to prevent its spread.
APHIDS, REDBERRY MITE

### Blackcurrants and jostaberries *(Ribes nigrum and Ribes x culverwellii)*
A jostaberry is a hybrid between the blackcurrant and gooseberry that suffers few, if any, of the blackcurrant's woes. Although it is a bit more vigorous and needs more space, it makes a good substitute. Stinging nettles growing nearby may benefit blackcurrants. Light blackcurrant crops result from dry conditions and low fertility, especially with old, large and unpruned bushes. Running off, when the topmost fruits fall off early, may just be down to viral or frost damage, or even poor pollination; prune and burn affected shoots. Heavy crops come from moist soil that is well mulched and enriched with nitrogenous manures – and from heavy pruning!

Blackcurrants are so healthy and so easy every garden should have them.

Special pruning of blackcurrants will give fantastic results and remove most problems. You want strong replacement shoots from ground level so all old, infected and infested growth is cut away. Prune before picking – that's right, before. Cut off old shoots at ground level (pick the berries at leisure) and leave a 'stool' of only five or so, best young shoots (legs) to grow on into next year.

## blackcurrant pests
Birds bother these plants less than other soft fruits, but netting is still needed. Bullfinches love to steal the buds. Aphids wither and wrinkle the tips, but this is rarely serious; the bushes need hard pruning anyway. Occasionally, a whitish, brown-headed caterpillar of the currant clearwing moth, or European currant borer, may hollow out the ends of the stems. They bend the stems in winter; infested, hollowed ones break off; cut them out low down and burn them. If the tips and leaves wither later in spring, it may be grubs of the currant shoot borer beetle: they are red, turning greenish, and also move into the fruits and ruin them. Prune out any dying stems in early spring and burn them. The cocoons are normally hidden in cracks in the bark in winter and the larvae may be lured into corrugated cardboard bands and destroyed later. Leaf midges cause leaves to distort in the same ways as after aphid attacks, but inside are whitish-orange grubs. Prune out and burn them and use plastic sheeting and mulches underneath to trap the pupae where the birds can get them. Sudden death or a slow, lingering one that is not otherwise explainable may just be caused by root aphids. Gooseberry saw-fly and gooseberry mildews (see pages 180-81) sometimes attack blackcurrants. All the currants can suffer from a capsid bug similar to the one attacking apples (see page 190). Blackcurrants may be attacked on

occasion by mussel scale (they were not pruned hard enough!), red spider mite in hot, dry conditions, and very rarely by weevils or looper caterpillars.

## blackcurrant diseases
The worst problem is when the leaves become darker green and stinging nettle shaped, with fewer veins, and yields drop – symptoms of currant reversion virus. This inevitably occurs on older bushes so these are rarely worth keeping beyond a decade or so. Total replacement by clean stock after burning all the old is required. A minute mite that is too small to see spreads the virus; it drifts in on the wind and causes buds to swell and

become disproportionately large but never open (big bud). Pick off the buds in mid- or late winter to slow the spread of both the mite and disease.

Often old, overgrown bushes are infested with coral spot, which needs pruning out and burning. Currants can suffer a leaf spot: sticky, brown patches that are shiny when wet cause leaf fall in midsummer and shrivelled fruits. Good, hygienic renewal pruning and heavy, rich mulches after leaf fall give relief. Bordeaux spray could be used. Black-currants may suffer from cluster cups, which are little, spotty forms of rust on leaves, but they are rare and cleared by hygienic pruning.
CORAL SPOT, CURRANT REVERSION VIRUS

Gooseberries will hang later and ripen further than the green hardballs sold in the shops.

### Gooseberries and Worcesterberries

(*Ribes uva-crispa* and *R. uva-crispa* 'Worcesterberry')

Gooseberries rarely last longer than fifteen or twenty years and are hard to rework from the roots because they are often grafted onto another rootstock. Occasionally a gooseberry bears yellow flowers; this is the Buffalo currant (*Ribes odoratum*) rootstock and needs removing. Gooseberries can be trained to most forms, but are best as cordons or goblet-shaped bushes on a short stem, or leg. Growing them as a stool, with many shoots from ground level, makes picking and pest control difficult. Prune in winter to short spurs on the main branches. Tomatoes and broad beans growing nearby are reputed to aid gooseberries. I underplant them with poached-egg plant (*Limnanthes douglasii*), which dies away and can be cleared just as the fruits benefit from bare soil underneath for ripening.

### gooseberry pests

Birds do least damage, but wasps make up for it, sucking the fruits dry to leave a bare skin. Bullfinches love to steal the buds. One significant problem is gooseberry sawfly. These first appear in late spring or early summer; if you watch daily, one leaf will suddenly have a dozen or two holes, each one the size of a match and being eaten by a wee, greenish caterpillar. Having eaten the first leaf, they disperse and each rapidly munches down a bit of the bush, until it is totally defoliated. Oddly, this is often worst in the third and fourth years after planting. Some years, there may be many broods, hatching one after another through summer. I have stopped many an attack on the first day with a finger and thumb. These pests hurl themselves off if shaken or disturbed, so quietly sliding a sheet of cardboard under the bush, then rattling it, will catch many. Banding the stem with sticky grease stops any escapees returning. Otherwise, they may be jetted off

with a hose and then handicapped by dusting them and the ground they have fallen on under the bushes with sieved wood ashes. This also benefits the plants, which are notoriously needy for potash and often show a deficiency with yellowish-brown leaf margins. Overwintering pupae may be trapped in mulch, laid in mid-summer over a plastic sheet and disturbed in winter to expose the pupae to birds. Some claim that growing broad beans with goose-berries keeps away sawfly.

Aphids may be troublesome, but effectively do the summer pruning for us. They often indicate ant activity, as do scale insects, which sometimes are found on older bushes. If the weather is warm and dry in late spring or early summer, and the leaves turn pale yellow, look scorched and drop off, check for red spider mites. Hose them off on sunny days. On drab, cold days, they hide on the lower leaves, so removing those leaves may help. Otherwise, gooseberries rarely suffer much, although they have almost all the same problems as black-currants (see page 178). Big bud does not harm them as much, the buds just turn brown and die, but the bush does not get reversion.

Capsid bugs may do more damage on gooseberries than on smaller currants; they cause corkiness and splitting of fruit skins. Sickly or weak plants, not explainable by, say, bad drainage, may well be suffering from root aphids. Examine a portion of the root system: if it has any white, woolly covering, dig up the plant in winter. If it is young, prune the roots, wash the remainder clean and replant elsewhere; if it is old, burn it. Old-time gardeners made a solution from elderberry leaves (*Sambucus nigra*) boiled in soft soap as a root drench to kill the aphids.

## gooseberry diseases

The other big problem with gooseberries is the mildew. American gooseberry mildew infects the stem tips and undersides of the leaves with a white felting, especially when the roots are dry; the mildew may spread onto the berries, leaving them at best suitable only for jamming (the mould may be scummed off). At worst, the berries split and rot and shoot tips wither. This is less of a problem if the plants have good airflow around them, are well pruned, well mulched and watered and early attacks are hygienically removed. (Some gardeners used sodium bicarbonate and sulphur-based sprays or dusts – which burn some cultivars – and they worked well, but sodium bicarbonate fungicide is not allowed under current UK legislation.) European mildew is similar but not as white and usually appears only on the top surfaces of the leaves. It responds to the same treatment as American mildew. Immune and resistant cultivars are available. Leaf spot can cause damage and requires the same treatments as for that attacking blackcurrants (see page 179).

Do not grow sedges near gooseberries – they are hosts to the annoying cluster cup fungus, which causes red and orangey blisters on the leaves and fruits. Treat it as for leaf spot.

GOOSEBERRY SAWFLY, MILDEW, WASPS

## Grapevines (*Vitis*)

The pruning of grapevines is an art in itself. Vines respond to vicious pruning in winter, ruthless de-shooting in spring, hard pruning and fruit thinning (bunch removal) in summer – by fruiting well. The key is limiting the number of buds left on last year's wood, and the number of new shoots, after the winter prune. These are then thinned to those bearing flowers and later stopped to direct energy into the fruits. In autumn, all shoots are then hacked back nearly to their bases, leaving a couple of buds on each stub. Most grapes are self-fertile, but the divine, all-female 'Muscat Hamburgh' needs a partner – 'Chasselas' works for me.

Choosing the cultivar is important: almost every one of forty or more that I have grown proved too disease-prone to recommend. 'Boskoop Glory', a black dessert grape, has proved one of the best in reasonable conditions for outdoors cropping; I recommend it if you have room for only one vine. Others that crop cleanly are rather often hybrids with some American (*Vitis labrusca*) blood, such as the strawberry grape (*Vitis* 'Fragola'), but their flavour is unfortunately usually inferior. Most involve a trade-off; superb flavour and texture is nearly always accompanied by difficulties. For example 'Siegerrebe' is fantastic, with rose-red, perfumed berries, but is miffy, prone to wasps, mildew and rot, sulks on lime, and is a poor cropper for many years – but it's gorgeous when you get some fruits.

## grapevine pests

Birds, birds, birds; then wasps and flies; then mildew and mould. Other than that, they are easy! Well, no. Vine weevil (see page 103)

Langley Gage, an old supersweet white variety.

Watch out for fly damage.

can weaken and kill vines. Luckily, in the UK grapes may be grown on their own roots from rooted cuttings because there are no phylloxera aphids to eat them. Most bought vines in the UK and all plants on the European continent are grown on resistant rootstocks. American (*Vitis labrusca*) hybrid cultivars seem naturally resistant and are huge croppers, but often of poor quality. Under cover, mealy bug, tortrix moths, scale insects and thrips require the usual remedies. I find hanging sprouting potatoes in the vines at bud break attracts many mealy bugs, which may then be removed and destroyed.

## grapevine diseases

Mildew is made worse by sudden changes in atmosphere and dryness at the roots, or humidity. It is fairly easily thwarted with sulphur, if this is dusted on as soon as the fruits or leaves get the first, whitish patches. Otherwise they go dusty, harden and split. The

Well worth growing in a tub.

Watch out for the birds.

various fruit rots and moulds are really only stopped by a dry spell in autumn, although they can be even worse in dry years, when more fruits are damaged by wasps and flies looking for moisture. Good hygiene, good pruning and air circulation, and not over-cropping all keep the amount of rot down. If there has been no obvious mildew to leave a powdery coating, but the fruits split, it is almost certainly caused by wet weather following dry or inconstant watering. Rotting bunches are probably the biggest loss after bird damage.

Black rot can cause blotches on the leaves that look a bit like scorch, but little black specks give it away as a fungus and the leaf withers. Hygienic tidying and disposal of the first attacks may stop it rotting the fruits and making them shrivel and dry up. Shanking makes the stem of the bunch of fruits die after turning brown and shrivelling. The fruits stop developing normally and, even if nearly ripe, they tend to be bitter. Both these rare complaints may be controlled with open pruning, good airflow and no sudden changes of temperature.
BIRDS, FLIES, MEALY BUG, MILDEW, MOULD, PHYLLOXERA APHID, SCALE INSECT, THRIPS, TORTRIX MOTH, VINE WEEVIL (P103), WASPS

## Kiwi *(Actinidia deliciosa)*

This climber is far too vigorous for most positions. It needs to be espaliered and spur-trained to bring it under control. Early flowers are often frosted, but the main reason for lack of crops is that both male and female plants are needed. Few self-fertile cultivars are currently grown, although only one male to every seven females is required. The male flowers are like soft, dusky roses and very, very beautiful *en masse*.

## Raspberries *(Rubus ideaus)*

Chlorotic leaves with interveinal patterning probably result from too much lime in too dry a soil. Thick mulches, especially of well rotted manures and leaf mould, counteract this and immediate relief may be had with seaweed-solution sprays that have added Epsom salts. Do not be confused by so-called summer and autumn cultivars. They are treated similarly in every way save for the time of pruning: summer-fruiting types are best pruned immediately after harvest to leave only the best young canes. Autumn-croppers have everything pruned to the ground in winter. Raspberries reputedly benefit from companion plantings of garlic, marigolds *(Tagetes)* and tansy *(Tanacetum vulgare)* grown nearby. Strawberries are mentioned in old literature as being planted under raspberries, but these would have been the true native, wild strawberry *(Fragaria vesca)* and not our modern cultivars.

## raspberry pests

Birds once again score highly on the annoyance list; netting is the best recourse. Wasps also suck the fruits dry. Aphids spread the dreaded mosaic virus (see below), but give few other problems and are hard to stop anyway. Brownish-yellow raspberry beetle is more of a problem; it is not a weevil as it is often miscalled. The fruits end up with scabby

Raspberry/blackberry hybrids are better value than either of their parents.

in the soil and emerge in early summer and are best drenched with soft-soap solution when they are tiny. Another grub, the raspberry cane borer, tunnels down the centre of shoots to the bases, causing them to wilt; cut out infested stems at the base and burn them.

### raspberry diseases

Yellow mottling, together with reduced vigour and low yields, is almost certainly caused by mosaic virus, for which there is no cure: eradication and burning are best. Raspberry stunt virus does just that, without any mottling; again, total eradication is required. Raspberry cane spot, or anthracnose, causes purple patches with whitish centres on stems, leaves and stalks that sink into cankers or go grey with black spots. The leaves may drop and the fruits become distorted and malformed and ripen unevenly; performance may be poor. This is best controlled by pruning into a good, open shape, heavy mulching after leaf fall, and training new canes away from the old so that spores do not fall on them.

Very similar is cane blight, with wilting and withering leaves, but the canes become brittle and break off easily just above ground level. This disease is soil-borne so is hard to eradicate; start afresh with new stock on new ground. The same goes for blue stripe wilt (a verticillium wilt, where bluish patches appear on stems, becoming stripy with interveinal yellowing like that of mineral deficiency, and the leaves wither and drop). Without the blue patches, and if the symptoms disappear with seaweed sprays, it could just be mineral deficiency. Blue stripe wilt also disappears with good manuring and feeding, so do not re-use the bed or propagate from the stools.

If dark purplish patches appear and the leaves are also blotched with brown splodges, it may be spur blight. The canes survive but the buds do not, so cropping is reduced.

parts and little white grubs. These may be scummed off, if the crop is used for jam, with little impact on the flavour or the grubs may be collected first by immersing the fruit under salty water and rinsing them. Raspberry beetle may also be controlled with thick mulches that are raked about in winter to allow birds to eat the pupae. Shaking the canes over sheets during flowering will catch the small adults. If there are a lot of tiny holes in the leaves and more on the stems and shoots, causing them to wilt or break, it could be red-legged or clay-coloured weevils. These lurk in loose litter and come out at night – when they may be caught. They will fall onto waiting sheets of sticky cardboard (sugar syrup will do), if a bright light or a shake disturbs them.

Withered and wilted shoots in spring may have been tunnelled by the reddish raspberry-moth grub; prune them out beneath the grubs and burn them. Place corrugated cardboard rolls in plastic sleeves at the stem bases from summer; many of the grubs will try to over-winter in them as brown chrysalises. Very rarely, some of the tortrix-moth and looper caterpillars that attack apples may appear on raspberries. Redberry mites cause poorly ripened berries (see page 191). Little pink grubs on the canes are raspberry cane midges, which often let in disease. They overwinter

Remarkably problem-free and a gourmet alternative to lemon juice.

Spur blight is worst in overcrowded beds in wet areas and responds well to good, open cultivation and heavy pruning to improve air circulation. The same overcrowded conditions, especially in shade, can cause mildew, which is obvious because of its powdery, whitish patches. Sulphur dust is effective, but really better conditions should be provided.

BIRDS, MOSAIC VIRUS, RASPBERRY BEETLE, WASPS

### Red- and whitecurrants *(Ribes rubrum)*

These currants are pruned more like trained apples, retaining a main framework (any form you want; I prefer espaliers) and cutting back all sideshoots in summer and winter, to form fruiting spurs. (Strangely, if kept dry and protected, the fruits will hang on until early winter in near-perfect condition.) Although the blackcurrants are useless after a decade, the red ones go on for ever; even if the top growth becomes worn out, a new plant can usually be worked up from the roots – although sometimes they are killed off by root aphids (see Gooseberries, page 181).

Redcurrants suffer far more from birds than most soft fruits and must be netted; white currants get away with it for longer. Fortunately, wasps rarely bother them, except in dry years. The plants will certainly get leaf-blistering aphids living underneath their leaves, which often pucker and contort with red and yellow mottling. This looks ghastly but rarely affects the cropping, especially if you summer prune. Remove three quarters of almost every new shoot – leaves, aphids and all – in the following weeks anyway, leaving the leading shoots alone so they can extend the framework. Otherwise, although they may have almost all the same problems as black-currants, these currants do not suffer much damage. If they get big bud, the buds just die and turn brown, but they do not get reversion.

BIRDS, LEAF-BLISTERING APHIDS

This may be your total crop if you don't follow my advice!

*Strawberries* (Fragaria x ananassa)
Strawberries suffer from a host of problems, but all are fairly unimportant compared to the big three: birds, closely followed by slugs and rots and moulds. Temporary covers, say of plastic sheeting or cloches, on plants in the ground keep off most problems. Outdoor crops also need netting, against birds. Netting is needed only for the brief period of cropping so may be temporary rather than a cage; this enables strawberry plots to be rotated to new quarters, evading many diseases and soil problems. On a small scale, jam jars or similar containers may be used to cover the flower trusses once they have set fruits. If you set them on their sides with the butts raised a bit, they stay dry, keep off birds, most other pests, most moulds and the weather – and act as tiny greenhouses to ripen your fruits earlier.

Scalded and small and shrivelled fruits and ones with soft, pink patches all indicate conditions that are too hot, dry and bright. Strawberries prefer it cooler, so provide shade netting in heatwaves. If your crops come too late in the year, get earlier crops outdoors by growing them on ridges covered in black plastic sheeting, and earlier still under clear plastic, but they will need careful ventilation.

Poor crops come for many reasons, mostly through age. Strawberries crop only for three years – hardly ever is it worth keeping older plants. Crowding also reduces the total crop, as does letting plants crop in the first year or letting them waste energy on runners. Start a new bed after two years so it starts cropping in the fourth. Better still, every year start a third of a new bed in midsummer, with healthy runners, and eliminate the oldest third of the old bed after it's finished cropping. Ideally, plant them a good stride apart before late summer and de-flower first-year plants and de-runner the others ruthlessly the following summer to get immense crops of immense fruits the next.

Straw is not essential but keeps the fruit clean.

They will be followed by two, at most three, years of slightly poorer and poorer crops.

Rogue out any odd-looking plants, pulling them up and disposing of them, with their roots and soil around them, before they infest the rest. The extra space will benefit the surrounding plants. Because a bed is short-lived, it is not worth putting in replacements and many pests and diseases are irrelevant to the amateur. However, if you do find any of the pests and diseases listed below, the answer is to dig up and burn all affected plants immediately, unless otherwise stated. New cultivars are worth trying and all stock should be replaced every five years anyway. A clean sweep and a fresh start is the best cure for all of them.

## strawberries under cover

Plants under cover permanently do not get the chilling they require, so perform badly and suffer red spider mite attacks, as they may do outdoors in hot, dry years. Runners may be potted in early summer, grown on and, in the next year, moved and cropped under cover – which gets round almost all the problems, but is a lot of work. A few plants in hanging baskets under cover can yield very clean crops months earlier than outdoors, even without heat. Keep them high up in the brightest light.

## strawberry pests

Some annoying pests are easily dealt with: put out saucers of fermenting fruit juice to trap slugs and some of the many sorts of strawberry beetles and weevils. The small, black strawberry blossom weevil damages the stem of the fruit, causing it to abort, and may attack other soft fruits, leaving telltale puncture marks cutting through the stalks. The strawberry rhynchites cuts through the leaf and fruit stalks, causing them to wilt and die. These can be thinned only by an autumn clean: remove all old leaves and runners and old straw mulches and regularly rake the soil to expose the grubs to the birds. Annoyingly, sometimes voles collect up fruits in little piles!

Leaves reddening and drying up, especially in dry weather, are signs of red spider mite; it can be reduced by misting the plants. Leaves that crinkle, pucker or yellow at the edges and die away could result from tarsonemid mite damage. The old boys cleaned their most valuable plants of the mite when moving them, by soaking them in water at 43.5°C (110°F) for twenty minutes and immediately cooling and planting them in a clean bed or pots.

Plants suddenly wilting and dying may be victims of vine weevil, another wingless weevil, leatherjackets, wireworms or chafer grubs eating the roots. Slow deterioration may be due to an eelworm infestation. Several (crown, leaf, bud, root and stem) eelworms attack strawberry crowns, causing stunting, thickening of leaf and flower stalks and corrugations in the leaves. Hot-water treatment (see above) may treat infested plants.

## strawberry diseases

Rotting fruits are attacks by all sorts of moulds: remove and burn or bury them to avoid infections. Strawing down reduces initial infections from soil splash and keeps the fruits clean. It may however increase the chance of frost damage, so beware. Mats or newspaper will also do, but not grass clippings or hay because they taint the fruits. If straw is used between the rows, burning it *in situ* in late autumn can clean the bed of a multitude of pests and diseases without harming the crowns much. A host of different viruses (crinkle, yellow edge, mosaic), mildews, leaf spots and leaf blotches are possible. One disease to watch for is red core – plants weaken and become unproductive and their leaves smaller with reddish tints. A sure sign is that the roots are withered and blackened, except for a red core. Dig and burn all plants and do not replant on the same site.
BIRDS, EELWORM, RED CORE, RED SPIDER MITE, ROTS AND MOULDS, SLUGS, STRAWBERRY BEETLES, TARSONEMID MITE, VIRUSES, VOLES

# fruit trees

Hand pollinating a peach tree is always worthwhile, undercover or outdoors, as pollinators are rare early in the season when they flower.

## trained and orchard trees

Unlike the short-lived, soft fruits or fruit-cage crops, these are more expensive plants, take more space, are slower to yield and can be productive for much longer, although peaches are often poor things after twenty years. So it is worth caring for them and attending to minor infestations before they spread and become worse. I may point out that getting rid of dead currant bushes is a lot less effort than digging up a dead plum or apple tree! Whereas soft fruits are remarkably obliging, tree fruits demand a bit more attention before they will crop well and cleanly. In particular, do plant them well, in a good, well dug hole, with well firmed-in roots, and make sure that they are well staked, well weeded and well watered. Do I make the point? A tree is there for decades, so do the job of planting really well.

## fruit production

Pollination is also trickier with tree fruits. A lack of fruit every year, or few fruits, when there are flowers and not a lot of hard, late frosts, indicates a need for a pollinator. No flowers create another problem, but if there are flowers get a branch or two from another tree, or two, that flower at the same time and hang these on your tree. If one bit gets fruits and no other, get a tree of the cultivar that you hung there. Often a wild relative, such as a crab apple or 'Morello' cherry, will do as a partner. Potted trees under cover will probably need hand pollination, as will the earliest flowering subjects outdoors, such as apricots. Biennial bearing is very common in tree fruits that exhaust themselves one year and are forced to take one or several years off to recover; then they eventually over-crop again. The answer is to thin the crops heavily every year. Pruning and training is crucial for all but standard and bush trees. Any cordon, espalier or fan must be regularly pruned. It is often best to do both a winter and a summer prune, and often several summer prunes. Keen fruit growers who do this, along with ruthless thinning of the crops, can achieve nearly 100 per cent clean crops of magnificent size and perfection – but not on any scale, because the labour is a bit intensive. However, it is worth it for favourites.

## potted orchards

These are an excellent idea because the pots control the vigour of the plants and so more cultivars may be housed in the same space. Potted orchards may be moved in and out of cover, so avoiding many pests and diseases and handicapping others. The cost is in more labour, especially with watering, and shorter-lived plants by comparison with those in the ground – but it is well worth it for the gardener who wants to grow the more difficult cultivars. For example, a small, frost-free greenhouse could house one vine and one peach planted in the ground with difficulty. However, you could easily get two peaches, two apricots and two vines in tubs in the same space. Moreover they need the cover only from late winter until late summer, then they go out, so the space is free from autumn until late winter for overwintering citrus and other tender fruit trees in more tubs. It gets overcrowded at changeover time in spring, when the new come in and the overwinterers can't yet go out, but that is only a temporary problem. The grapes, being so hard-pruned, need much less space until they have regrown.

Handle them gently if you want them to keep.

## Apples *(Malus domestica)*

No crop suffers as many different problems as apples, yet many, many gardens have an old tree that has cropped since time immemorial with no care or attention. Some problems do bother most apples, but the majority of them are rarely seen or do little real harm. Most apples crop in surplus anyway and, if the table and store are filled, it doesn't matter if the leftovers are rotters or perfect – after all, the birds don't mind. With hundreds of cultivars to choose from, it makes sense to grow sorts that are relatively free of pests and diseases. I suggest that you choose more late-season storing apples than earlies and mid-season croppers, unless you want to process them.

Unless you live in a remote place, pollination is rarely a difficulty although apples are tricky – there are so many trees about that they are usually served. Apples flower late in spring when pollinating insects are plentiful, but trees that flower at extreme ends of the season may not have a partner near enough for the pollinators to reach. If your tree flowers well but never fruits, plant nearby a crab apple, or a multi-grafted 'family' tree, on a dwarfing stock, to act simply as a pollinating partner. Several, if not all, cultivars are prone to biennial bearing so require thinning; all apples respond well to heavy thinning of the fruitlets anyway, not just in years when they set far too many.

Those few cultivars known as tip bearers (mostly early sorts such as 'Beauty of Bath') may be pruned into unfruitfulness very easily. They do not form flowering spurs like most apples but bear the fruits near the tips of the stems, so leave on last year's growth to flower. Thus tip bearers can easily be grown only as unpruned trees and are not suitable for cordons or other trained forms.

June drop is not a disease or a pest attack, but looks disastrous. The tree suddenly drops a large number of surplus fruitlets, leaving fewer

to swell and ripen. This normally occurs around midsummer and the number of fruits dropped depends on the number of fruits set and the tree's reaction to seasonal conditions. Most drop in dry seasons after mild springs or following years that carried exceptionally heavy crops.

Bitter pit is not very common, but sometimes found on old trees on worked-out soils, especially acid soils. Basically, a shortage of water causes lots of small, brown spots to appear in the fruits' flesh, mostly just under the skin. Mulch to bolster the moisture and micro-life of the soil. Applying lime, especially calcified seaweed, and spraying with seaweed solution also helps on acid soils. Water core or glassiness is another physiological disorder, where the core of the fruit seems to be water-logged. It is worst in young, over-fertilised trees in high temperatures and with extremes of water stress. Picking and cooling the fruits in a dry place can restore some fruits to normalcy. I find 'Charles Ross' particularly prone.

Apples are said to benefit from penstemons to keep sawflies away, chives and garlic to discourage fungal diseases and alfalfa or lucerne (*Medicago sativa*) to bring up nutrients from deep down in the soil.

### apple pests

Birds and wasps (see pages 112 and 110) are the major problems in many gardens. Wasps also rely on birds to start holes for them and our friends the blue tits and blackbirds are common culprits, pecking holes in ripening fruits to test them. Do not be over-tidy; leave some windfalls and cut them in half to fob off these pests.

Very corky or distorted fruits may have suffered from capsid bugs – they do a lot of early damage to fruits that is often attributed to other causes when it becomes apparent later. The pests make small punctures in the leaves and shoots (brown or black marks), then in

the fruits. Their punctures cause corky patches that expand with the fruit, making them unsightly and prone to other problems. Capsid bugs hatch in spring from eggs buried under the bark, moult five times and get bigger, eventually grow wings and depart. Until then, if they are shaken or jetted off, they have to climb back up the trunk so can be stopped by sticky bands. Apply a vegetable-oil emulsion with a brush in winter to choke their eggs.

Aphids of several strains are often evident, but seldom do much harm, although heavy infestations cause leaf curling and distortion and honeydew moulds. Hose them down or spray with soft soap – but not on a bright day, please. Apple suckers, a type of psyllid, look much the same; occasionally, they may cause severe damage to opening flower buds that is easily confused with frost damage. Check for frost damage on other flowers and foliage; if there isn't any, suspect suckers and treat as for aphids. Woolly aphid is remarkably common in old, overgrown orchards and rare in open, well pruned ones. The insect nestles in 'cotton wool' in cracks in the bark, especially where it has been broken or cut or where canker has ulcerated it. A stiff brush and soapy water clears it from old wood; use a soft sponge more gently on less robust growths. A North American wasp, *Aphelinus mali,* is used to control this pest, but I'm not aware of it being currently available in the UK. Growing trailing nasturtiums in profusion under the trees is reputed to drive woolly aphids away. Neat pruning and using a wound sealant reduces potential places for them to lurk and breed.

Holes and 'maggots' in the apples are probably those of the codling moth or apple sawfly. The moth has a pinkish caterpillar with a brown head and the sawfly a dirty-whitish caterpillar with a brown head. They both make big, rotten holes in the middle of the fruit and a tunnel to the side or near the flower end. A sawfly caterpillar is worse as it may leave one fruit and start on another or even several apples. It attacks when the fruit first swells until early summer, about the time of the June drop; through summer and early autumn, it's the codling-moth caterpillar's turn. So thin fruits in three or more stages, removing and destroying all infested fruits. Any fruits that redden or ripen very early and most that drop are likely to be infested, so collect and destroy those, as well as any with obvious holes. Pheromone traps may reduce the numbers of codling moths or indicate their presence. Codling-moth caterpillars over-winter under loose bark and may be trapped in corrugated cardboard bands, or sacking wraps, put on in early summer and burnt in winter. Sawfly pupate in the soil under the tree; put a layer of mulch on top of a plastic sheet to catch them, remove it in winter and thoroughly compost it or spread it thinly so birds can eat the cocoons.

In hot, dry conditions, red spider mites occasionally cause trouble, browning leaves and bringing on autumn colour early in summer. They are hard to spot in summer, but their winter egg clusters are bright red and found in cracks in the bark and may be scrubbed out. During the growing season, hose down the tree regularly in dry weather to discourage and blow off as many mites as possible. Tiny, black bryobia mites may also do similar damage.

Several weevils attack parts of apple trees, but rarely badly. The apple blossom weevil causes some flower buds to go brown and to stay shut; lift off the 'cap' to reveal the grub within and discount frost damage. The twig cutter weevil does just that to the ends of twigs, which fall off, and an even rarer weevil causes tiny holes to appear in the fruits as if someone has pressed a ballpoint pen into them. Apple bud weevil often attacks pears more severely, but causes dead buds and shoot-tip damage. All these weevils are hard to control other than by hand, with corrugated cardboard traps or with natural predators such as birds and wasps.

Several different caterpillars are likely to eat the foliage, often with little permanent damage – excepting ones that attack *en masse*. Lackey-moth caterpillars (bluish-grey with red and whitish or yellowish stripes) are easy to deal with: they spin themselves silk tents in a crotch at midsummer; remove at night and burn them. The eggs are laid in an obvious ring around a stem and may be pruned out in winter. Vapourer-moth caterpillars (hairy yellow tufts on their backs) also leave bundles of yellowish or reddish-brown eggs attached to a silk cocoon; prune them out in winter. Set out corrugated cardboard and sacking bands in early summer and check monthly to control the caterpillars. (If hand picking the caterpillars, wear gloves, goggles and mask because the hairs can irritate.) Caterpillars of tortrix and several other moths also eat foliage and buds and damage the surfaces of fruits. They wriggle backwards if touched and mostly hide in silk nests formed between leaf surfaces. These may be squished; browntail and ermine-moth nests are much like those of the lackey moth and may be disposed of similarly. A browntail caterpillar is blackish with brown tufts and two red spots near the tail; ermine caterpillars may be bluish, greyish or whitish with rows of black spots.

Three more moth maggots – the winter, March and mottled umber – are all looper caterpillars and move by bending their middle segments and moving the front and rear parts independently. They damage foliage and fruit from early in the season and then fall to the ground to pupate. Trap them in deep mulches laid over plastic sheets for winter eviction or apply sticky, non-setting bands around the trunk (and any stake!) in midwinter; keep

Do not let any of these remain on the tree through winter. As small as they are, they seriously infect the new crop.

These needed ruthless thinning, they'll distort and crush each other and none will make any size.

bands topped up until summer to stop females (which can't fly) crawling onto the trees.

Mussel, San José and oyster scale insects are all occasionally found on old trees and in overgrown orchards and particularly on wall specimens. Individually, these pose no problem, but en masse they weaken the trees; scrub them off in winter with a strong soft-soap solution.

Rare but not often worrying are apple fruit miners, which make multiple, wee tunnels under the skins, causing sunken patches; control them as you would codling-moth caterpillars. Be on your guard if rowan or mountain ash trees (*Sorbus aucuparia*) are in the vicinity – they are hosts to this pest. As rare is pear slugworm (see page 196).

### apple diseases

Mildew commonly attacks young leaves and shoots, leaving them narrowed, distorted, curled or even withered, and covered with a powdery growth. Similar looking to aphid attacks but usually earlier in the season, mildew may be disregarded – unless it is rampant. If flower buds are damaged, they yield poorer fruits, if any. Dead but infected shoots appear grey in winter; prune out and burn them, as well as any affected shoots seen in spring. Sulphur dusts work but damage some cultivars. The old boys used a spray of soft soap and washing soda to good effect. Cultivars, such as 'Cox's Orange Pippin' and 'Bramley's Seedling', are notorious.

Cankers are serious diseases, often much worse in dank, stagnant, overgrown conditions than in drier, open, sunny orchards. The spores enter through wounds, even leaf scars. They cause sunken spots that rot and ulcerate the bark, exposing wood and making it swell around the lesion until it rings the twig, limb or even trunk and the tree dies. It often attacks only for a season, then gives up at that site so often the limb does not die but is weakened

and prone to breakage and further woes. Cankers are best pruned out if possible – if not, cut out and sterilise the wound, then painting it with wound sealant may allow the wound to heal and will exclude other problems. It is important to burn the prunings and any small, mummified fruits. Bordeaux sprays give relief and seaweed sprays help the tree to recover. Strangely, some cultivars get attacked often whereas others are rarely bothered; even a different rootstock can make a tree more or less susceptible. 'Cox's Orange Pippin' and 'James Grieve' are particularly troubled. Heavy, badly drained soils and over-fertilisation aggravate attacks; failing to control scab or woolly aphids allows damage that enables canker to spread further.

Often greenish, scabby patches that turn dark on the fruits usually result from scab. The infected spots sink and become corky and black, sometimes perfectly round in shape. They may proliferate on stored apples. This fungus attacks every bit of the tree; it is common and varies in severity according to conditions and cultivar. 'Cox's Orange Pippin' of course suffers badly, whereas 'Charles Ross' and 'Beauty of Bath' are rarely touched. Scab often lets in canker. If scab attacks early on, it distorts the fruits and cracks even appear; if late, they develop normally with only skin damage. Remove all mummified fruits in winter and prune out all shoots with obvious scabby spots and lesions; the cleaner the trees are, the cleaner they stay. Both Bordeaux mixture and sulphur may be used, but with care since some cultivars are sensitive.

Very similar to scab, but not so serious, is sooty blotch. Dark patches that make the fruits look as if they are touched with soot are often worst in damp years and develop further in overly humid storage conditions. Treat as for scab (see above). Do pick fruits on a dry day and dry them well before storing to prevent

It seems a waste, but better these go so the remainder swell bigger.

any attack from worsening with keeping.

Brown rot is another disease of the fruits that, like scab, may also attack the leaves. It is not the brown rot of decay, but rough, raised rings on the skin of a yellowish hue that slowly mummify the fruit. Any wounds, or rough treatment causing bruising, may get a simple rot that's brown and brown rot; the latter may either dry out the fruit or, especially in store, turn it black with a white fluff that allegedly infects surrounding fruits. Brown rot is controlled by limiting wounds by careful handling and good pest control as well as picking fruits for storage with their pedicels (little stalks) intact. Hygienic collection and disposal of mummified and blackened fruits is essential.

Blossom wilt is a disease where the blossoms die, then the stem behind them; even the branch dies back. Pruning out and hygienic disposal of affected stems are essential as soon as it is spotted. Cultivars such as 'Bramley's Seedling' and canker-resistant cultivars also resist brown rot and blossom wilt. Rare but worrying is rubbery wood, an aptly named virus seen in old specimens of a few cultivars, particularly 'Lord Lambourne'. The wood is soft and in bad cases stems become weeping; yields drop. Mosaic virus causes pale patterns in the leaves and reduces the tree's vigour and crop. Another virus causes Chats, where the fruits stay smaller than crab apples, ripen and fall early; they are of little use. Star crack is often confused with capsid-bug damage, but is a virus infection with no control; the tiny, star-shaped, corky patches become indented as the fruit expands. If any of these viruses are confirmed, the trees must be destroyed to prevent the viruses from infecting others.

APPLE SAWFLY, APPLE SUCKERS, BIENNIAL BEARING, BIRDS (P.112), BITTER PIT, BLOSSOM WILT, BROWN ROT, CANKER, CAPSID BUGS, VARIOUS CATERPILLARS, SCAB, SCALE INSECTS, SOOTY BLOTCH, VARIOUS VIRUSES, WASPS (P.110), WATER CORE, WOOLLY APHID

... except possibly an English grown peach.
RIGHT Dabbing olive oil in the eye of the fig
helps speed final ripening.

Nothing better than an English grown apricot...

## Apricots, nectarines and peaches
*(Prunus armeniaca, Prunus persica* var. *nectarina* and *Prunus persica)*

All three suffer more from frost losses of bloom than everything else and the fruitlets are sensitive for weeks after setting. Since the trees flower so early, there may also be few pollinators about, so lightly brushing the flowers helps immensely. Wasps and rots spoil peach crops, whereas weather affects nectarines, which need better summers to perform, and apricots escape peach leaf curl; otherwise, these trees are similar in many ways, as are their ornamental forms. Although these stone fruits love lime, too much leads to a shortage of available iron and can cause pale green, yellow-tinged leaves. Regular sprays and drenches with seaweed solution help, as will thick mulches of rich, well rotted manure.

Apricots tend to get dieback, which needs pruning out. Pruning trained peaches and nectarines is tedious, so they are easiest grown as bushes, are productive for two decades,

then expire when they get leggy and dead in the middles. If they are trained on walls, they can live longer. Apricots are different and fruit on spurs more like apples, so although they may crop as bushes they're most reliable if fan-trained on warm walls.

All three of these stone fruits do very well grown in big tubs, housed outdoors until mid- or late winter, brought under cover for flowering and fruiting, then going out again for autumn and into winter. This gets round most of their problems and much of the pruning. Permanent housing under cover is not recommended because they do not get a winter chill and fail to thrive – to say little of the pests that proliferate! Plums that are small and hard make good jam, but small, hard peaches or apricots do not. If you want succulent, luscious globes of dessert fruits or ones that are good for jam, thin early, thin often and never leave two fruitlets closer than a hand's width apart. Be especially vigilant at splitting doubles because they rarely swell cleanly if left.

## peach pests
Several aphids cause similar symptoms to peach leaf curl (see below), but all are easily spotted and soft-soap sprays will see them off; the flexible shoots may be dipped instead. Sometimes other orchard pests occur, such as winter and tortrix moths, web-spinning sawflies, capsid bugs and, on walls of course, red spider mites and mussel scale. Shot holes start as brown spots in leaves and become holes, and later form scabs and spots that may ooze gum on shoots and fruits. Hygienic pruning and thick mulches reduce attacks.

## peach diseases
The biggest problem is peach leaf curl, when the leaves curl, spot, redden and pucker. This fungus gets in as the buds open and swell and may be stopped by a couple of sprayings of Bordeaux mixture at this stage. It is worse in wetter areas and may be kept off entirely by keeping the shoots dry. Permanent housing under cover gets round this problem although inviting many others. Small bushes, flat- and wall-trained forms outdoors may be protected by being covered with a plastic sheet from midwinter until the buds open. Once trees reach full size, they often shrug off attacks anyway. Mildew may cause powdery patches on the leaves and shoots as well as stunted growth and yields; prune it out, spray with Bordeaux mixture and mulch after leaf fall.

Watch for mosaic virus, which mottles the leaves yellow, is unaffected by seaweed sprays and is incurable. A shortage of lime in the soil often causes soft or split stones, which as the name suggests split and usually open the flesh at the flower end, encouraging infestation by earwigs. Earwigs only eat out the kernel and the flesh is often fine – mind you, if you don't spot the smaller split, you may have the macabre experience of biting into sweet flesh that is suddenly overrun with earwigs!
PEACH LEAF CURL, RED SPIDER MITE, MOSAIC VIRUS, MUSSEL SCALE, SPLIT STONES, WASPS

## Figs (Ficus carica)

Few problems bother figs – save the birds. The main reason that most trees do not crop well is cultural. They tend to run to growth rather than fruit. Then when they do fruit, figs try to crop three times a year and this over-exertion allows no crop to do well. So never feed or manure them in open ground; they benefit from cramped roots in restrictive boxes. (I find stainless-steel drums from washing machines set in the ground perform well because they allow moisture, air and small roots through, but if the roots try to swell they cut themselves off.)

Prune figs in late winter to remove lush, soft growth with big gaps between joints and leave short-jointed wood to fruit; thin the fruits that set. Most importantly, remove all fruits and fruitlets that are still on outdoor figs in early winter. This allows the next set of embryonic figs to develop in spring and to crop in summer – thin these figs in early spring and remove any others that appear afterwards. Beware the milky sap, which can irritate.

In tubs and on hot walls, red spider mite (see page 108) may be a problem. However, figs are the most amenable of all fruits to tub culture and are then small, compact and productive. They do not need be housed under cover in winter, although you may wish to bring them in to gain another season of cropping.

BIRDS, RED SPIDER MITE (P.108)

This filbert nut is totally enclosed by the husk.

### Hazelnuts *(Corylus avellana and Corylus maxima)*

These trees suffer from big bud (buds swell and distort without opening), various critters munch the leaves and others make empty shells of the nuts, but the only problem is squirrels. They take the lot. Control these animals and don't worry about anything else. Trim back the proliferation of shoots around the base. I find that squirrels bury most nuts in soft soil around the trees, so I heavily mulch under them with thin, sandy, gravelly material in which the squirrels obligingly hide many nuts. (Don't use manure or compost since hazelnuts thrive on dry, stony ground and do not need it too rich.) As the nuts ripen a rough rake-over soon reveals recently buried nuts.

Burying wire baskets of sand proves fairly productive because they can be lifted out and shaken clean, but demand too much work overall. Interestingly, if you simply pick the hanging or fallen nuts the percentage of dead or rotten nuts is much higher than that of the buried nuts – the squirrels bury only good ones. Empty shells with wee holes have been eaten by the nut weevil; collect them on plastic sheets overlaid with thin mulches as they fall and burn them.

BIG BUD, NUT WEEVIL, SQUIRRELS

### Mulberries *(Morus nigra)*

Mulberries that are reluctant to fruit are invariably too dry. Although age is thought necessary for fruiting, I've seen one cropping the year after planting (it is bad practice to let that happen – 'twas not mine!) Odd-shaped leaves are common, especially after heavy pruning, which the trees will withstand, if required.

### Pears and quinces *(Pyrus communis and Cydonia oblonga)*

Quinces are closely related to pears and experience the same problems, although quinces are tougher, need moist soils and flower later, usually missing the frosts. A complete lack of fruit despite flowering is almost certainly because of the absence of a pollinator. Some pears, such as 'Conference', produce odd, banana-shaped fruits if they are only self-pollinated. Poor numbers of fruits are more likely to result from drought; poor growth usually is caused by competition from a grass sward underneath, which most pears resent. They like a thick mulch over a rich, moist soil. Most important is a prompt harvest – if left on the tree until they drop, pears go soft and woolly. Handle them gently and ripen them in warmish (not cold) and not too dry conditions; inspect them daily to catch them before they go over. Pears tend to upright growth and the branches often need to be bent down to induce fruiting, so espalier forms suit them. Thinning the crops is as beneficial as with apples.

### pear pests

Along with infrequent attacks from most of the pests that attack apples (see pages 190–3), pears have a few of their own. Lots of small fruits dropping off may just be June drop, as with apples (see page 188), but it may be pear gall midge, which fills the blackened fruitlets with wee, white maggots that escape when the fruitlets drop to the ground. Pick up and burn the dropped fruits or rake the soil from early to midsummer when they are falling to expose the maggots to the birds. Or expose them by putting down plastic sheeting. Tents formed in the leaves in summer by caterpillars that exude red fluid are signs of the social pear sawfly and need removing and burning. If the leaves are looking patchy and skeletonised, look for slug-like, green or blackish slugworms (sawfly grubs) grazing the tops of the leaves and hand pick or dust them.

Nearly invisible mites cause leaf blistering with yellowish spots. They were traditionally treated with a lime-sulphur wash that is no longer available; I find that soft-soap sprays work. Aphids rarely bother pears, nor do capsid bugs.

### pear diseases

The commonest problem on pears is blackening and browning of the leaves, which is often simply cold or wind damage, but if the flowers and leaves wither and go brown, it may be fireblight: cut it out and burn it before it spreads. Pear scab causes small spots on leaves that fall early and corky spots on fruits; although similar to apple scab, it is a different species. It may cause entire twigs to wither and a bad attack will let in pear canker as well. Pear canker is the same fungus as apple canker with the same symptoms. Some cultivars are more prone, such as the popular 'Williams' Bon Chrétien', 'Conference' and 'Doyenné du Comice'. Both scab and cankers

Pears are hard to ripen well and often picked too late.

are best treated with remedial pruning and burning
of the infected material, treating wounds with a sealant compound and applying heavy mulches after leaf fall. Bordeaux mixture may be used against both with some success.

Any apparent capsid-bug damage is more likely to be stony pit or dimpled pears – a virus. The fruits are smaller with dimples or pits and hard and gritty at the bases, where they are usually darker green. 'Doyenné du Comice' is one of several cultivars that are often attacked. Once infected, trees do not recover and must be eradicated. If only the odd fruit is affected, it may well be capsid-bug or even weather damage.

CANKER, DROUGHT, FIREBLIGHT, JUNE DROP, PEAR CANKER, PEAR GALL MIDGE, SCAB, SLUGWORMS, SOCIAL PEAR SAWFLY, STONY PIT

### Persian and black walnuts (Juglans regia and Juglans nigra)

Squirrels do their usual and rob you blind of walnuts. However, walnuts are big trees and often stand apart from others, so may have a squirrel funnel wrapped around the trunks. Like a rat funnel, this stops squirrels climbing the trunk and, if they can't jump on from another tree, they can't get at the walnuts – neat! Some nuts may be dead inside, but this is as often a result of the season being too dry as from any disease. Surprisingly, you may find a maggot in your walnut; they are attacked rather rarely by the same codling moth that haunts apples. Consider it an interesting curiosity. Equally curious is the blister mite, which causes leaf blisters although they very rarely cause any losses.

Walnuts suffer a leaf blotch or spot disease that creates yellowish-brown patches that are greyish on the undersides of the leaves and later go brown. The patches may also appear on the shuck, or fruit covering. Collect and burn or cover leaves with a thick mulch. If the patches are made up of lots of spotty bits rather than single plain blotches, they are more likely to be bacterial blight. This disease also causes black streaks and dieback on the shoots and spotting of the fruits, which rot inside. Prune, burn and mulch. Bordeaux sprays are barely worth the effort.

Be warned: walnut leaves and especially the shucks of the fruits, as they soften, will stain your skin and clothes indelibly. Walnut leaves, especially those of the American black walnut, are especially harmful to any plants they fall on and are said to inhibit many crops, if grown near them.

BACTERIAL BLIGHT, BLISTER MITE, CODLING MOTH, LEAF SPOT, SQUIRRELS

Plums often come in unusable gluts.

***Plums and related fruits*** (*Prunus domestica*)
Closely related to plums are other stone fruits
such as bullaces, damsons, gages and
mirabelles (*Prunus insititia* cultivars); all may
be treated similarly. Plums make bigger trees
than are normally required, because of their
brittle, upright growth, a reluctance to be
trained or to crop well in tubs, and small
numbers of dwarfing stocks available compared
to apples. They need more space and sometimes give huge surpluses when the flowers
miss the frosts. Thus almost all of the plum's
woes could be ignored except for silver leaf
disease (see below). Frost takes more flowers
and therefore crops than all other problems.
In years that escape the frosts, all the plum
family tend to crop so heavily that the brittle
branches break and exhaust the tree. With
secateurs or shears if necessary, ruthlessly
hack off masses of fruiting stems along with
their fruitlets (preferably well before the fruits
swell) or prop up the branches if it's too late.

## plum pests
The commonest problem is maggots in the
fruits: if they are red, it's the red plum maggot
(larvae of the plum fruit moth); if whitish with
a brown head, it is the plum sawfly. Both are
hard to treat although the moth maggot may
be thinned with pheromone traps and caught
in corrugated cardboard bands in late summer.
Otherwise, practise good hygiene and remove
and dispose of every infested fruit – they often
ripen and drop early – and use plastic sheeting
and mulches to trap over-wintering pupae.
Birds and wasps are always troublesome on
the sweeter cultivars, but kindly leave us the
sour and unripe! Aphids, especially mealy
plum aphids that coat the undersides of the
leaves, can attack heavily, but do little serious,
long-term harm other than withering a few
shoots. One aphid also attacks asters so don't
grow them near plum orchards. Leaf gall mites

Beware of this. Suckers coming from plum roots will slowly sap the crop of the main tree. Very bad, Bob.

may cause odd, little protuberances on the leaves, but are rarely a problem.

Whole branches and limbs dying or with tunnelled bark and wood, often with an odd smell, are infested with shot-hole borer – a beetle that may attack almost any fruit tree, although it mostly prefers stone fruits. Promptly prune out and burn all affected parts; if the trunk has been invaded, push hot wax into and over the holes to suffocate the beetles. Most of the leaf-eating caterpillars that bother apples (see page 190) also attack plums and occasionally an errant codling moth will attack the plums. A red-legged weevil may even wander over from currants and other fruits, but predominantly from raspberries.

## plum diseases

Poor growth, dieback and poor cropping indicate silver leaf disease, but the confirming sign is a silvery look to the leaves in summer (caused when air gaps form under the leaf membranes). Fungi later appear on affected branches, which need pruning out and burning. *Trichoderma virides*, a fungus that is parasitic on others, may be used on plum trees to prevent silver leaf, but is not available to amateurs in the UK. In countries where *Trichoderma* preparations (injection, wound paste or root drench) are allowed, employ a professional to get the maximum benefit from this innovative treatment. The important thing is to avoid pruning any stone fruits or ornamental *Prunus* at any time other than in summer in dry conditions, to prevent the fungus from gaining access. Any winter damage should be pruned back immediately; I prefer to cauterise the wounds with a blowtorch before sealing them with a suitable compound, such as beeswax, melted and applied with a brush. Buying trees on the most dwarfing rootstock available and leaving them unpruned, except for remedial work, is

safest. Choice cultivars that you must have may be cropped in big tubs: they are not long-lived and require inordinate care with feeding and watering, but it's worth it, especially since they may be moved under some sort of cover on frosty nights.

Plums can get a similar leaf curl to peaches (page 194) and need similar treatment. Bacterial canker causes stunted shoots, yellowing and withering leaves, other leaves with shot-hole-like spots, and cankers ulcerating limbs as on apples (see page 192). The ubiquitous 'Victoria' is often badly attacked, as is 'Czar'. Remedial pruning and mulches are essential and Bordeaux mixture may be used. If there is dieback and no large canker but only tiny hairs or jellylike pimples are visible, it may be branch dieback, but prune and burn it out in the same way. Brown rot and blossom wilt cause the same interrelated nest of problems as they do on apples – withered shoot tips, cankers and mummified fruits (see page 193). Often plums with brown rot also get whitish bubbling.

Mottled leaves indicate a mosaic virus; it has no cure and burning is the only option. Plum pox is a similar virus, causing mottling and bluish or reddish, depressed rings and spots on the fruits, again with no cure. In wet years, rounded, brownish blemishes may occur, especially on light-skinned fruits; this sooty blotch is made worse by poor drainage and stagnant conditions, but easily rectified by improving conditions with more sun and air. Similarly, fruit gumming is caused by stressful conditions such as hot and dry weather – fruits ooze a clear, chewy gum in droplets and have gummy lumps when cooked.

BACTERIAL CANKER, BIRDS, BLOSSOM WILT, BROWN ROT, CODLING MOTH, FRUIT GUMMING, LEAF CURL, PLUM SAWFLY, RED LEGGED WEEVIL, RED PLUM MAGGOT, SILVER LEAF, SOOTY BLOTCH, VIRUSES, WASPS

Sweet and acid cherries (*Prunus avium* and *Prunus cerasus*)

### Sweet and acid cherries (*Prunus avium* and *Prunus cerasus*)

A total absence of fruit may easily result from a lack of pollination – cherries are most tricky. However, a 'Morello' may pollinate almost any sweet-cherry cultivar, except the earliest flowerers. Blossoms are often ruined by wet weather; they rot and let in several diseases. The fruits also split easily if rain follows a dry spell while they are still swelling.

Cherries may be grown in large tubs, but often fail to set fruit. However, since the dwarfing rootstocks for cherries do not keep the trees small enough to net easily, growing them in tubs may well be more productive. Cherries do not like it hot, so if they are under cover give them the coolest, well ventilated spot.

### cherry pests

The only problem worth considering is birds. Nothing much keeps them off other than total exclusion, but this is not easy – most established cherries are on vigorous rootstocks and make huge specimens that are too big to cover with netting. Cherries like the open ground, so the only solution is to buy the most dwarfing form available. Don't plant it in rich, deep soil but poorer, preferably thin and chalky, soil and keep it moist with a nutrition-less mulch such as straw. Thus the tree may remain small enough to cover. One disadvantage of netting is the birds do not control caterpillars and other pests. The cherry-fruit-moth caterpillars are clear green with brown heads and enter the flower buds and eat them and the fruitlets, doing much damage. If our climate warms more, the cherry fruit fly will lay its white maggots in the fruit, which rot inside with a soft, brown patch at the stalk end. The maggots drop out and pupate in the soil; they need careful picking and destroying, along with any windfalls. Like apples, they get capsid bugs (see page 190), mussel scale (see page 192); and the same sawflies that bother pears (see page 196).

Cherries crop despite often suffering devastating attacks of a blackfly (aphid) that does little damage even though it messes up the shoot tips, causing them to blacken and shrivel. The aphid attack soon turns into a feast for ladybirds, which go on to patrol the garden, and it summer-prunes the tree for us!

### cherry diseases

Ideally, do not winter prune cherries, because it lets in the fungal disease silver leaf (see page 199). Summer pruning is safer if branches need removing to keep the tree down to size. Gummosis, gloop oozing from cracks in the bark, may result from bacterial canker. It is often made worse by waterlogging, especially on acid or heavy soil. Infection occurs in autumn through wounds and kills twigs, stems and even branches, in the same way as cankers in plums and apples. The first sign may be yellowing, withering leaves that often curl upwards. Sunken, cracked areas appear on the bark and ooze more gum. Susceptibility varies with the cultivar. Treatment, if early enough to be effective, requires immediate hygienic pruning; sterilise all wounds and use a wound sealant, especially for cuts made after summer. Restore vigorous growth with feeding, liming and draining. Bordeaux sprays may also help to clean up the tree, if applied frequently.

The fruits and flowers are vulnerable to the same brown rot (see page 193) as apples and bacterial canker (see page 199) as plums. 'Morello' cherries in particular are often badly attacked by blossom wilt (see page 193); the flowers and leaves die with no obvious cause or canker and need immediate, hygienic pruning.

Rarely, the leaves suffer leaf scorch, turning yellow then brown and hanging on all winter to reinfect the next spring. The fruits get small, hard, black spots in the flesh. Hygienic removal of all infested leaves from big trees is difficult, but get what you can. Mulch fallen leaves with thick layers of moisture-retentive material over a dressing of lime and wood ashes. Use seaweed sprays throughout the season. The same treatment may be given to cherries that sometimes suffer from interveinal yellowing, due to a shortage of available manganese in the soil. Leaf curl is similar to peach leaf curl (see page 194) and may be treated the same way, but also causes witches' broom in cherries – a dense proliferation of distorted stems arise from a stunted leading bud.

APHIDS, BACTERIAL CANKER, BIRDS, BLOSSOM WILT (P.193), BROWN ROT (P.193), CAPSID BUG (P.190), MUSSEL SCALE (P.192), SAWFLIES (P.196), SILVER LEAF (P.199), WITCHES' BROOM

# getting the best out of your garden

How to help your garden to fix itself ● Making and placing: bird boxes, pools, ponds and water features, newt lodges, toad holes, wildlife refuges, log piles, rock piles, hedgehog boxes, ladybird nests and lacewing hotels ● Companion plants and native plants ● Don't waste it all ● How to have flowers fresh for longer on your table ● Harvesting vegetables, salads and fruits only when they are perfect ● Simple solutions for storing and preserving your produce

# how to help your garden fix itself

Friends come in many sizes.

## befriend wildlife

If we encourage a greater variety of wild creatures of every size, our garden benefits because they control each other and contribute their wastes and bodies to the general fertility. The more things that eat each other in turn make the richest, most healthy ecosystem for our plants. One way to achieve this is by allowing some pests as food sources for others! Left to themselves, they will soon be controlled by something, it's just that it may happen only after our flowers or crops are spoilt. However, we can ensure that a balance is reached sooner by encouraging garden predators and parasites by supplying more food sources and water and by making and placing refuges, micro-habitats, nest boxes and hibernation sites.

### bird boxes

A shortage of next sites is most often the limiting factor for the small, insectivorous birds that we love and that help we gardeners. However, don't make any of the common mistakes in putting up nest boxes. Don't put them where cats can get at them or below head height, don't face the entrance towards the sun or the prevailing wind, and don't fail to clean them out before midwinter. Birds often choose their sites during late winter so put up new boxes early.

### pools, ponds and water features

The best way of encouraging more wild life is to have some water in the garden. Don't forget to make sure that there is a muddy edge, which is so good for many critters; if there is a steep edge, put in several ramps or safe ways out – too many hedgehogs and other creatures drown otherwise. Provide damp areas with marginal plants and some upright stems such

Spot the frog.

as bulrushes in the water for dragonfly larvae to use when they emerge from the water. Don't expect wildlife if you have fish and don't expect more than mud if you get ducks.

Newts like to get under damp or wet, cool slabs and toads also need deep, damp holes. Make places for them around a pond's edge with hidden and half-buried, half-submerged flowerpots and buckets. You can combine these hiding places with a small rock or log pile to look like a natural feature yet provide for an immense number of critters.

### wildlife refuges

It turns out that about the best place in the garden to find all sorts of creatures big and small is the wild area of long grass and weeds next to the compost heap. From the wildlife point of view, it is worth having more than one compost bin, with one for the usual wastes

Old prunings = ladybird hotel.

and another for the really slow and woody stuff – this will act much like a little nature reserve. Patches of long grass that are only a few feet square – it doesn't matter much what sort or where – encourage ground beetles and other useful creatures.

A very good way of getting lots of beetles and other creatures is to stack logs in damp, shady places and not too closely, with many gaps. Old, rotting logs are better than new firewood for this. We want all sorts of rots and small, processing creatures to come in to feed the bigger creatures that can then move out to police the rest of the garden. Brush piles are similarly useful.

Rock piles and ones of bottles, plates, tiles and so on can be good for numerous, small creatures, especially if they are sited in damp shade and have plenty of gaps. Conversely, another rock pile in the sun might be excellent

Geese make better guard dogs than dogs and keep your lawn free of weeds.

Ready-made ladybird nests and lacewing hotels may also be bought. However, any collection of hollow stems cut and bundled together and hung in dry places will do the same job admirably and for free. I find bundles of dried sweetcorn stems and leaves particularly appeal. Corrugated cardboard may be rolled up around rose and other prunings and they make snug little shelters when set inside an evergreen or dense hedge. It takes time for the insects to discover a place, but then they reuse it each year.

### native plants for native critters?

Of course there are specific companions between some plants, and between some plants and certain creatures, that are worth noting, mostly for vegetable crops. But from the point of view of most wildlife, well, they haven't read the manual. They don't know if a flower or a tasty leaf is a native or not; if they can use it, they will. For example, they may take advantage of clumps of teasel (*Dipsacum fullonum*), lady's mantle (*Alchemilla mollis*) and lupins, which all catch water in their leaves. So although we are willing to plant this or that to encourage certain forms of wildlife, in general all we really need to do is to have as many different flowers and plants as possible (which goes against aesthetic principles, but there it is). If we want masses of predatory wasps and flies, lacewings and ladybirds, we need to plant masses of all sorts of flowers blooming over as long a period as possible – that's it. We can improve and tweak it here and there, but diversity and lots of dense plant growth seems to be the most important factor. However, I am very sure that some carefully discovered plant combinations will prove remarkably efficacious – when we finally work them all out.

for other wildlife such as snakes and lizards (don't panic – snakes are very good rodent controllers). Even a small bank of sand will become populated by many critters.

### wildlife hotels

Hedgehog boxes are well enough known now to be sold commercially, but a dry spot under a shed that is made secure, filled with leaves and given an entrance tunnel is as likely to be colonised quickly. (Take care that your efforts to help hedgehogs do not encourage rats.)

# don't waste it!

## what friends are for

Having gone to all the effort of growing your flowers and produce, don't let them go to waste. If you do not want them or have more than you can eat or store, invite friends – not to take it off your hands since they will never appreciate your generosity anyway. No, invite them over for meals. They will undoubtedly come, you do after all have real food, and what will they bring? Bless its pointed little head. There you go, it's nearly a miracle: turn your watering into wine. And you don't have to drive home…

## how to keep cut flowers fresh

Cut the flowers in the morning, as soon as the dew has dried upon them and they are still cool, or in the cool of the evening. Never cut them in the heat of the day unless you just have to. Plunge them into water straightaway. If there is a delay, cut the ends off afresh and then plunge them. You can try to fill hollow stems with water, plug them with cotton wool and invert them in the water; it really helps. Congeal the sap of stems like those of poppies over a small flame from a match or lighter. Removing the leaves always keeps cut flowers fresher; especially remove those that would be below the water line and soon go smelly.

There is little point adding anything to water to make the flowers last longer, but it is worth changing it regularly and shortening stems by a tad each time. Some claim sugar, aspirin or soda helps the flowers to last longer; perhaps they do, they can do little harm. A piece of charcoal will stop the water going sour, though. A few flowers, such as hibiscus, stay open all day regardless, but most others wilt if they are too warm. All cut flowers are best kept as cool as possible. Remember, a piece of tastefully set fern or foliage will enhance the flowers magnificently.

# enjoying the harvest

## food for the year

Successful harvesting and storing are as important as growing the crops in the first place, especially in temperate climates, which have a short growing season. In such regions, most crops can be sown only in early and late spring and most of them have to be harvested before the autumn frosts. The majority of shrubs and trees have no leaves from autumn until spring and no fruits except from midsummer to autumn. Apart from some hardy winter greens and a few salads if we have the greenhouse space, we are forced to grow almost all our year's supplies in less than six months of frost-free weather and everything to keep us going through the lean months must be stored. (Of course, we could always go and buy some imported substitutes, but they never taste the same.)

Harvesting is the most glorious job of the year and we all enjoy getting in our crops, whether it is on a grand or modest scale. Digging potatoes is like searching for buried gold, while cupboards filled with preserves and the deep freezer become our treasure chests. While all the cups are overflowing, do remember that soon there will be an almost bare garden and little chance of replenishment for another six months. So use your harvest diligently – store only the best, eat fresh the rest, compost what's left. Do not give away all of your best too casually so that you are left only with the poorer and misshapen ones. Have friends and neighbours round for a meal and share your produce with them that way.

## harvesting vegetables and salads

Vegetables usually have a long season so can be picked as required and many store very well. However, it always pays to plan well ahead and think about when you will gather and process the surplus, to avoid too much running to and fro at the last minute. For example crops such as petit pois ripen and go over rather rapidly; plan to harvest some for use on the day and process the rest all in one efficient swoop, otherwise it's tough peas or save them for drying. Many vegetables are easier to store than fruits because they are less prone to rot. Indeed some, such as brassicas, leeks, parsnips and most other roots, are best stored undug in the ground if they are protected against hard frosts. Some vegetables, like the squashes and the onion tribe, just need careful drying and keeping in an airy, frost-free place.

It is not widely appreciated just how quickly valuable nutrients diminish in food once it is picked. Time spent wilting in poor conditions can halve the vitamin content as well as spoil the texture and flavour. Harvesting herbs to be used fresh is best done at the last minute. If storing herbs, do pick them at their peak – often just before they flower – and do not leave them to go over. Always pick crunchy salad crops at dawn with the cool dew on them to get maximum crispness and keep them in the refrigerator until required.

## the perfect time to pick fruit

While the time to harvest most vegetables is not often that critical, most fruits are more demanding and only thoroughly enjoyable when perfectly ripened. The morning sun is stronger than in the afternoon because the air is cleaner, so on any fruit bush or tree the morning sunny side ripens first. Of course fruit ripens earlier if extra warmth is supplied – look for early fruits next to a wall, window, chimney or heating vent, or just close to the soil. Likewise, you may find some late fruits hidden in the shade after all the rest have ripened. Watch carefully for ripe fruits on the sunny side of most fruiting plants: when they are ripe, the rest of the crop is probably perfect for storing or processing.

The best time for picking each fruit will also depend on the cultivar, the soil, the site and the season – factors that all vary considerably and can be determined only by experience. However, the sequence in which different crops mature usually remains the same, so if one crop is late because of current conditions, other crops will be delayed as well. Most store best if picked when they are just under-ripe; they may keep much longer if picked even younger, but this will be very much at the cost of flavour and sweetness. Melons are improved by chilling first, but most fruits are tastiest when warmed by the sun and eaten straight off the plant. A few fruits, such as pears, must be watched until they are nearly ripe, picked a tad early and brought to perfection in a warm, not too dry, dim room – inspect them daily and eat them before they go over. Long-keeping fruits like apples need extremely careful picking, to avoid bruising them, if they are to last ten months in storage.

## selecting produce for storage

We occasionally store some crops such as pears for a period to improve their eating quality, but we store most of them predominantly to extend the season for as long as possible. We can keep most crops for longer if we choose and store them well. Choose cultivars that are suitable for storing; many early croppers are notoriously bad keepers! There is absolutely no point in trying to store anything that has any blemish or bruise to let in moulds; use it up straightaway or process it into juice, jelly, chutney or purée. Use only perfect produce and do not store early and late

cultivars together or any that may cross-taint.
Vegetables need to be kept separate from fruits!
Remember, if only one in ten goes off every
month, you have to start with two trays just to
allow for the rots and end up with one tray after
six months! So do not store everything for ages
merely for the sake of it, just to have to compost
it all anyway, but select and store well the fruit
and vegetables that you will actually use.

## simple storage solutions

Waxing fruits is undoubtedly good for extending
their shelf life, but could help shorten yours.
Some will keep as well wrapped in clean
paper or oiled (vegetable) paper. Another early
method of mould deterrence was dipping fruits
in a solution of sodium bicarbonate and drying
it off before storing. It worked well, but left
each fruit with a powdery appearance. Common,
long-keeping fruits and vegetables such as
apples and potatoes may be stored at home
for months, even up to a year. The major
problems apart from moulds are shrivelling,
through water loss, and the depredations of
rodents and other large pests.

A conventional store is too large for most of
us and the house or garage is too warm, cold or
dry. I find dead deep freezers and refrigerators
make excellent, compact stores. They are dark,
maintain the contents at a constant temperature
and easily keep out frosts. Most useful of all, they
are rodent-proof! Some ventilation is needed
and may be obtained by cutting small holes
in the rubber door or lid seal. Condensation
usually indicates insufficient ventilation, but too
much draught will dry out fruits.

The unit may stand somewhere dry outdoors since it needs no power, although it is
out of sight in a shed and better protected
against the cold – it may even get too warm.

A dry place for ripening seeds and sets is very useful.

Obviously, it is not a good idea to put your store in the same place as strong-smelling things or substances such as paint! Likewise, although straw makes a convenient litter, if it gets damp it taints; shredded newspaper is safer although it also has a slight whiff; dried stinging nettles are reckoned good, but are dangerous to handle. In extremely cold conditions or frosts, put a sealed bottle of warm water inside the unit each night and morning for extra protection. To save space (provided that the water table is low), sink a dead chest freezer into the ground and paint the lid.

When putting crops in store, it is usually best to leave them to chill at night in trays or bags and then to load them into the store in the morning, when they have dried off but before they are warm. Similarly, it is helpful to chill and dry off many crops initially by leaving the store open on cool, dry nights and closing it during the day for a week or two after putting the food in the store. Always inspect stored crops regularly; they can go off very quickly. Most fruits are best removed from the store some time before use so that any staleness may leave them.

If you can't eat them all at once, make jam.

## preserving the pleasure

Although many crops may be stored in their virgin state, some will go off too quickly and are best processed to preserve them for longer. There are several ways to do this, varying in complexity and cost in equipment, energy and time. As well as fresh crops, almost every pickle, sauce, chutney and confectionery I enjoy is homemade and the time taken is freely given – especially the eating bit! Herbs and fruits are the most valuable crops to process; vegetables take more effort and have generally less cash value, but you can never have too much frozen asparagus. Preserved vegetables can be very hazardous once they have gone off, whereas bottled or jammed fruit is rarely as harmful even if it has gone mouldy. So if you are not meticulous and attentive to detail, stick to processing fruits!

### jams and jellies

Almost any fruit can be jammed or jellied to preserve the fruit in a sugary gel and many fruits are palatable only if so treated. Remember that it is far quicker and easier to make four by two pound batches of jam than one big eight pound batch! Large batches have a low heating and evaporating surface compared to their volume and take much longer to process so the fruit degrades more. You get better results from quickly cooking up a small batch than from standing around watching some great cauldron bubble all day!

Jellies are made from fruits that are simmered and then strained to a juice so that they set clear and bright and are appreciated by many people because there are no seeds or skins in them. Fruits are easy to pick for jellies since the odd sprig, hard or underripe fruit or bit of leaf is not a problem once the juice has been strained. The juice is too over-augmented with overdone squeezings of the fruit pulp reheated with some water. The diluted juice then requires proportionately more sugar for it to set.

Many prefer the textures of jams, which contain pieces of or whole fruits along with the seeds and skins – and don't forget the nutritional value. A conserve is just an expensive jam, usually with more fruit and less sugar or filler. (Freezer jams are conserves made with so little sugar that they go mouldy quickly unless they are kept frozen and used from the refrigerator.) However, jams require much more careful picking and preparation. My solution for, say, blackcurrants is carefully to pick the very finest berries first, and then more roughly pick the bulk of the fruit to jelly. Since the bulk is going to be jellied and strained, there is no need to take so much care to keep out the sprigs. *Before* the juice of the bulk is set with sugar, the finest berries are added and quickly cooked.

### setting jams and jellies

White sugar is traditionally used for jamming and jellying. Brown or organic sugar can be used but add a caramel flavour, which may overpower delicate preserves. Honey is not really successful because its flavour is strong and it goes off when heated as much as is needed for jam. Similarly, concentrated juices can add too much flavour. To make a setting gel for most fruits, add the same weight of sugar. The amount of fruit may be increased and the sugar decreased according to your skill and the amount of jam you eat!

Ideally, simmer down the fruit with the minimal amount of water; strain it if it is for jelly; add the sugar and bring to a boil; skim off any scum and pot. It is important to use sterile containers and conditions. Heat clean jars and lids in boiling water or in the oven so that you can pot up the jam and seal it *immediately* for best results. Store the jars, once cold, in a dark, cool place.

Some fruits are difficult to set, particularly strawberries in a wet year. Adding chopped apples to the jelly fruits or apple purée to the jams supplies the pectin needed to make any fruit set. Lemon juice gives extra acidity for a pleasing tartness that brings out the piquant flavour of some jams. Whitecurrant, and even better, redcurrant juice make good substitutes, providing good colour and helping to set difficult jams. Their flavour is tart yet mild so their jellies make good carriers for more strongly flavoured fruits in short supply, especially for raspberries and cherries.

### chutneys, sauces and pickles

These preserves are almost just jam-making with vegetables! But we add vinegar and salt to the sugar, or even replace the sugar entirely, because vegetables are so prone to go off. Many vegetables are combined with fruits in chutneys – truly a feast of goodness, if well made. Tomato sauce is ripe tomato jam with vinegar and spices, and many other sauces are based on this preserve, with more or less chilli, tamarind or pepper. The vegetables may be salted first, but are often almost raw in pickles such as piccalilli (wee bits in a mustard sauce). What healthier food is there?

Almost ready, the black ones could
be picked individually.

## juicing

Juices may be drunk as they are, as squashes
diluted with water and in cocktails, as well
as used in cooking. I find juices are the very
best way of storing fruit, other than turning
it into wine – but that's another book! Not all
crops may be easily juiced. Harder fruits and
vegetables are easier to pulp with electric
machinery. Many others may be squeezed to
express the juice or heated or frozen to break
down the texture and then strained. Add
sugar or salt to taste and improve the colour,
flavour and keeping qualities. Vegetable juices
should only be consumed fresh for safety.

Grapes are the easiest to press and the
most rewarding and you can still ferment the
pips and skins afterwards. Such wine tastes
no worse than most of my regular vintage,
although that is faint praise. It is best to crush
the grapes first to break the skins; most of the
currants and berries may be squeezed in the
same way. Apples and pears must be crushed
and then squeezed; they will go through the
same equipment but more slowly than juicier
fruits. Simmer pulpy, firm fruits such as plums
with water until they soften, then strain off
the juice; repeat the process and add sugar
to the combined juices to give the basis for
jellies. Raspberries, strawberries and other
fruits with delicate flavours are best frozen,
then defrosted and strained, to obtain a pure
juice unaffected by heat.

Suitable presses and crushers for processing
large amounts are widely available if the
quantities are too large for kitchen tools;
they are usually sold and hired for home and
small-scale wine makers. Fruit juices ferment
rapidly in the warm, last longer if kept cool in
the refrigerator and keep for months or years
if they are deep-frozen. They take less space

Beans keep best in the haulm hanging in a dry airy place.

in a freezer than the crop they come from and are as good afterwards, until they ferment. I freeze mine in the wax cartons and plastic bottles that milk comes in, leaving a wee space in each container for expansion. I have two freezers: one for juices and one for everything else because I want to drink my own apple or grape juice, not the stuff that comes out of my tap.

## drying fruits and vegetables

Many foods may be dried if they are simply sliced thinly and exposed to warm, dry air. This traditional method does lose some flavour, but concentrates the food in a much smaller volume so use dried herbs sparingly. However, in temperate climates such as those of the UK and much of maritime Europe and North America, the air is too humid and drying does not happen quickly enough. It is further slowed by the low temperatures in those regions. Making solar-powered dryers (simply wire trays under glass with good ventilation) usually allows fruit to dry, but in regions with high humidity the food may still go mouldy before it dries. And of course flies and other creatures must be excluded! I slice the food thinly and hang the pieces, separated by spaces equivalent to at least half their sizes, on long strings over my cooking range. It provides the dry warmth and ventilation needed to desiccate most foods within a day or two, or even just overnight for the easier crops such as apples.

Oven-drying with artificial heat is risky because it can cook the food and destroy its value, texture and keeping properties. It is possible if the temperature is low and the door kept partly open. Oven-drying is convenient nonetheless for finishing off partly dried samples after you have done other baking; the decaying heat desiccates well with little risk of caramelising or burning. Dried foods keep for long periods if sealed in dark containers and kept cool and dry; they may be eaten dried or reconstituted when required.

Herbs for drying are usually best gathered once the dew has dried off them. Hang them upside down in small bunches in a very airy place. Bright light bleaches out the colour so some shading may be necessary. Once they are completely dry, the herbs may be crushed and put in jars or sealed in paper bags in a tin.

## freezing

This technique captures flavours that may be lost by drying. It is particularly good for herbs, especially parsley and basil, which may be frozen and need almost no time to defrost. These can even be conveniently frozen in water or oil as handy portions in ice cubes. Most fruits freeze easily with little preparation, unlike vegetables, which need blanching first. Chop up the vegetables and immerse them in boiling water for a few minutes or more and then chill them again before freezing. It is extra work and uses fuel, but then you can eat your own in any month of the year. Only the very best is worth freezing since few things are improved by the process.

With most fruits and blanched vegetables, merely putting them in sealed freezer bags or boxes is sufficient; however, they tend to freeze in a block that is inconvenient to use later. Place the food pieces loose on wire trays or greased baking trays to freeze them and pack them afterwards. Fruits that are cut or damaged must be drained first or, if you have a sweet tooth, they may be dredged in sugar to absorb the juice. Stone fruits are best de-stoned before freezing because the stone can give an almond taint. Remove tough skins of fruits such as tomatoes or plums after freezing and before use by carefully squeezing the frozen fruit under very hot water – the skins should slip off easily.

Foods lose value slowly in the freezer; the longer they are frozen, the less nutritional value they have. Fruits do not deteriorate as badly or as quickly as vegetables or meats and fatty products. However, most fruits turn to soggy lumps in pools of juice when defrosted, which is not as appetising as the fresh product. They are still packed full of sweetness, flavour and vitamins and are well worth having for culinary use, especially in tarts, pies, sauces and compotes. A mixture of frozen fruits is marvellous if they are partly defrosted, so that they retain their frozen texture like pieces of sorbet, and are served with cream.

# the yearly diary

Spring comes with the first blooms.

Draining pots after soaking.

## a stitch in time saves nine

This principle is true in almost everything
and particularly in gardening. Many a pest
outbreak may be quashed early on by a little
squishing between finger and thumb long
before any eggs hatch or maggots move over
the plants. The 'good old boys' were skilled
and relaxed, largely because they knew the
timing for each and every operation. Many
gardeners may just attend to whatever happens
to take their notice at any time, but then
things get missed. A few years' experience
of doing the right thing at the wrong time –
or the wrong thing at the right time – gives
equally mixed results, but it doesn't matter
as long as you learn from the experience
and do better next time.

It is much like learning to drive: initially
it is all panic, but soon things make some
sense and before long you are looking farther
ahead and it all becomes automatic. Until
then, here are some methods and reminders
of what must be done when. There is a right
time for everything in gardening and it was
last week or, worse, last month! In order not
to fall into this error, keep a diary of missed
opportunities, as described earlier (see page
13) as well as referring to my yearly diary on
the following pages. Everything in gardening
comes round and round again. To make it
easier to cope with each job in it's turn, we
can break down the tasks into those that
need doing really frequently, those that need
doing regularly, and those that are seasonal
and only come round once or so a year.

## the daily round

Make a daily inspection of your garden and
make notes, listing pending and pressing jobs
(such as sowings, potting-up or prunings due)
so you may plan at leisure. As you proceed,
the most important thing is to water whatever
needs it and to harvest whatever is wanted
for the kitchen or store. As you go, collect and
dispose of any litter, gather up other junk, tools,
toys and so on and put them away. If you
have a cold frame or greenhouse, adjust the
ventilation according to the season and, if
necessary, check the min/max thermometer
to ensure that the plants are being kept at
suitable daytime and night-time temperatures.

## the weekly routine

The vital tasks are daily ones; you should
complete them before starting on weekly
chores. The most important task is to take
advantage of any window for sowing and
transplanting that is due – next week will be
too late! Afterwards, sharpen your hoe and
weed the beds and borders. Then clip the
lawn edges and mow the grass. Collect all
suitable materials together for composting
and move them to the heap. Have a break,
sit down and look through your notes for any
seasonal tasks that may be due, such as fruit
thinning or compost turning.

## the seasonal cycle

Along with the regular jobs such as the
watering, weeding and grass cutting, there
is a variety of activities in the garden that
need to be tackled only once each year, such
as harvesting in autumn and preparing for
winter. These are often easier to overlook than
more frequent tasks, so I've included crucial
seasonal tasks in the yearly diary. Obviously,
the exact timing will vary according to your
locality, site and soil, and you may not grow
exactly the same plants as anyone else, but
most plants have similar requirements at much
the same season. The gardener's year naturally
starts off in darkest, coldest late winter.

# calendar of pastimes

## late winter

**E**mpty insect traps and old bird boxes and hang up new bird boxes so that they are ready when the birds need them. Put out bird food, hang up fat and provide sources of water.

**M**ake sure that no weeds get a hold – they pull up easily at this time. Hoe whenever it's dry enough.

**S**pray peaches and almonds when the buds are swelling with Bordeaux mixture against peach leaf curl.

**C**ut the grass if no frosts are likely; set the blades high and return the clippings.

**P**ut down impenetrable sheet mulches on top of new ground or green manures. Spread loose mulches under and around everything, preferably immediately after a period of heavy rain.

**P**lant out hardy trees and shrubs if the ground is workable. Firm in the roots of autumn plantings after hard frosts.

**C**heck ties and stakes after gales.

**F**inish any major pruning work that needs to be done, but leave alone stone fruits or evergreens unless they are damaged by winter storms.

**C**hit early seed potatoes on trays in a light, frost-free place.

**T**idy sheds and greenhouses and repair and clean tools and equipment.

**I**f necessary, order seeds and plants and plan where you will put them.

**C**heck your food stores and remove anything that is starting to rot before it infects others.

## early spring

Put out food, hang up fat and provide water for birds.

To stop any weeds getting away, hoe at least every other week and top up thin, weedy mulches.

Spray peaches and almonds for a second time with Bordeaux mixture. Examine every plant in the garden and under cover for pests, diseases and dieback before they start to leaf up.

Cut the grass at least fortnightly, preferably weekly, and return the clippings or put them as mulch around trees and bushes. Move, lay, sow and repair turf in non-frosty weather.

Once the soil becomes workable, plant out evergreens, soft fruit, artichokes, asparagus and rhubarb.

Spray the entire garden with diluted seaweed solution.

Hand-pollinate early-flowering plants under cover.

Cover blossoms and young fruitlets with net curtains or sheets to protect them from frost damage on still, cold nights.

Prune tender plants, evergreens, herbs and hollow-stemmed shrubs such as buddleias.

Outdoors, plant garlic, onion sets, shallots, potatoes.

Sow plants to be grown under cover: tomatoes, cucumbers, aubergines, peppers, hardy and half-hardy annuals.

Outdoors, sow in warm soil under cloches: peas, broad beans, onions, leeks, beetroot, kohlrabi, cabbages, cauliflowers, lettuce, spinach, turnips, carrots, chards, salsify, scorzonera, parsnips, herbs, radishes, spring onions, sweet peas and hardy annuals.

Check your food stores and remove anything that is starting to rot before it infects others.

## mid-spring

Plant out potatoes, onion seedlings and perennial herbs.

Spray everything with diluted seaweed solution; spray anything showing deficiency symptoms more heavily.

Firm in roots of earlier plantings after any hard frosts.

De-flower new fruit plants to give them time to establish.

Protect blossoms and young fruitlets from frost with net curtains, plastic sheeting or newspaper.

Feed and top-dress all plants in pots.

Tie in new growths of vines and climbing plants.

Once their flowers die, prune and cut back most early-flowering shrubs.

Cut the grass weekly and return the clippings or put them as mulches around trees and bushes.

Hoe weekly to ensure that no weeds get a hold.

Examine each plant for early signs of pests and diseases. Put out slug pubs and pheromone traps. Make night-time searches of your garden for pests – especially in sowing and propagation areas.

Sow plants under cover to plant out later: tomatoes, ridge cucumbers, gherkins, courgettes, marrows, pumpkins, sweetcorn and half-hardy flowers.

Outdoors, sow: peas, broad beans, most brassicas, lettuces and saladings, herbs, spinach, turnips, carrots, swedes, salsify, scorzonera, radishes, kohlrabi, fennel, leeks, parsnips, sweet peas and hardy annuals.

Use up stored fruits and vegetables and clean out stores once empty.

## late spring

Hoe frequently to ensure that no weeds get away. Top up weedy mulches.

Examine every plant for pests and diseases, especially for aphids, caterpillars and, indoors, red spider mite or whitefly. Make night-time searches of your garden for pests – especially in sowing and propagation areas.

Cut the grass at least fortnightly, preferably weekly, and return the clippings or put them as mulch around potatoes.

Pot up any plant needing repotting.

Establish a daily watering round for all pot-grown plants. Feed indoor pot plants with comfrey liquid or seaweed solution weekly.

Spray everything with diluted seaweed solution; spray anything with deficiency symptoms more heavily.

Protect blossoms and young fruitlets from frost damage on still, cold nights.

Tie in and support climbers and the tallest herbaceous plants.

Cut back most flowering shrubs once their flowers die.

Harden off and plant out under cover; tomatoes, peppers, aubergines, melons, sweetcorn, ridge cucumbers, courgettes and marrows or plant them outside under cloches only if you are sure that the last frost is over.

Outdoors, sow in situ under cloches once you are sure that frosts have passed: tomatoes, ridge cucumbers, gherkins, courgettes, marrows, pumpkins, French beans, runner beans, sweetcorn and half-hardy flowers.

Sow outdoors without cloches: peas, most brassicas, lettuces and saladings, herbs, spinach, turnips, carrots, swedes, salsify, scorzonera, kohlrabi, fennel, leeks, parsnips and hardy annuals and biennials.

Harvest and use or store and preserve any crops.

### early summer

**M**aintain good weed control so that no weeds get a hold; hoe fortnightly or weekly.

**E**xamine every plant for pests and diseases, especially aphids, caterpillars and, indoors, red spider mite or whitefly.

**C**ut the grass at least fortnightly and preferably weekly, but raise the height of cut of the mower.

**P**ot up anything needing repotting.

**I**ncrease frequency of watering for all pot-grown plants to at least thrice daily!

**I**ndoors, feed pot plants with comfrey liquid or seaweed solution weekly.

**P**lant or move out tender plants in pots for the summer.

**S**pray everything growing with diluted seaweed solution; spray anything with deficiency symptoms more heavily.

**D**eadhead roses and cut back most flowering plants after their flowers die.

**T**hin raspberry canes.

**P**rune grapevines, cutting back stems to three or five leaves after a flower truss.

**T**ie in new growths of climbing plants to their supports.

**F**ruit thinning, first stage: remove every diseased, decayed, damaged, misshapen, distorted and congested fruitlet. Compost or burn rejected fruitlets immediately and protect the remainder from birds.

**O**utdoors, sow: lettuces and saladings, beetroot, kohlrabi, swedes, turnips, spinach, chicory, endive and herbaceous biennials and perennials.

**H**arvest and use or store and preserve everything that is ready, before it goes over.

### midsummer

**H**oe fortnightly to ensure that no weeds get away.

**M**ake night-time inspections of your garden to catch pests on the prowl.

**C**ut the grass at least fortnightly and preferably weekly, but raise the height of cut of mower even more.

**W**ater all pot-grown plants at least thrice daily. Indoors, feed pot plants with comfrey liquid or seaweed solution weekly.

**S**pray everything growing with diluted seaweed solution, and anything with deficiency symptoms more heavily.

**D**eadhead roses and cut back most flowering plants after their flowers die.

**I**f it is warm and humid, spray main crop potatoes with Bordeaux mixture.

**P**erform summer pruning: remove approximately one half to three quarters of each new shoot, except for leaders, of all red and white currants, gooseberries and all trained fruits. Prune grapevines, cutting back stems to three or five leaves after a flower truss; if there is no flower truss by the sixth leaf, cut it back anyway and mark it for removal during winter pruning. Take out old, fruited wood on blackcurrants and raspberries. Stone fruits are traditionally pruned now to avoid silver leaf disease.

**T**ie in new growths of climbing plants to their supports.

**C**ut back evergreens and conifer hedges.

**F**ruit thinning, second stage: remove damaged fruits. Harvest and eat or preserve ripe fruits and protect remaining fruit from birds and wasps.

**S**ow: lettuces and saladings, carrots, swedes, turnips, Chinese cabbage, winter spinach, kohlrabi, Florence fennel, chards.

**H**arvest and use or store everything that is ready for picking.

### late summer

**H**oe fortnightly to ensure that no weeds get away.

**M**ake night-time inspections of your garden to catch pests on the prowl.

**P**rotect every ripening fruit from the birds and wasps.

**C**ut the grass at least fortnightly and preferably weekly, but reduce the height of cut of the mower a little.

**D**ecrease watering for pot-grown plants to at least twice daily. Feed pot plants with comfrey liquid or seaweed solution weekly.

**S**pray everything growing with diluted seaweed solution, and anything with deficiency symptoms more heavily.

**D**eadhead roses and cut back most flowering plants after their flowers die.

**F**inish pruning all stone fruits to avoid silver leaf disease.

**T**ie in new growths of climbing plants to their supports.

**P**lant new strawberry plants, if you can get them.

**O**rder hardy trees and shrubs for autumn planting.

**S**ow under cover: winter lettuces and saladings, early carrots.

**O**utdoors, sow: winter lettuces and saladings, Japanese and spring onions, winter spinach, turnips, Chinese greens and hardy and biennial flowering plants.

**S**ow green manures and winter ground cover on bare soil that is not mulched.

**H**arvest and eat, store or preserve everything that is ready.

## early autumn

Hoe fortnightly or top up mulches to maintain good weed control.

Cut the grass at least fortnightly and preferably weekly; collect the clippings with any fallen leaves and put them around trees and bushes. Raise the height of cut again.

Decrease watering for all pot-grown plants, but still check them daily.

Transplant biennial flowering plants that are pot-grown, with a decent rootball.

Cut back herbaceous plants as their stems wither.

Remove old canes of all the berrying fruits and tie in new stems.

On still, cold nights, protect tender bedding plants from frost damage with sheeting.

Bring indoors tender plants in pots.

Collect and dry seeds.

Plant: garlic, daffodils and most other bulbs.

Sow hardy annuals to overwinter.

Sow green manures and grass.

Harvest and use or store everything before it goes over.

## mid autumn

Control weeds by hoeing fortnightly or topping up mulches.

Cut the grass at least fortnightly and preferably weekly; collect clippings and fallen leaves together or rake them into rings around trees and bushes. Aerate and spike the grass if needed, brushing in sharp sand and grass seed if you are a workaholic.

Decrease watering again as growth slows more.

If necessary, make new beds and borders and move turf.

Spread mulches under and around everything possible.

Outdoors, plant: garlic and bulbs, deciduous shrubs, trees and soft fruit (preferably bare-rooted).

Check ties and stakes if gales are forecast.

Cut back herbaceous plants as their stems wither.

Winter-prune: apples, pears, grapes and non-stone fruits and other plants, once they drop their leaves.

Order seed catalogues and anything to plant soon. Collect and dry seeds and berries for sowing next year and to feed the birds.

Check food stores and remove anything that is starting to rot before it infects others.

Harvest and store late fruits and tender root vegetables.

## late autumn

Continue to hoe fortnightly or top up mulches to maintain weed control.

Cut the grass at least fortnightly; collect fallen leaves with the clippings or rake them onto now empty or dormant beds and borders.

Water all pot-grown plants only as needed.

Lime the vegetable beds.

Make and turn compost heaps and sieve and store finished compost.

Plant out bare-rooted deciduous shrubs, trees and soft fruit – if the soil is in good condition and the plants are dormant.

Winter-prune any plant that still needs it.

Check ties and stakes after any gales.

Take cuttings of hardy plants as they drop their leaves.

Harvest and store root vegetables under cover in cold areas. Check food stores and remove anything that is starting to rot before it infects others.

Take all hosepipes, plastic cans and so on under cover before hard frosts make them brittle.

## early winter

**C**ut the grass if the weather is still mild; collect the fallen leaves with the few clippings and bag them up to make leaf mould. Lime most tough grass swards every fourth year, but not among ericaceous or lime-hating plants.

**D**ecrease watering to a minimum as plant growth almost ceases.

**P**lant out hardy trees and bushes, provided that the soil is still in good condition and not frozen.

**C**heck ties and stakes after each gale.

**C**lean out gutters and drains once the last leaves have fallen. Clean the greenhouse, cold frames and glass and plastic cloches.

**P**rune hardy trees and bushes, including any major work necessary on trees and bushes (but not on stone fruits or evergreens.) Make a bonfire of diseased and thorny material.

**G**et in your seed orders early so that you get the best choice and they arrive in time for the new season. Order potatoes, evergreen and herbaceous plants for spring.

**C**heck food stores and remove anything that is starting to rot before it infects others.

## midwinter

**M**ake bird boxes, slug pubs, insect traps, hibernation quarters and plastic bottle cloches.

**O**n clear bright days, make a health and hygiene check: examine every plant for damage and dieback, scale insects and mummified fruits. Collect up and destroy hibernating snails.

**C**lean and repair the mower so it's ready to roll in the spring!

**C**heck ties and stakes after any gales.

**M**ake sure that your seed orders are in.

**C**heck food stores and remove anything that is starting to rot.

**R**elax, take it easy for a while: note your successes and mishaps of the year, enjoy the fruits of your labours and plan the pleasure of next year and doing even less work.

# bibliography

*John Cushnie,* **Ground cover: A Thousand Beautiful Plants for Difficult Places**, Kyle Cathie, 1999
*John Cushnie,* **How to Prune**, Kyle Cathie, 2007
*John Cushnie and Marianne Majerus*, **Trees for the Garden**, 2004

Well, you might find John Cushnie's book on pruning useful and his books on trees and ground cover give plenty of good choices, but really what you want are:

*Bob Flowerdew's* **Complete Book of Companion Gardening**, Kyle Cathie, (revised ed.) 2004
A substantial textual feast illuminated by subtle and artistic photography and a seminal work of genius – seldom has there been such a work of profound significance, scholarly insight and practical application.

*Bob Flowerdew's* **Complete Fruit Book:** *A Definitive Sourcebook to Growing, Harvesting and Cooking Fruit,* Kyle Cathie, (new ed.) 2000
In over two dozen editions in more than a dozen languages, this book had to be retitled The Complete Book Of Fruit for the politically correct in order not to offend complete fruits. Anyway, this book is gorgeously written and lavishly produced with photographic masterpieces and has all you could ever wish to know about growing and eating every fruit and nut, from the common and the garden to the wild and exotic.

*Bob Flowerdew's* **Organic Bible:** Successful Gardening the Natural Way, Kyle Cathie, 1998
A comprehensive tour de force by this modest genius, this manual contains all you could ever want to know about organic gardening and the wonderful results of working with nature, growing flowers and produce and tending the harmonious space that they share with us. All the photographs in this book were taken in Bob Flowerdew's garden.

*Bob Flowerdew*, **The Companion Garden**, Kyle Cathie, 1994
The UK edition is sadly now out of print, but was retitled for the Americans, as **Good Companions: A Guide to Gardening with Plants that Help Each Other**, Summit Books, 1992
Beautifully written and elegantly produced, with excellent illustrations. A concise introduction to the way plants may be grown together to help each other thrive.

*Bob Flowerdew*, **The Gourmet Gardener:** Everything You Need to Grow and Prepare the Very Finest of Vegetables, Fruits and Flowers, Kyle Cathie, 2005
Gardening with the emphasis on quality, taste, flavour, texture, cultivar and seasonality, while concentrating on your favourites and indulging them! Not for the novice, except as an aspirational read or on a cold night.

*Bob Flowerdew*, **The No-Work Garden:** Getting the Most out of Your Garden for the Least Amount of Work, Kyle Cathie, 2004
The book you've really been waiting for, on how to save effort and stress while gardening both effectively and organically! It is also a good read, quite funny and just solid enough to play cards on.

*John Cushnie, Bob Flowerdew, Bunny Guinness, Pippa Greenwood, Anne Swithinbank*, **Gardeners' Question Time: All Your Gardening Problems Solved**, Orion, 2002

*Matthew Biggs, John Cushnie, Bob Flowerdew, Bunny Guinness*, **Gardeners' Question Time Plant Chooser**, Kyle Cathie, 2003

*Matthew Biggs, John Cushnie, Bob Flowerdew, Anne Swithinbank*, **Gardeners' Question Time: Techniques & Tips for Gardeners**, Kyle Cathie, 2005

*Bob Flowerdew*, **Organic Gardening Basics:** Five Easy Steps to Growing Organically, Hamlyn, 2007 (formerly published as **The Organic Gardener**, 1993, and **Go Organic!**, 2002)

*Bob Flowerdew, contributor to Basil Caplan (ed.)*, **Complete Manual of Organic Gardening**, Headline, 1992

Bob also writes regularly for the weekly magazine *Amateur Gardening*, and monthly publications *BBC Gardeners' World Magazine, Gardens Monthly, Kitchen Garden* and *Organic Life*.

## picture acknowledgements

All photography by **Francesca Yorke**
except pages: 11, 14-15, 22, 23, 27, 28, 36, 39, 47 (top left), 48, 49 (left), 57, 70 (right), 82 (right), 87, 125 (bottom right), 137, 150 (top), 152, 154, 157 (middle & right), 160, 161, 166, 168, 169 (right), 173 (right), 175, 176 (right), 186, 195, 196, 209, 220 (right): Pete Cassidy; 98 (middle): Kay Truepenny/Alamy; 103 (right) Martin Fowler/Alamy; 105 (left): Anderw Darrington/ Alamy 105 (middle and right), 107 (right), 118 (left), 119: Holt Studios International Ltd/Alamy; 118 (right) John Glover/Alamy; 119: Bob Flowerdew; 121: Kevin Howchin/Alamy; 147 (right): Elizabeth Whiting & Associates/Alamy; 187 Arco Images/Alamy

# index